DOUG
MCNISH

The
Classics
Veganized

OVER 120 FAVOURITE

COMFORT FOOD RECIPES FOR

A VEGAN LIFESTYLE

DOUG McNISH

PENGUIN

an imprint of Penguin Canada, a division of Penguin Random House Canada Limited

Canada • USA • UK • Ireland • Australia • New Zealand • India • South Africa • China

First published 2020

www.penguinrandomhouse.ca

LIBRARY AND ARCHIVES CANADA CATALOGUING IN PUBLICATION

Title: The classics veganized : over 120 favourite comfort food recipes
for a vegan lifestyle / Doug McNish.
Names: McNish, Douglas, author.
Identifiers: Canadiana (print) 2020017293X | Canadiana (ebook) 20200172956 | ISBN 9780735237063
(hardcover) | ISBN 9780735237070 (HTML)
Subjects: LCSH: Vegan cooking. | LCGFT: Cookbooks.
Classification: LCC TX837 .M36 2020 | DDC 641.5/6362—dc23

Cover and interior design by Five Seventeen

Cover and interior food photography and styling by Nicole Axworthy

Lifestyle photography by Walker Jordan with styling by Carol Dano

Printed and bound in China

10 9 8 7 6 5 4 3 2 1

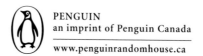

PENGUIN
an imprint of Penguin Canada
www.penguinrandomhouse.ca

To my wife, Candice. I'm not sure I could make any of this happen without you. Thank you for always believing in me and in us.

To my son, Ewan. You have taught me more about life, love, silliness, and happiness than I could have ever imagined. I know life has lots of magic in store for you.

Lastly, for the animals. I live a vegan lifestyle for them in the hope that one day we will look back and say, *Can you believe we used to eat animals?*

Contents

1 Introduction

2 About this Book

6 Cooking Tips

7 Deep-Frying 101

9 Stocking a Vegan Pantry

18 Essential Equipment

Appetizers

23 Crispy Mushroom Calamari

24 Boneless Wings

27 French Onion Soup with Melted Mozzarella

28 Cashew Mozzarella Sticks

31 Cheesy Garlic Bread

32 Cheesy Tex-Mex Quesadillas

35 Mile-High Loaded Nachos

36 Stuffed to the Rim Skins

39 Gooey Cheese Fondue

40 Fiesta Seven-Layer Dip

43 South of the Border Jalapeño Poppers

44 Blooming Onion

45 Creamy Tomato Bisque

47 Creamiest Cream of Mushroom Soup

48 Un-Chicken Noodle Soup

51 Crispy Corn and Squash Hush Puppies

52 Caprese Stacks

55 Killer Crispy Latkes with Sour Cream and Chives

57 Classic Poutine

58 Baked Crab Dip

Sides and Salads

63 Twice Baked Vegan Taters

64 Perfect French Fries and Seasoning Salt

67 Smashed Taters

68 Maple Baked Beans

70 Herbed Holiday Stuffing

71 Creamy Risotto

73 Creamed Garlic Spinach

74 Crispy Dillies with Ranch Dressing

77 Slow-Cooked Southern-Style Collard Greens

78 Buttermilk Onion Rings

81 Deviled Eggs

82 Cobb Salad

85 Creamy Caesar Salad

87 Waldorf Salad

89 Greek Salad

90 Chopped Salad

Brunch

95 Buttermilk Blueberry Pancakes

96 Peanut Butter Fudge and Chocolate Waffles

99 Stuffed and Stacked French Toast

100 Muesli and Cashew Yogurt Parfait

102 Cage-Free Cheesy Omelette

104 Breakfast in Bed Scones

105 Seitan Bacon

107 Quiche Lorraine

108 Count of Monte Cristo

109 Croque Monsieur

113 Brunch Club Sandwich

114 Sunny Side Up Vegan Eggs with Yolks

115 Perfect Vegan Scramble

116 Downhome Fries

117 Buttermilk Fried Chicken

118 Cage-Free Eggs Florentine

120 Dirty South Sausages and Biscuits with Gravy

121 No Bull Breakfast Links

122 Cheesy Scramble Biscuits

123 Shakshuka

125 Ultimate Vegan Caesar

The Main Deal

129 The NY Strip
130 Home-Style Meatloaf
133 Chickpea Pot Pie
134 Beer Battered Tempeh and Chips
137 Bacon Double Cheeseburgers
139 Meatball Sub
143 White Widow Mac and Cheese
144 Sharp Cheddar Mac and Cheese
145 Bangers and Mash
146 Chickpea Salisbury Steak
148 Lentil Ragout with Cheesy Rice
149 Stuffed Grilled Cheese Sandwiches
151 Reuben Sandwiches
152 Philly Cheesesteak Sandwiches
154 Smoked Carrot Lox Pinwheel Wrap
157 Spaghetti and Meatballs
158 Fettuccini Alfredo
161 Mushroom and Spinach Lasagna
162 No-Beef Stroganoff
165 Shepherd's Pie
166 Holiday Ham
167 Hickory Smoked Ribs
171 Butter Tofu
172 General Tso Tofu
175 Drunken Vegan Chicken Stew
176 Crab Cakes with Remoulade Sauce
179 Fiesta Chili
180 Tortilla Bake
183 Eggplant Parmesan
185 Change Your Life Chana with Tandoori Cauliflower

Sweet Sinful Desserts

189 Apple Crisp
190 Crunchy Chocolate Chip Cookies
192 Pineapple Upside Down Cake
195 Everyday Pound Cake
196 Molten Lava Chocolate Brownie Cake
199 New York Style Cheesecake
200 Coffee Cake
202 Chocolate Fudge Cake with Buttercream Frosting
203 Carrot Cake with Cream Cheese Frosting
205 Luscious Lemon Meringue Pie
206 Bodacious Blueberry Pie
207 Pecan Pie
208 Deluxe Banana Split
211 Peanut Butter Buckeyes
213 Churros with Salted Caramel Sauce

Pantry Staples and Condiments

216 Almond Milk Cheddar Cheese
217 Almond Milk Cheese Curds
218 Cashew Mozzarella
219 Swiss Cheese
220 Blue Cheese
221 Feta Cheese
222 Cream Cheese
223 Mac and Cheese Sauce
224 Nacho Cheese Sauce
225 Tartar Sauce
226 Hollandaise Sauce
227 Honey Garlic Sauce
227 Buffalo Sauce
228 Anytime Gravy
229 Whipped Butter
230 Garlic Butter
231 Sour Cream
232 Creamy Mayo
233 Classic Vinaigrette
233 Ranch Dressing
234 Russian Dressing
235 Best Banana Soft Serve

237 Acknowledgments
239 Index

Introduction

Flash back to fifteen years ago and you would have seen me, a classically trained chef, working the grill at a steakhouse cooking hundreds of steaks a night. What this younger me wasn't aware of just yet was the cruel life of factory farmed animals raised for food, the negative health effects associated with a diet built around animal products, and the environmental degradation that raising animals for food creates. I was in my early twenties when these things came to light for me and when I decided to become vegan and dedicate my professional efforts to creating compassionate vegan cuisine.

Prior to my vegan cooking, I was lucky enough to work for and with some amazing chefs in all facets of the culinary world. I have been part of award-winning catering teams, was trained in traditional fine dining, and worked at a large Mediterranean-inspired bistro, in French cuisine, and at the aforementioned steakhouse, a country club, a professional sports arena, and more. I did not know it at the time, but all of these influences and experiences would help mould my palate and lead me to understand how truly amazing vegan cuisine can be.

Initially it was just for fun. I tried to re-create vegan cheese recipes I would see in books and magazines. I let my co-workers and friends sample my creations, and while there were a lot of hits, there were also a lot of misses along the way. It was the misses that helped form the foundation for what I do now. I don't think you can become a good home cook or chef unless you make mistakes, and lots of them. They are our true-life teachers.

Anytime I set out to veganize a recipe, I try to look at how the original version was made. I not only look at the physical makeup of the recipe, but also bring back a memory of a taste or an experience associated with the original animal-based food I made. These past experiences are what inspire me to re-create something as close to the traditional version as possible.

Vegan cuisine is exploding all over the world, and now more than ever people are adopting a plant-based diet or vegan lifestyle. Not only are they starting to understand that you do not need animal products to survive, but with new science-based evidence and research coming out all the time, people are understanding that you can actually thrive eating a healthy plant-based diet. I am both excited and honoured to be a part of this growth, and I hope that through the recipes in this book, you will understand how truly amazing vegan cuisine can be.

My approach to cooking is always about two things: good flavour and good texture. If I can achieve both, the dish is always a winner in my eyes. I've applied this philosophy to every recipe in this cookbook to create an awesome collection of more than 100 vegan recipes that reinvent classic comfort foods with a modern spin! I truly hope you can taste, sense, feel, and experience the love that has gone into each and every bite along the way!

About This Book

My goal for this book was to re-create familiar recipes and turn them into standout vegan dishes that no one would know are meatless. Not only do they taste amazing, but I have worked hard to ensure that the appearance and texture of the dishes are what you would expect from great food. I use traditional techniques with a modern approach in my cuisine, which I know will have you coming back to this book for years to come. I have broken the book into six sections and done my best to cover every type of dish you could make at home.

I start with appetizers because, really, is there any better way to start a meal? There are some comfort food favourites like the classic Crispy Mushroom Calamari (page 23), Boneless Wings (page 24), Cashew Mozzarella Sticks (page 28), and South of the Border Jalapeño Poppers (page 43). Some of my personal favourites, and dishes I love to eat any time of the year, are the French Onion Soup with Melted Mozzarella (page 27), Creamiest Cream of Mushroom Soup (page 47), and Baked Crab Dip (page 58). Whether you are an omnivore, a long-time vegan, or new to this way of eating, I know these apps will make their way to your dinner table.

And of course, no meal is complete without a side dish or fresh salad. There are so many classic sides that are always hugely popular—a classic never goes out of style! Vegan sides? No problem at all. I have created sides like Creamy Risotto (page 71), Creamed Garlic Spinach (page 73), Maple Baked Beans (page 68), and Smashed Taters (page 67) that go well with virtually any dish. In most instances, nearly any side in this book can be paired with any other dish. For a more indulgent side dish, try my Perfect French Fries and Seasoning Salt (page 64), Buttermilk Onion Rings (page 78), or Crispy Dillies with Ranch Dressing (page 74).

I've included four of my favourite salads—classical takes on their traditional counterparts. Whether it's the Creamy Caesar Salad (page 85), Waldorf Salad (page 87), Chopped Salad (page 90), or my Greek Salad (page 89), I am sure there are one or two you will come back to over and over again and make a regular part of your meals.

Vegan brunch is near and dear to my heart. It is something I am known for, and have worked on for so many years. I have always challenged myself to keep inventing new and amazing dishes to celebrate this special meal, which is not quite breakfast and not quite lunch.

One of the things I love so much about brunch is that it's one of the only meals where it is not only acceptable but encouraged to mix sweet and savoury. Of course, you will find Buttermilk Blueberry Pancakes (page 95) piled high, light and fluffy. A brunch section would not be complete without waffles, so I have included my Peanut Butter Fudge and Chocolate Waffles (page 96), which feature chunks of peanut butter fudge and chocolate sauce.

On the savoury side, there is my Cage-Free Cheesy Omelette (page 102), Buttermilk Fried Chicken (page 117), Count of Monte Cristo (page 108), and vegan eggs, complete with yolks that run! Make sure to try your hand at my (world-famous) Sunny Side Up Vegan Eggs with Yolks (page 114). And, to end the brunch section, I have included what I think is the Ultimate Vegan Caesar (page 125). Brunch is meant to be shared, and I've made these recipes with that in mind.

Moving on to main course dishes, I have worked hard to re-create some hearty dishes that most would not ever imagine could be vegan. Recipes like Hickory Smoked Ribs (page 167), The NY Strip (page 129), Holiday Ham (page 166), and Reuben Sandwiches (page 151) are not only possible, but also delicious and filling! Classics like Chickpea Pot Pie (page 133), Bangers and Mash (page 145), Drunken Vegan Chicken Stew (page 175), and Eggplant Parmesan (page 183) help round out the recipes in this section.

Dessert has always been crucial to me. Not only does it put the finishing touches on a meal, but it is a way to end a memorable dining experience. Desserts are really just science when you break them down, and it's super easy to make them vegan! Vegan butter, like my Whipped Butter (page 229), or margarine work just as their traditional dairy counterpart does. Sugar (make sure it is vegan, as some is processed with bone char), maple syrup, and agave nectar all work well for sweetness, and tofu, baking powder, and baking soda all help make things rise in the oven while baking.

The recipes in the dessert section are not only classics but easy to throw together with basic ingredients. Some of my favourites are the Pineapple Upside Down Cake (page 192), Molten Lava Chocolate Brownie Cake (page 196), New York Style Cheesecake (page 199), and Apple Crisp (page 189); they are the perfect way to end your meal.

What kitchen is complete without a nicely stocked pantry? I have created the recipes in the Pantry Staples and Condiments section so that you can have a wide array of staples to choose from every single day. Recipes like Creamy Mayo (page 232), Cashew Mozzarella (page 218), Sour Cream (page 231), and Cream Cheese (page 222) will hopefully become a regular part of meals for you and your family.

Other recipes like Nacho Cheese Sauce (page 224), Anytime Gravy (page 228), and Blue Cheese (page 220) may have more specific uses, but they can be used in many ways other than simply for nachos, meatloaf, or salads. As an example, the nacho cheese sauce is great on burgers, as a topping on rice bowls, and even for dipping your favourite sandwich. All of the recipes in this section can be made and stored in the fridge for at least one week, and in many cases keep even longer.

One of the things I love most about cooking is that there are never really any set rules. Everything is open to interpretation in one way or another, and things can be adjusted to suit your preferences. Salt can be increased or decreased in most recipes, as can the amount of oil. Personally, I like my food on the saltier side, and the same goes with oil—I generally like to use a little more oil than most. There are exceptions, of course, and you should use your judgment when following or altering recipes.

I use vegan bacon, ham, chicken, and beef throughout the book, and of course suggest using my homemade recipes for each. But even though my homemade recipes are great, you can definitely use any other type of vegan meats in most of the recipes. In a pinch, I like using store-bought seitan bacon; tempeh bacon; seitan chicken, beef, or ham; or any of the multiple types of premade vegan meats that are hitting the market.

In many of my recipes, I reference bacon, sausage, wings, chicken, burgers, and so on. In vegan cuisine, we often refer to meats. To those new to this way of eating, making a *burger* out of lentils or *meatballs* out of walnuts can seem strange at first. These terms are used to help people understand what to expect when eating a dish in terms of flavour and texture. I loved the taste of meat and find pleasure in making vegan versions that taste just as good or better! Veganism is generally an ethical choice not to eat animals. Usually it is not that vegans don't enjoy the taste of meat, but rather that they find the idea of eating animals to be wrong and so abstain from it.

I also use vegan mayonnaise, butter, cream cheese, and sour cream in recipes throughout the book. I have provided easy-to-make recipes for all four of these staples, but feel free to use your favourite store-bought version if you get a last-minute inspiration to make a dish or simply don't have time to make one of the base recipes from scratch. Life is busy, so I get it and sometimes do the same myself!

Throughout the book, I also use tamari but mention soy sauce as an alternative. I highly recommend using tamari if you can. Although it's a bit more expensive, a little goes a long way and it is packed with flavour. Tamari provides a depth of flavour (or umami) that soy sauce does not. In some of my recipes, I have recommended using *only* tamari, and I suggest you stick with that if you can—it really makes a difference. However, in most recipes I give you the option of using tamari or soy sauce. Of course, in a pinch soy sauce will work in all of the recipes if you do not have tamari on hand.

Vegan cuisine has come so far over the years. From its roots of brown rice, sprouts, and tofu, the way in which vegan cuisine is viewed has changed dramatically. In the last couple of decades restaurants and chefs all over the world have been creatively defining a genre and style of cuisine that is new and fresh. These trends have inspired so many to follow suit at home. Long gone are the crunchy-granola juice bars and wheatgrass shots. Things that have never been done before are being showcased in luxury and style, and the world is paying attention. It is truly an exciting time to be living and working in this world of growth and change. Cooking is an art, and you really need to take your time when making a dish. Good food happens only when you give it the love, patience, and time it requires.

Cooking Tips

1. Don't crowd your pan when cooking. When you crowd a hot pan with food, you steam your food instead of layering each ingredient and creating caramelization and depth of flavour. It's a common mistake to crowd the pan and cook over high heat, but then you are left with a soggy mess that tastes *just* okay. It's not only okay to change the temperature of a pan and adjust as needed, but also recommended! Pay attention to the level of heat used for the best outcome.

2. Always try to use the best ingredients you can find. Although this may seem simple, people often buy the cheapest ingredients for everything. Of course, cost is a factor for most items, but keep in mind that if you start with a poor-quality ingredient, chances are you will have a poor-quality result. Think about cooking like anything else in life. The more you put into it, the more you get out of it. I recommend using high-quality tofu, beans, spices and herbs, cooking oils, and more.

3. Cooking times are only guidelines and should not be followed to a T. In the recipes, I have provided a visual or physical description of what to look for, and I recommend using these visuals as a guide. No two ovens, stoves, pots, pans, baking sheets, or appliances are the same. Use your judgment; if something needs more time, let it have more time. If something needs a little more salt, add a bit more salt.

4. My portions are not small. In assigning portion sizes, I have assumed that you are a good eater. With nearly every recipe, except for the baked goods, expect a nice plate of food for each suggested serving.

5. Feel free to add your own flair to my recipes. If there is something you do not like—chipotle pepper, for example—try omitting it or substituting smoked paprika or sweet paprika. Cooking is an art form and should be treated as such.

6. Confidence is key when cooking. The kitchen can be an intimidating place, but it can also be a place of great success and achievement. This can happen only when you are confident and able to overcome your fears. As I always say, just go for it and make it happen!

7. Just as confidence is crucial in any kitchen, so is making mistakes! I can assure you that no great chef or home cook has ever become great without making mistakes. It is okay to screw up a recipe and try again—that is how we get better.

8. In the last fifteen years, high-powered blenders have become much more popular, and rightfully so. Even though they are considered expensive, I highly recommend getting one for your kitchen. They make every item silky smooth and can do what other pieces of equipment cannot.

9. Soft herbs like dill weed or fresh basil should never be chopped too much. They oxidize and turn brown very easily, which makes them lose their flavour. When chopping, try not to bang the blade of the knife on the herbs; instead, rock it back and forth until the herb is cut small enough.

10. In professional kitchens we use the French expression *mise en place*, which means everything in its place. In English it refers to having everything ready before you start to cook. I cannot stress enough how important this is to not only save time, but also ensure that recipes come out as they should, and that you are not stressed while making them. Having all of your ingredients pre-cut, pre-measured, and ready to go will not only set you up for success, but also help you embrace your time in the kitchen!

Deep-Frying 101

Deep-frying food is an art and can yield some really amazing results when done properly! Although using either a commercial or a countertop deep fryer will almost always yield the best results, I completely understand that not everyone has access to one. Having said that, these days you can pick up some rather inexpensive countertop deep fryers from kitchen supply stores or online.

Here are some advice and techniques that can help you be successful when deep-frying.

1. I recommend using either a heavy-bottomed pot or a Dutch oven to fry in. Ideally you want whatever you use to hold at least 16 cups (4 quarts/4 L) to allow enough room for the food to be fully submerged in the oil.

2. While deep fryers have a maximum fill line, pots do not. A general rule is to never fill a pot more than halfway with oil. This allows enough room for the oil to bubble and expand when you put in the food. For example, if the pot holds 16 cups (4 quarts/4 L), only put in 8 cups (2 quarts/2 L) of oil.

3. Do not overcrowd the deep fryer or pot. This is a common mistake that many make. When you add too much food to hot oil, the temperature of the oil drops and the food absorbs too much oil. This makes the food soggy and unappetizing. When in doubt, fry your food in smaller batches to prevent the temperature from dropping too much.

4. If you do end up using a smaller pot, put in less oil and still fill it only halfway. Fry your food in smaller batches so that it remains crispy and cooks properly.

5. If you are deep-frying in a pot, I recommend investing in a candy thermometer. You can clip it to the side of the pot, and it will help you gauge the correct temperatures when frying. If you are using a countertop fryer, it should have a thermometer built in.

6. Season your food right when it comes out of the hot oil! I can't stress this enough. If you wait to add salt or any other seasoning until after the food has cooled down, it will not stick to it.

7. Use metal tongs if frying in a pot. They are the best utensil to use for flipping and removing food. You can also use a slotted spoon, but you will not have as much control with a spoon as you would with a set of metal tongs.

8. Hot oil can lead to grease fires, so it is best to ready. Make sure to have a mini fire extinguisher or baking soda on hand in case of an emergency. Baking soda can stop a small grease fire by smothering the flames. Never put water on a grease fire, as it will only spread the flames and make the fire worse.

Stocking a Vegan Pantry

Herbs and Spices

Allspice

Black peppercorns

Caraway seeds

Cardamom, whole and ground

Cayenne pepper

Chilies, dried

Chili powder

Chinese five-spice powder

Chipotle powder

Cinnamon, sticks and ground

Cloves, ground

Coriander seed, whole and ground

Cumin, whole and ground

Curry powder

Fennel seed, whole and ground

Fenugreek seeds

Garlic powder

Ginger, ground

Hot pepper flakes

Nutmeg, whole and ground

Onion powder

Paprika, sweet, hot, and smoked

Turmeric, ground

Oils, Vinegars, and Seasonings

EXTRA-VIRGIN OLIVE OIL Extra-virgin olive oil is the oil that comes from the first pressing of the olives. Generally, this is the oil you want to use for salads and in creating recipes where low heat is used to cook the food. A good example of this would be when making a simple tomato sauce or lightly cooking some asparagus.

OLIVE OIL After extra-virgin olive oil has been made, olives continue to be pressed and their oils are extracted. This oil is better for cooking.

VEGETABLE OIL Vegetable oils are fats that are extracted from seeds, legumes, or some vegetables. They usually have a higher smoke point and are better for cooking over high heat.

BALSAMIC VINEGAR Balsamic vinegar is vinegar made from crushed grape skins, seeds, and stems. It is dark, rich, and great for dressings and marinades.

RED WINE VINEGAR Red wine vinegar is vinegar made from red wine. It is great for sauces, dressings, and marinades.

TOASTED SESAME OIL Toasted sesame oil is the oil made from roasted sesame seeds. It has a unique, nutty flavour and is commonly used in Asian cuisine.

UNPASTEURIZED APPLE CIDER VINEGAR Unpasteurized apple cider vinegar is a vinegar made from fermented apple juice. It is great for marinades, sauces, and dressings. I prefer to use unpasteurized apple cider vinegar rather than pasteurized apple cider vinegar in most of my recipes. The living bacteria in it provide a better taste and overall better end product. It can be found in most grocery stores, health food and natural food stores, and online.

WHITE WINE VINEGAR White wine vinegar is vinegar made from white wine. It is great for sauces, dressings, and marinades.

DIJON MUSTARD Dijon mustard is a paste made from ground mustard seeds, vinegar, and sometimes wine. It is creamy in texture and great to use in dressings, sauces, and marinades. I use it in many recipes to create a creamy texture without having to add large amounts of fat. It is also a great emulsifier and helps to hold together recipes in which a fat and a liquid bind together.

DRY YELLOW MUSTARD POWDER Dry mustard powder is ground mustard seed and can be added to sauces, gravies, and marinades for a nice bite or tang.

HOT SAUCE Hot sauce can be a wonderful addition to many recipes. I like to use one that is spicy but also flavourful. Some of my favourites are made from chili peppers like habanero and jalapeño, and not only cayenne pepper.

MISO Miso is a Japanese condiment made from fermenting soybeans. It can also be made using rice, chickpeas, barley, and sometimes other grains. Miso is salty and provides a rich, deep, earthy flavour. Miso comes in forms that are light, and these are typically referred to as shiro miso. The medium style of miso is a little darker and higher in salt and is referred to as shinshu miso. Dark miso is commonly referred to as aka miso. Typically, the darker the miso, the deeper and richer the flavour. Generally, I like to use light miso to make vegan cheeses or light cream sauces. Dark miso is great for gravies, soups, and marinades.

PURE VANILLA EXTRACT Pure vanilla extract is made from the seeds in a pod of vanilla. Generally, it is made by extracting the flavour using alcohol.

SEA SALT Sea salt is salt that has been produced through evaporation of ocean or saltwater lakes, usually with little processing or anything added. I prefer to use sea salt because of its texture and ability to dissolve easily. Unless otherwise stated, I use fine sea salt in my recipes.

VEGAN WORCESTERSHIRE SAUCE Most Worcestershire sauces contain fish in the form of anchovy. Vegan Worcestershire sauces are available at specialty stores or online. Some lower quality Worcestershire sauces are vegan by nature, so make sure to read the label before using.

Sweeteners

AGAVE NECTAR Agave nectar is the syrup produced from an agave cactus. It has a rich, viscous texture and is much sweeter than sugar. Be sure to start with a little when using and add more as needed.

BROWN SUGAR Brown sugar is sugar that has been either not refined or partially refined and contains molasses. It is great in baking, desserts, sauces, marinades, and more.

COCONUT SUGAR Coconut sugar is sugar that has been made by processing the sap from a coconut palm. It is great in baking, desserts, sauces, marinades, and more.

MAPLE SYRUP Maple syrup is syrup that is made from the sap of a maple tree. It has a thinner body than agave, so the two cannot be interchanged in recipes. It is great in dressings, sauces, marinades, and more.

MOLASSES (FANCY AND BLACKSTRAP) Molasses is made by refining sugar cane or beet molasses. It is a thick, viscous sap that can be used in baking, dressings, marinades, sauces, and more. Fancy molasses is more commonly used in baked recipes like cookies and cakes, because it is sweeter and lighter in flavour and texture. It is made from condensed juices directly from sugar cane, so it is also used sometimes as a topping on pancakes or waffles. Blackstrap molasses is usually made after the third boiling of the sugar cane juice and is much thicker and less sweet than fancy molasses. It is considered a good source of iron and high in other trace minerals. It is mildly bitter and should not be used as a substitute in recipes that call for fancy molasses. Blackstrap molasses can be used in some baking recipes that call for a dark flavour, such as gingerbread cookies, pumpkin pie, raisin cookies, and tarts. And blackstrap molasses is also used in some soups and stews in some cultures.

WHITE SUGAR White sugar is commonly referred to as sugar. It is refined, generally from sugar cane or beets. It has had all molasses and other impurities removed. It is great in baking, desserts, sauces, marinades, and more.

Specialty Items

AGAR Agar is used in vegan cooking as a form of gelatin and generally comes in powder or flakes. The powder form dissolves very easily when cooked and is great to set almost anything up. Agar is natural and comes from seaweed. If you are using flakes, the ratio is 1 tablespoon (15 mL) of flakes to 1 teaspoon (5 mL) of powder. If using flakes, soak them in about four times the amount of very hot water before adding to your recipe, as this will help them dissolve more easily.

BLACK SALT Black salt (also referred to as Kala Namak) is salt that comes from volcanic ash. It contains sulphur, which gives it a flavour similar to eggs. It is great to use in vegan recipes that are mimicking eggs. It can be found in most well-stocked grocery stores, health food and natural food stores, or Indian specialty stores.

CITRIC ACID Citric acid is a weak acid that is most commonly produced from citrus fruit such as lemons and limes. It has a strong tart flavour and is a great addition in making vegan cheeses and other sauces. Make sure to look for food grade citric acid when purchasing.

LIQUID SMOKE Liquid smoke is the flavour of smoke that has been distilled and condensed into a seasoning. It is available in most grocery stores, in health food and natural food stores, or online, where it usually can be purchased in a small bottle. A little goes a long way, so make sure not to add too much to a recipe or it can overpower the flavour.

NUTRITIONAL YEAST Nutritional yeast is inactive yeast that is grown on beet molasses. It is pasteurized, rendering it not living and thus making it different from traditional bread yeast. It is generally fortified with vitamins and minerals and is typically valued for its high levels of vitamin B_{12}. It is used to make vegan cheeses, sauces, dips, spreads, and more.

VEGAN BUTTER AND MARGARINE Vegan butter is now widely available in most grocery stores. It is generally made using oils such as canola, soy, and coconut and is available in the refrigerated section. It can be used for baking, sauces, gravies, and more.

VEGAN CHEESE While I always recommend making your own cheese from scratch, I realize that in today's world we aren't always able to make the time for such things. Some of my favourite vegan cheeses that melt well in recipes like poutine, pizza, or lasagna—where melted cheese is needed—include Daiya cheese shreds, Follow Your Heart cheese shreds, Emborg cheese shreds, and Miyoko's Kitchen fresh mozzarella.

VEGAN CREAM CHEESE Vegan cream cheese is now widely available in most grocery stores. It is generally made using soy-based ingredients to create the creamy texture.

VEGAN LACTIC ACID Lactic acid typically comes from animal products but can also be made from cornstarch, potatoes, or molasses, and it is becoming easier to find. Vegan lactic acid is available in specialty grocery stores or online and comes in a powder form. It is used to give a sour flavour to foods such as sourdough bread, kimchi, or cheeses.

VEGAN MAYONNAISE Vegan mayonnaise is now widely available in most grocery stores. Vegan mayonnaise is made without the use of eggs. Other ingredients such as soy are generally used to create the product.

VEGAN SOUR CREAM Vegan sour cream is now widely available in most grocery stores. It is generally made using soy-based ingredients to create the creamy texture.

VITAL WHEAT GLUTEN FLOUR Vital wheat gluten flour is the protein found in wheat. Wheat berries are stripped of most of their starch, and what remains is the protein gluten. It is often used in commercial bread baking to improve the texture by making it more tender and adding some more elasticity. Vital wheat gluten flour is also used to make a vegan meat substitute called seitan. It can be found in health food stores and in most large grocery stores.

Soy Products

SOY LECITHIN Soy lecithin helps bind together the fats, proteins, and liquids in recipes to help create an emulsification and is commonly referred to as an emulsifier. Lecithin is used in commercial salad dressings, mayonnaises, and other sauces so that these products do not appear to be split or broken in the container.

SOY SAUCE Soy sauce is a Chinese-based sauce made from fermented soybeans. Typically, wheat (or other grains) is added, as is a higher concentration of salt.

TAMARI Tamari is a Japanese-based sauce made from fermented soybeans that is also gluten-free. Traditionally, tamari is a byproduct of making miso. Tamari has a bolder, more robust flavour than soy sauce, as it is generally made only from soybeans, water, and salt. Soy sauce generally contains a grain such as wheat. I prefer to use tamari in my recipes, especially when used as an ingredient in sauces, dressings, dips, and marinades. Soy sauce will work as a substitute for tamari, but the flavour will not be as rich and pronounced.

TEMPEH Tempeh is made from whole soybeans and is sold in the fridge or freezer section of your local grocery store or health food store. It is made by steaming whole soybeans and then cutting them into small pieces. The pieces are formed into a block and a fungus is added, and then it ferments. Tempeh is a great meat substitute, as it is high in protein. I prefer unpasteurized tempeh for its meaty, firm texture.

TOFU Tofu is a high-protein ingredient made from soybeans. Tofu is coagulated soy milk in the same way that cheese is coagulated dairy milk. It is generally made by making milk from the soybean and setting it with an acid such as calcium chloride or nigari. Tofu comes in four textures: soft, medium, firm, and extra firm. Soft tofu is best for dips and spreads or can be roasted in the oven until crisp. Medium-firm tofu can be used for stir-fries and other dishes but be sure to drain the water out of it before cooking to prevent oil splattering. Firm and extra-firm tofu are great for stir-fries, for roasting, and in dishes like casseroles, soups, and stews where meat would normally be used. They can also be used to make vegan cheeses. Generally, three types of tofu are available to purchase:

Vacuum-packed tofu Vacuum-packed tofu is packaged in vacuum-packed plastic, not in water. It is generally higher in protein and better to use for stir-fries, roasting, searing, and sautéing.

Water-packed tofu Water-packed tofu comes packed in water. It is generally lower in protein and good for roasting, pan-frying, scrambled tofu, dips, and spreads.

Silken tofu Silken tofu is sold in an aseptic box and is shelf stable, meaning it does not require refrigeration. It is good for dips, spreads, purées, and sauces but generally not good for stir-fries or pan-frying.

TVP (TEXTURED OR TEXTURIZED VEGETABLE PROTEIN) TVP is a high-protein soy product made from defatted soybeans. It is a great meat substitute for dishes that call for ground meat. It comes in various sizes and shapes—from small flakes to large chunks—and is usually sold dry and needs to be reconstituted in water before using.

Coconut Products

Coconut oil can be purchased in two different forms. One is deodorized coconut oil, commonly referred to as refined; the other is virgin coconut oil.

CANNED COCONUT MILK Canned coconut milk is made from the meat from mature coconuts. The meat is blended with water, heated, and strained. I prefer to use full-fat coconut milk when possible to give better mouthfeel and flavour.

CANNED COCONUT CREAM Coconut cream is made from the meat from mature coconuts. The meat is blended with water, heated, and strained. It is higher in fat and creamier than coconut milk, as it contains less water.

DEODORIZED (REFINED) COCONUT OIL Deodorized coconut oil, also called refined coconut oil, is coconut oil that has had the flavour of coconut removed. It works well in vegan recipes like mac and cheese or creamy sauces that would typically call for butter or other higher fat products.

SHREDDED COCONUT Shredded coconut is made from the meat from mature coconuts. It can be purchased sweetened or unsweetened. It is most commonly used in baking or desserts but can be used in savoury applications as well.

SLICED COCONUT Sliced coconut is made from the meat from mature coconuts. It can be purchased sweetened or unsweetened. It is most commonly used to make bacon in vegan cuisine, referred to as coconut bacon.

VIRGIN COCONUT OIL Virgin coconut oil is made from the first pressing from mature coconut meat. It has a coconut flavour, so be cautious when using it if you do not want your food to taste like coconut. Because it is high in saturated fat, it firms up when cold and can be used in various applications in vegan cuisine, especially desserts.

Flours, Starches, and Other Baking Ingredients

ALL-PURPOSE FLOUR All-purpose flour is made from grinding high-protein hard wheat and low-gluten soft wheat into a powder. It is most commonly used for breading, baking, and thickening.

ARROWROOT FLOUR OR STARCH Arrowroot flour is a finely ground white flour derived from various types of tropical South American plants. It is a common ingredient used in gluten-free baking to help bind and hold together other gluten-free flours.

BROWN RICE FLOUR This common ingredient is made from finely ground brown rice and is great in baking and for breading.

CAKE FLOUR Cake flour is made from finely grinding soft winter wheat grains into a powder. It is lower in protein than pastry flour, and it is bleached. This makes it ideal to use for making very moist cakes.

PASTRY FLOUR Pastry flour is made from grinding soft winter wheat grains into a powder. It is lower in protein and good for use in cookies, pie crusts, and biscuits.

TAPIOCA FLOUR OR STARCH Tapioca is commonly used in gluten-free flour blends, baked goods, cakes, and pastries. It provides a chewy texture in baked goods and a nice crispness in pastries. It can also replace cornstarch in equal parts.

WHOLE WHEAT FLOUR Whole wheat flour is made from grinding whole wheat grains into a powder. It provides more fibre and nutrients than all-purpose flour but can be used in place of all-purpose flour. Whole wheat flour makes heavier bread and baked goods.

BAKING POWDER Baking powder is a fine powder made from baking soda, cream of tartar, and a moisture-absorbing agent. It is most commonly used in baked recipes to help leaven where yeast is not used. It works by releasing carbon dioxide into a recipe, which helps create air pockets and leaven the final product. Baking powder is similar to baking soda except that it has an acid component, so it begins to work as soon as a liquid is added to it. Recipes that call for single-acting baking powder will need to be made as soon as it is added; those that use double-acting baking powder allow a little more time for the baking powder to work, as it will increase again in volume once heat has been added.

BAKING SODA Baking soda is a common leavening agent used in baked goods, pancakes, and more. It begins to release carbon dioxide as soon as it comes into contact with something acidic (such as vinegar or lemon juice) and a form of liquid. This reaction creates air pockets and leavens the final product. Recipes that call for baking soda must be made as soon as it is added or they can fall flat.

CHOCOLATE CHIPS Look for vegan chocolate chips that have no milk added. They come in various sizes, so choose what suits your recipe best.

COCOA POWDER Cocoa powder is a dark, deeply rich powder that has been made by milling whole raw cacao beans. It has been defatted of much of the cacao butter (the fat found in chocolate), making it powderlike in consistency. It is great to use in baking and in desserts for a chocolate flavour.

XANTHAN GUM Xanthan gum is a finely ground white powder made by fermenting the sugars most commonly found in corn. It is used as a thickener and binder in baking, as well as a stabilizer in other recipes. A little goes a long way, so make sure to follow recipes and add only what you need. Typically, ⅛ teaspoon (0.5 mL) or even a pinch of xanthan gum is enough.

Grains and Pseudograins

BROWN RICE Brown rice is a whole grain that has had the outer shell removed. It comes in short-grain and long-grain forms. Only the husk has been removed in brown rice, meaning that it retains much of its nutrition.

JASMINE RICE Jasmine rice is a whole grain that can come in either white or brown forms. The refining process is the same as for regular white or brown rice. It is most commonly used in Indian cuisine.

MILLET Millets are small, yellow, naturally gluten-free grains that resemble cornmeal. In some markets it can be white, yellow, or red. It is an ancient grain that is great for cereals, soups, and stews or as a replacement for rice in many dishes. When millet is cooked until soft, it can be a great ingredient to bind recipes like veggie burgers and meatballs.

OATS Oats are white and beige in colour. Quick cooking rolled oats are oat groats that have been lightly roasted, steamed, cut in half, and then pressed to make them cook more quickly. Large flake oats have been pressed even flatter to make them cook even more quickly. All types of oats are perfect for cereals, breads, and desserts.

QUINOA Quinoa, a complete protein and naturally gluten-free, comes in three colours (white, red, and black) but is most readily available in white. All three types can be used in soups, stir-fries, stews, and chilies, and virtually anywhere rice is used. White quinoa is softer and fluffier than red and black quinoa when cooked, so it is better for replacing rice in most dishes and in stir-fries. Red and black quinoa have a denser texture and a nutty flavour.

WHITE RICE White rice is a whole grain that has had the husk, bran, and germ removed. It comes in short-grain and long grain forms. After it is hulled, it is generally polished, giving it a white, shiny look.

Corn Products

CORNMEAL Cornmeal is made from ground and dried pieces of corn. Cornmeal most commonly comes in three different sizes: fine, medium, and coarse. I like to use all three sizes in my recipes to attain different textures for a crispy gluten-free breading. Stone-ground cornmeal refers to cornmeal that has been milled without the use of heat, retaining the authentic corn flavour.

CORNSTARCH Cornstarch is a finely ground starch derived from corn. It is often whisked with cold water to help thicken and bind sauces. The mixture of cornstarch and water is commonly referred to as a slurry.

CORN TORTILLAS Most commonly, corn tortillas are available as 6-inch (15 cm) rounds but can come in other sizes as well. I like to use them for wraps or to toast them and then use them with my favourite dip or spread.

Tomato Products

Canned tomatoes, whole or diced
Sun-dried tomatoes

Tomato paste

Legumes

Black beans
Chickpeas
Kidney beans
Lentils, green and red

Lupini beans
Mung beans
Navy beans
Pinto beans

Nuts and Seeds

Almonds
Cashews

Flaxseed, whole and ground
Walnuts

Other Tips and Tricks for Pantry Items

GRINDING FLAXSEED To grind flaxseed for most recipes, you will need to pulverize them into a powder. The easiest way to do this is with a dedicated coffee grinder that you use for flaxseed or spices. Since most coffee grinders are small, you will want to use at least 3 tablespoons (45 mL) of whole flaxseed. Grind until powderlike. Always refrigerate or freeze any leftover ground flaxseed to prevent it from becoming rancid.

MAKING A FLAX EGG When you mix 1 tablespoon (15 mL) of ground flaxseed and 3 tablespoons (45 mL) of hot water and allow it to sit for about 10 minutes, this is commonly referred to as a "flax egg." In most recipes, a flax egg has the same binding properties that a traditional egg would provide, but it does not leaven in the same way traditional eggs do.

SOAKING AND PURÉEING CASHEWS For recipes that include puréed cashews, you can use cashew pieces. Since they are blended, it does not matter what the nuts look like; plus, cashew pieces are usually cheaper.

MINCING GARLIC For recipes that call for minced garlic, the garlic should be very fine, pretty much like a paste. One of the best ways to mince garlic is to place whole cloves on a work surface and lightly smash them with the back end of a knife. Roughly chop the smashed garlic, then sprinkle a little bit of sea salt on it and drag the back end of the knife over it, applying firm pressure, until it becomes a paste.

WORKING WITH JALAPEÑO PEPPERS OR OTHER HOT PEPPERS Most of the heat in jalapeños or other hot peppers is in the seeds and ribs. If you like heat, leave the seeds and ribs in the jalapeños. If you like the flavour of jalapeños but not as much heat, remove the seeds and ribs.

MAKING A CORNSTARCH SLURRY A mixture of cornstarch and water is commonly referred to as a slurry and is used to thicken many different types of sauces, especially Asian-style sauces. Always use cold water when making a slurry, and if the cornstarch clumps together, use a whisk to make the slurry smooth before adding it to your sauce.

Essential Equipment

KNIVES A good set of kitchen knives is integral to success in any kitchen. The most useful knives to purchase are a good-quality French knife, also called a chef's knife, and a paring knife. These two knives are the most important ones anyone can have, in my opinion. I recommend investing in good-quality knives once, and then you most likely will never have to again.

POTS AND PANS A good set of pots and pans is important in any kitchen. I like to have at least one nonstick sauté pan, a couple of pots for soup, and some other pans for everyday use.

BAKING DISHES A good set of baking dishes is key not only to roasting and cooking ingredients in savoury applications, but also to baking. I recommend oven-proof glass dishes in various sizes.

BAKING PANS Baking pans are essential in many applications. I recommend having a few different sizes and having at least one with a nonstick surface.

CUTTING BOARD A cutting board made of wood is ideal, as a plastic one will dull the edge of kitchen knives much more quickly. Look for a cutting board that is made of solid wood and at least 2 feet (60 cm) long. This will allow you to prepare your food, leave it in piles on the edges of the cutting board, and seamlessly go back to the work you were doing. Always wash a cutting board with a wire scrub brush to clean the natural grooves created by the wood.

FOOD PROCESSOR A food processor is used to process ingredients, generally ones that contain less liquid, into very small pieces. Although they do not blend ingredients until silky smooth, they can make recipes very smooth. I always recommend a food processor with a 10-cup (2.5 L) bowl and an S-shaped blade, which is the most common attachment. Most food processors also have slicing and shredding attachments.

BLENDER A good blender is necessary to make a silky-smooth purée for soups, sauces, and more. A blender is generally used instead of a food processor when the recipe contains ingredients that have a higher moisture content. In fact, a blender requires a certain amount of liquid in order to blend and make ingredients smooth.

HIGH-SPEED BLENDER The main difference between a regular blender and a high-speed blender is the strength of the machine. A high-speed blender has a motor that can reach as high as 3 horsepower! These blenders make quick and smooth purées from ingredients like cashews, coconuts, seeds, and more. Although they are expensive, I highly recommend purchasing one.

STAND MIXER A stand mixer is a machine used in baking to mix dough or other ingredients. Typically, they come with a paddle attachment and a whisk attachment.

ELECTRIC HAND MIXER An electric hand mixer is used to mix together butter and sugar (commonly called creaming) in baking or to mix other ingredients in smaller amounts than would be required by a stand mixer.

MANDOLINE A mandoline is a tool that has a slicing blade attached to a flat surface that you grip. It allows you to run an item along the blade, slicing it to the same length, width, and size repeatedly.

COLANDER A colander is a bowl that contains many small holes along its underside and is generally used to drain liquid from ingredients, like when draining cooked pasta or washing fruits and vegetables.

MIXING BOWLS A good set of mixing bowls is great to have in any kitchen. These bowls can be used for mixing, cleaning, seasoning, and more. It is important to have various sizes of bowls for different recipes. I prefer bowls made of stainless steel.

MEASURING SPOONS AND CUPS I like to keep a good set of stainless steel measuring spoons and cups on hand at all times. Certain ingredients need to be measured accurately and precisely, and to do this you will need a solid set of spoons ranging from ⅛ teaspoon (0.5 mL) to 1 tablespoon (15 mL) in size. Measuring cups are important as well and can be found in sets ranging from ¼ cup (60 mL) to 1 cup (250 mL).

FINE MESH STRAINER A fine mesh strainer is used to strain out small particles of food. The holes are much smaller than those in a colander and can catch items as small as a grain of rice or even quinoa.

COFFEE GRINDER A coffee grinder is a great little tool that can be used to grind spices freshly for any recipe. They are generally fairly cheap and can be applied to any whole spice. I like to keep one coffee grinder on hand for spices and another for grinding flaxseed.

FINE TOOTH GRATER A fine tooth grater (such as the ones made by Microplane) is a good tool to finely grate items like garlic or ginger and to remove the outer layer of skin from citrus fruit.

METAL TONGS I always recommend a couple of good sets of tongs in any home kitchen. Ideally, you should have a few pairs: a longer pair for using in the oven, a medium pair for the oven and cooking, and a smaller pair for salads.

SPATULAS Having a good set of oven-proof spatulas helps with mixing ingredients and removing ingredients from a mixing bowl.

Appetizers

Crispy Mushroom Calamari

This one is for vegans, or anyone, who love the taste and texture of seafood. Marinating the mushrooms in fresh dill and lemon juice gives them that fresh ocean flavour, but make sure to slice the mushrooms properly or they may fall apart when you fry them. Keep up the tradition by dipping them in my tangy Tartar Sauce (page 225).

SERVES 4

Prep ahead
Tartar Sauce (page 225)

Mushroom Calamari
6 large king oyster mushrooms

2 cups (500 mL) water

½ cup (125 mL) roughly chopped fresh dill

¼ cup (60 mL) freshly squeezed lemon juice

1 tablespoon (15 mL) Dijon mustard

1 tablespoon (15 mL) tamari or soy sauce

1 teaspoon (5 mL) sea salt

4 cloves garlic, lightly crushed

Breading
1 cup (250 mL) brown rice flour

1 cup (250 mL) medium or coarse grind cornmeal (see Tip)

1 tablespoon (15 mL) garlic powder

½ teaspoon (2 mL) sea salt

2 cups (500 mL) ice-cold water (see Tip)

—

4 to 6 cups (1 to 1.5 L) vegetable oil, for frying

1 batch Tartar Sauce, for serving

1. **PREPARE THE MUSHROOM CALAMARI** Place the mushrooms on a work surface. Using a knife, remove about ½ inch (1 cm) of the bottom of each stem and discard. This part of the stem is very tough and not edible. Remove the caps and save to use in another recipe.

2. Using a knife, cut the remaining stems into ½-inch (1 cm) thick rounds. You should get about 4 to 5 rounds per stem.

3. Using an apple corer or the tip of a pastry bag, cut little holes in the middle of the mushroom rounds, remove the centres, and discard. Transfer the mushroom rounds to a medium bowl.

4. In a separate medium bowl, mix together the water, dill, lemon juice, mustard, tamari, salt, and garlic. Pour over the mushrooms and marinate for at least 30 minutes or overnight, covered, in the fridge. You can use this marinade one more time before discarding it.

5. **MAKE THE BREADING** In a medium bowl, whisk together the brown rice flour, cornmeal, garlic powder, and salt. Add the water and mix until well combined. Use the batter immediately if possible; if it sits, it will thicken. If the batter is too thick, add more water, 1 tablespoon (15 mL) at a time, to make it a little looser. The batter should have the same texture as a thick pancake batter.

6. Heat the vegetable oil in a large pot or small deep fryer to a temperature of 375°F (190°C).

7. **COOK THE CALAMARI** Remove the mushrooms from the marinade and shake off any excess, then pat dry with a kitchen towel or paper towel. Dip the mushrooms into the breading and mix until evenly coated. Dip in the hot oil and fry until golden brown and crisp, using metal tongs to turn the mushrooms as necessary, 4 to 5 minutes total. Remove the calamari from the oil using metal tongs. Serve immediately with tartar sauce for dipping.

TIP

1. Use medium or coarse grind cornmeal. The coarse grind gives a better texture on the outside of the calamari. Fine grind cornmeal will work, but it will not be as crunchy. **2.** Using ice-cold water will help make the mushrooms very crispy when frying them.

Boneless Wings

I love to fry these bad boys until they are crispy on the outside and tender in the middle. Vital wheat gluten flour and a broth with nutritional yeast give each *meaty* piece the chew and flavour of chicken. When nice and crispy, toss them in my signature Buffalo Sauce (page 227), Honey Garlic Sauce (page 227), or your favourite barbecue sauce and serve them with some fresh carrot and celery sticks with homemade Ranch Dressing (page 233). After all, wings really are for flying and not frying!

SERVES 2

Seitan (Wings) Dough

1 cup (250 mL) vital wheat gluten flour

3 tablespoons (45 mL) nutritional yeast, divided

1¼ teaspoons (6 mL) garlic powder, divided

½ teaspoon (2 mL) sea salt, divided

¾ cup (175 mL) + 2 tablespoons (30 mL) water

1 tablespoon (15 mL) vegetable oil

1½ teaspoons (7 mL) Dijon mustard

Broth

8 cups (2 L) water

¼ cup (60 mL) nutritional yeast

2 cloves garlic

1 teaspoon (5 mL) sea salt

3 to 4 sprigs fresh thyme

Breading

1 cup (250 mL) all-purpose flour

½ cup (125 mL) cornstarch

2 teaspoons (10 mL) sweet paprika

1 teaspoon (5 mL) garlic powder

¼ teaspoon (1 mL) sea salt

———

8 to 10 cups (2 to 2.5 L) vegetable oil, for frying

1. **MAKE THE SEITAN DOUGH** In a medium bowl, whisk together the wheat gluten flour, 2 tablespoons (30 mL) of the nutritional yeast, 1 teaspoon (5 mL) of the garlic powder, and ¼ teaspoon (1 mL) of the salt.

2. In a blender, combine the water, the remaining 1 tablespoon (15 mL) nutritional yeast, vegetable oil, mustard, the remaining ¼ teaspoon (1 mL) salt, and the remaining ¼ teaspoon (1 mL) garlic powder. Blend on high speed until smooth.

3. Pour the water mixture into the flour mixture and, using your hands, mix until well combined. Remove the dough from the bowl and place on a work surface. Knead only a few times to make it a little firmer and to make sure no dry patches of flour remain. Do not overknead or the dough can become tough. Shape the dough into a round and cut into 2 equal pieces. Place both pieces of dough in a large pot.

4. **COOK THE DOUGH IN THE BROTH** Cover the dough with the water, nutritional yeast, garlic, salt, and thyme. Bring to a boil, uncovered. Reduce the heat to a simmer and cook for 35 to 40 minutes. Remove from the heat and allow the seitan to cool in the broth, about 1 hour. Make sure the seitan is cooked in the middle by cutting off a small piece and feeling the middle. It should not be gummy in texture, but firm and slightly spongy. When the seitan is cool enough to handle, remove from the broth and transfer to a work surface. Discard the broth. Using your hands, tear the cooled seitan into bite-size pieces.

5. Heat the vegetable oil in a large pot or small deep fryer to a temperature of 375°F (190°C).

6. **PREPARE THE BREADING** In a medium bowl, whisk together the flour, cornstarch, paprika, garlic powder, and salt.

7. **FRY THE WINGS** Toss the torn pieces of seitan in the breading until evenly coated. Fry the pieces until crisp and golden, 5 to 6 minutes. Using metal tongs, remove from the pot or fryer and shake off any excess oil. Toss the wings in your favourite sauce.

TIP

Make the wings ahead! Once you have fried the wings, allow them to cool completely. Place them in a single layer on a baking sheet lined with parchment paper, cover tightly with plastic wrap, and store in the freezer for up to 2 months. Bake from frozen on a baking sheet lined with parchment paper at 350°F (180°C) until crisp, about 20 minutes.

French Onion Soup with Melted Mozzarella

When I was young, my dad would take me out for French onion soup at our local diner. So, it had to be one of the first dishes I tried to re-create with an equally delicious vegan version! It's still one of my favourite hearty soups to this day, because I definitely succeeded. Traditionally, French onion soup is made using veal stock, but in my version, tamari is a stellar substitute, giving it the same rich and salty background flavour. The key to this soup is slowly caramelizing the onions over low heat until they are as sweet and golden brown as I am after a couple of weeks in Cuba.

SERVES 4

Prep ahead

Cashew Mozzarella (page 218)

Ingredients

2 tablespoons (30 mL) vegetable oil

12 cups (3 L) thinly sliced white onions

½ teaspoon (2 mL) sea salt

2 tablespoons (30 mL) finely minced garlic (see Tip)

2 tablespoons (30 mL) chopped fresh thyme leaves

½ cup (125 mL) dry white wine, such as Chardonnay

8 cups (2 L) water

½ cup (125 mL) tamari or soy sauce

1 tablespoon (15 mL) unpasteurized apple cider vinegar

4 pieces day-old bread

1 cup (250 mL) Cashew Mozzarella, sliced

1. In a medium pot, heat the vegetable oil over high heat. Add the onions and salt and cook, stirring frequently, until the onions start to brown on all sides, 4 to 5 minutes. Reduce the heat to low and continue cooking, stirring occasionally, until the onions are soft, brown, and caramelized, about 1 hour. Be careful not to cook them over too high heat or they will burn. If the heat is too high, add a splash of water and reduce the heat.

2. Add the garlic and thyme to the caramelized onions and cook, stirring constantly, until the garlic is fragrant, 2 to 3 minutes.

3. Add the white wine and cook, stirring frequently, until most of the liquid has evaporated, 3 to 4 minutes.

4. Add the water and tamari. Bring the soup to a boil, uncovered, then reduce the heat to a simmer. Cook until the liquid has reduced and the soup is rich and flavourful, about 15 minutes. Remove from the heat and stir in the apple cider vinegar. Season with salt to taste.

5. Preheat the broiler to high or the oven to 400°F (200°C).

6. Place 4 bowls on a baking sheet. Divide the soup among the bowls. Top each bowl with enough bread so it mostly covers the soup and then about ¼ cup (60 mL) of sliced cashew mozzarella. Place under the broiler until the cheese is golden brown and bubbling, 3 to 4 minutes. If baking, bake until the cheese is melted and bubbling, 10 to 12 minutes.

TIP

To mince the garlic, place whole cloves on a work surface and lightly smash them with the back end of a knife. Roughly chop the smashed garlic. Sprinkle a little bit of sea salt on the garlic and drag the back end of the knife over it, applying firm pressure, until it becomes a paste. Chop more if you want the paste to be completely smooth.

Cashew Mozzarella Sticks

Like most people, just thinking about battered, deep-fried cheese makes my mouth water. Who doesn't get pleasure from sinking their teeth into something so crispy and golden brown on the outside, creamy and gooey in the middle? Trust me, my Cashew Mozzarella Sticks won't disappoint! The contrasting textures and comforting flavours are undeniably good, and my Cashew Mozzarella (page 218) works perfectly. It melts and stretches in the same way dairy cheese does, except it's easy to make yourself and doesn't require kidnapping any baby cows. These are great to make ahead of time, too. Simply bread them and then store them in the freezer until you're ready to fry them! I love dipping them into my Mac and Cheese Sauce (page 223) or even just my Creamy Mayo (page 232). But, honestly, they don't even need dip—they are that good.

SERVES 4

Prep ahead

Cashew Mozzarella (page 218)

Ingredients

½ batch Cashew Mozzarella

1 cup (250 mL) dark beer such as an IPA or stout (see Tip)

1 cup (250 mL) all-purpose flour

½ cup (125 mL) + 2 tablespoons (30 mL) nutritional yeast, divided

1½ teaspoons (7 mL) garlic powder, divided

1½ teaspoons (7 mL) sea salt, divided

4 cups (1 L) panko crumbs

1 tablespoon (15 mL) sweet paprika

1 teaspoon (5 mL) dried thyme

—

4 to 6 cups (1 to 1.5 L) vegetable oil, for frying

1. Cut the cashew mozzarella into twelve 3-inch (8 cm) × ½-inch (1 cm) sticks. Place on a baking sheet lined with parchment paper and store in the fridge until firm and cold, about 15 minutes.

2. In a medium bowl, combine the beer, flour, ½ cup (125 mL) of the nutritional yeast, ½ teaspoon (2 mL) of the garlic powder, and ½ teaspoon (2 mL) of the salt. Using a whisk, mix until no lumps remain and the mixture is smooth.

3. In another medium bowl, combine the panko, remaining 2 tablespoons (30 mL) nutritional yeast, paprika, remaining 1 teaspoon (5 mL) salt, remaining 1 teaspoon (5 mL) garlic powder, and thyme. Using a whisk, mix until well combined.

4. Using your hands, gently roll the cheese sticks in the beer batter. Then roll them in the seasoned panko until coated on all sides and you can no longer see the cheese. Arrange in a single layer on the baking sheet lined with parchment paper that you used to refrigerate the cheese sticks, and place in the freezer for 1 hour to firm up.

5. Heat the vegetable oil in a large pot or small deep fryer to a temperature of 350°F (180°C).

6. Remove the cheese sticks from the freezer, pat dry with a kitchen towel or paper towel. Dip in the hot oil and fry until golden brown and crisp, using metal tongs to turn the cheese as necessary, 4 to 5 minutes. Remove the cheese sticks from the oil using metal tongs. Serve immediately with your favourite dipping sauce.

TIP

1. If you do not like or consume alcohol, substitute an equal amount of alcohol-free beer for the dark beer. **2.** Not all beer is considered vegan. Some use animal products like isinglass or gelatin in the refining or clarification process. Make sure to look for beers that have no animal products. I like to use the website barnivore.com to double- and triple-check! I like to use the website barnivore.com to double- and triple-check! **3.** Traditional mozzarella sticks are long and cylindrical. Don't worry if you do not cut the sticks to the same size as traditional ones; any shape will do for this recipe.

Cheesy Garlic Bread

Much of my youth was spent going to restaurants with my mom. She was what they call a "foodie." We would eat everywhere from the most unassuming greasy spoons to classy Japanese joints, and every imaginable establishment in between. But no matter where we went, the one dish I could never do without was cheesy garlic bread. This version is made with my protein-filled Cashew Mozzarella (page 218), so it browns and melts like dairy mozzarella cheese. To me, this is nothing less than the epitome of comfort food—and bonus, no cows were harmed in the making!

SERVES 4

Prep ahead
Whipped Butter (page 229)
Cashew Mozzarella (page 218)

Ingredients
¼ cup (60 mL) vegetable oil
1 cup (250 mL) minced garlic (see Tip)
1 cup (250 mL) Whipped Butter, at room temperature
2 teaspoons (10 mL) garlic powder
2 teaspoons (10 mL) lemon zest
1 cup (250 mL) loosely packed finely chopped flat-leaf parsley (see Tip)
1 large crusty baguette
1 cup (250 mL) Cashew Mozzarella

1. In a medium pot, heat the vegetable oil over medium heat. Add the garlic and cook, stirring constantly, until it is fragrant and just starting to brown, 2 to 3 minutes. Remove from the heat and set aside to cool slightly.

2. In a food processor fitted with a metal blade, combine the whipped butter, cooked garlic, garlic powder, and lemon zest. Process until smooth. You will need to stop the machine once and use a rubber spatula to scrape down the sides of the bowl. Transfer the mixture to a medium bowl. Stir in the parsley until well combined.

3. Preheat the broiler to high or the oven to 400°F (200°C).

4. Cut the baguette in half lengthwise. Spread the whipped butter mixture evenly over the surface of the baguette. Top with the cashew mozzarella in a thick, even layer and broil until the cheese is golden brown and bubbling, 3 to 4 minutes. If baking, bake until the cheese is melted and bubbling, 8 to 10 minutes. Serve immediately.

TIP

1. For this recipe, place the peeled garlic cloves in a food processor fitted with a metal blade and process until broken down into small pieces. You will need to stop the machine once or twice and use a rubber spatula to scrape down the sides of the bowl to get uniform pieces of garlic. **2.** Flat-leaf parsley can turn brown if you chop it too much or too hard. To keep the colour and flavour, run a sharp chef's knife through it several times until it is broken down into small pieces.

Cheesy Tex-Mex Quesadillas

For me, the perfect quesadilla is all about how the various textures, flavours, and aromas come together to make one epic dish. A crunchy shell encases soft, gooey cheese and seasoned ground meat that, when combined, makes for a scrumptious, satisfying, yet simple meal. I use firm tofu that's crumbled and spiced Tex-Mex style before being cooked as a kickass ground beef replacement that could fool even the staunchest meat eater!

SERVES 4

Prep ahead

Almond Milk Cheddar Cheese (page 216)

Sour Cream (page 231)

Tex-Mex Tofu Filling

1 pound (450 g) firm vacuum-packed tofu, crumbled

1 tablespoon (15 mL) roughly chopped chipotle peppers in adobo sauce (see Tip)

1 tablespoon (15 mL) tamari or soy sauce

1 tablespoon (15 mL) melted deodorized coconut oil

1 tablespoon (15 mL) chili powder

1 tablespoon (15 mL) garlic powder

1 tablespoon (15 mL) nutritional yeast

¾ teaspoon (4 mL) ground cumin

½ teaspoon (2 mL) sea salt

¼ teaspoon (1 mL) black pepper

Pinch of cinnamon

2 tablespoons (30 mL) vegetable oil

Refried Pinto Beans

2 pounds (900 g) dried pinto beans

8 cups (2 L) water, more as needed

1½ cups (375 mL) roughly chopped white onion

1½ cups (375 mL) roughly chopped tomato

16 cloves garlic

3 tablespoons (45 mL) tamari or soy sauce

1 tablespoon (15 mL) ground cumin

1 tablespoon (15 mL) smoked paprika

1 tablespoon (15 mL) chili powder

2 teaspoons (10 mL) ground coriander

2 teaspoons (10 mL) sea salt

1 teaspoon (5 mL) onion powder

1 teaspoon (5 mL) sugar

1½ teaspoons (7 mL) chipotle powder

½ cup (125 mL) vegetable oil

4 large flour tortillas

1 cup (250 mL) Almond Milk Cheddar Cheese

Vegetable oil, for cooking

For serving

Salsa

Sour Cream

Thinly sliced romaine lettuce

1. **MAKE THE TEX-MEX TOFU FILLING** In a medium bowl, mix together the crumbled tofu, chipotle peppers, tamari, coconut oil, chili powder, garlic powder, nutritional yeast, cumin, salt, black pepper, and cinnamon.

2. In a medium pot, heat the vegetable oil over medium-high heat. Add the crumbled tofu mixture and cook, stirring constantly, until browned and fragrant, about 10 minutes. Remove from the heat and set aside.

3. **MAKE THE REFRIED PINTO BEANS** In a medium pot, combine the pinto beans, water, onion, tomato, garlic, tamari, cumin, paprika, chili powder, coriander, salt, onion powder, sugar, and chipotle powder. Bring to a boil, uncovered. Reduce the heat to a simmer and cook until the beans are soft and most of the liquid has evaporated, about 1 hour. Some dried beans take longer to cook than others and can require more water. While cooking, check to make sure the beans are covered with water and add up to ½ cup (125 mL) more water at a time, as needed.

4. Remove the pot from the heat and in a slow, steady stream add the vegetable oil and blend with an immersion blender until the beans are creamy and smooth. You want them to have a bit of texture, but no large pieces of bean should remain. If you need more water to help make the beans smooth, add 2 tablespoons (30 mL) at a time.

5. **ASSEMBLE THE TORTILLAS** Working with 1 tortilla at a time, along one half of the tortilla layer about ½ cup (125 mL) of the refried pinto beans, ⅓ cup (75 mL) of the Tex-Mex tofu filling, and ¼ cup (60 mL) of the almond milk cheddar cheese. Fold the other half of the tortilla over the filling, and gently press the 2 sides together.

6. Heat a large nonstick skillet or sauté pan over medium heat. Add enough vegetable oil to coat the bottom of the pan. Add a quesadilla and cook until golden brown and crisp, 3 to 4 minutes per side. Repeat to cook the remaining quesadillas. Serve with salsa, sour cream, and lettuce.

TIP

The liquid in a can of chipotle peppers is called adobo sauce. Make sure to add a little bit of the adobo sauce with the chipotle, as it is full of flavour.

Mile-High Loaded Nachos

These loaded nachos are great for every occasion, whether it's watching the big game, munching down on a Saturday night, or indulging a sudden urge to excite your senses. The Nacho Cheese Sauce (page 224) deliciously coats crispy corn tortilla chips, traditionally topped with creamy refried beans and guacamole. Pile 'em high, and dig in to every bite!

SERVES 2 TO 4

Prep ahead

Tex-Mex Tofu Filling
(see page 32)

Refried Pinto Beans (see
page 32)

Nacho Cheese Sauce (page 224)

Sour Cream (page 231)

Ingredients

1 package (12 ounces/300 g)
yellow or blue corn
tortilla chips

1 cup (250 mL) Tex-Mex Tofu
Filling

1 cup (250 mL) Refried Pinto
Beans

½ cup (125 mL) Nacho Cheese
Sauce

1 medium avocado, peeled and
pitted

3 tablespoons (45 mL) freshly
squeezed lime or lemon
juice

2 cloves garlic, minced

¼ teaspoon (1 mL) sea salt

½ cup (125 mL) finely diced
tomatoes

2 cups (500 mL) finely sliced
iceberg lettuce

¼ cup (60 mL) Sour Cream

2 tablespoons (30 mL) thinly
sliced green onion (white
and light green parts only)

Hot sauce (optional)

1. Preheat the oven to 350°F (180°C). Line a baking sheet with parchment paper.

2. Evenly spread the tortilla chips on the prepared baking sheet. Layer the Tex-Mex tofu filling, refried pinto beans, and nacho cheese sauce over the chips. Bake until the cheese is bubbling and golden brown, 10 to 12 minutes.

3. Meanwhile, in a small bowl, mash together the avocado, lime juice, garlic, and salt until no large pieces of avocado remain.

4. Remove the nachos from the oven and top with diced tomatoes, mashed avocado, lettuce, sour cream, green onion, and hot sauce, if using. Serve immediately.

Stuffed to the Rim Skins

Despite their appetizer status, these underestimated potato skins are pretty much a meal in themselves. They're cheesy, salty, smoky, and can never go wrong. If you're into life hacks, make them a couple of days in advance and store them in an airtight container in the fridge. When planning to enjoy, pop them into the oven at 400°F (200°C) and bake until they are crisp and golden, 15 to 20 minutes.

SERVES 2

Prep ahead

Almond Milk Cheddar Cheese (page 216)

Seitan Bacon (page 105)

Sour Cream (page 231)

Ingredients

8 to 10 cups (2 to 2.5 L) vegetable oil, for frying

2 medium russet potatoes, baked and cooled (see Tip)

½ cup (125 mL) Almond Milk Cheddar Cheese

4 to 6 strips Seitan Bacon, cut into small pieces

½ teaspoon (2 mL) sea salt

½ teaspoon (2 mL) garlic powder

¼ teaspoon (1 mL) freshly ground black pepper

¼ teaspoon (1 mL) smoked paprika

2 tablespoons (30 mL) Sour Cream

1 green onion, thinly sliced, for garnish

1. Heat the vegetable oil in a large pot or small deep fryer to a temperature of 400°F (200°C). Line a baking sheet with parchment paper.

2. On a work surface, using a sharp knife, cut each cooled potato in half lengthwise. Using a spoon, scoop out most of the potato flesh into a medium bowl. Set aside.

3. Cook the potato skins in the hot oil until golden brown and very crisp, 5 to 6 minutes. Remove from the oil using metal tongs and transfer to a plate lined with paper towel to help absorb some of the excess oil. Cool completely, about 10 minutes.

4. To the bowl with the potato flesh, add the almond milk cheddar cheese, seitan bacon bits, salt, garlic powder, pepper, and paprika. Using a potato masher, mash until well combined. It is okay to have a few bigger pieces of potato.

5. Preheat the oven to 400°F (200°C).

6. Place the cooked potato skins on the prepared baking sheet. Spoon the potato and cheese mixture into the potato skins and bake until golden brown and crisp, 10 to 12 minutes.

7. Garnish with sour cream and green onions and serve immediately.

TIP

To cook the potatoes, place them on a baking sheet lined with parchment paper and bake in the oven at 350°F (180°C) until soft in the middle, 45 to 60 minutes, depending on the size of the potatoes.

Gooey Cheese Fondue

Perhaps the classiest crowd-pleasing classic that I've veganized is this exquisite gooey cheese fondue. It's perfect for dipping your favourite vegetables, breads, vegan meats, and basically any other edible you could imagine. Make sure you use arborio rice and potatoes, as the starch found in both gives this dish the characteristic texture of traditional gooey cheese fondue. There is something irresistibly fun about dipping and twirling your favourite foods in hot, bubbling lava full of flavour. For a sophisticated experience, serve in a traditional fondue warming dish complete with serving forks.

SERVES 4 TO 6

Ingredients

4 cups (1 L) water

2 cups (500 mL) peeled and chopped white potatoes, such as russet

¾ cup (175 mL) nutritional yeast

⅓ cup (75 mL) + 2 tablespoons (30 mL) dry white wine, such as Chardonnay, divided

1 tablespoon (15 mL) + 1 teaspoon (5 mL) unpasteurized apple cider vinegar, divided

¼ cup (60 mL) chopped white onion

¼ cup (60 mL) arborio rice

¼ cup (60 mL) raw cashews

2 tablespoons (30 mL) dried red lentils

1 tablespoon (15 mL) Dijon mustard

1½ teaspoons (7 mL) sea salt

2 to 3 cloves garlic

¼ teaspoon (1 mL) vegan lactic acid powder (optional; see Tip)

For serving

Toasted bread

Broccoli florets

Snow peas

1. In a medium pot, combine the water, potatoes, nutritional yeast, ⅓ cup (75 mL) of the white wine, 1 tablespoon (15 mL) of the apple cider vinegar, onion, rice, cashews, lentils, mustard, salt, and garlic. Bring the mixture to a boil, then reduce the heat to a simmer and cook, uncovered, stirring occasionally, until the rice is soft, 30 to 40 minutes. Remove from the heat and allow to cool slightly, uncovered, about 10 minutes.

2. Position an oven rack so that the fondue will be close to the broiler but not touching it and preheat the broiler to high heat or the oven to 450°F (230°C).

3. In a high-speed blender, fill the blender jar halfway with the potato mixture. Blend until completely smooth, with no lumps. Add the remaining 2 tablespoons (30 mL) white wine, the remaining 1 teaspoon (5 mL) apple cider vinegar, and lactic acid, if using. Blend until smooth.

4. Divide the fondue mixture evenly among medium oven-proof ramekins or cast-iron skillets. Broil or bake until the tops are golden brown and the mixture is bubbling, 6 to 8 minutes. Serve immediately with toasted bread, broccoli florets, and snow peas for dipping.

TIP

Vegan lactic acid is great for making vegan cheeses and adding to other non-dairy recipes. Most animal-derived bacteria, like the ones found in cheese, give recipes an explosion of flavour in the mouth. Vegan lactic acid does the same thing and makes flavours stand out and pop! Although it is not as easy to find in traditional grocery stores, it is available online and in specialty stores. I highly recommend picking it up and trying it out for yourself.

Fiesta Seven-Layer Dip

Dishes like this are designed to be fun, and finger-licking good. I mean, who doesn't love scooping their food? There's something comforting about crunching into salty chips slathered in a mouth-watering combination of melted cheese, fresh salsa, creamy guacamole, and hearty beans. The different flavours come together, complementing each other like the best friend you never had compliments your questionable new haircut.

SERVES 4 TO 6

Prep ahead

Refried Pinto Beans (see page 32)

Nacho Cheese Sauce (page 224)

Sour Cream (page 231)

Salsa

2 cups (500 mL) diced tomatoes

½ cup (125 mL) finely diced white onion

½ cup (125 mL) loosely packed roughly chopped fresh cilantro leaves

⅓ cup (75 mL) finely diced jalapeño peppers

3 tablespoons (45 mL) freshly squeezed lime juice

2 tablespoons (30 mL) extra-virgin olive oil

½ teaspoon (2 mL) sea salt

Guacamole

2 medium avocados, peeled and pitted

⅓ cup (75 mL) freshly squeezed lemon juice

3 cloves garlic, minced

½ teaspoon (2 mL) sea salt

For assembly

1 batch Refried Pinto Beans

1 cup (250 mL) Sour Cream

2 cups (500 mL) Nacho Cheese Sauce

2 cups (500 mL) thinly sliced romaine lettuce

½ cup (125 mL) thinly sliced green onion (white and light green parts only)

1 package (12 ounces/300 g) yellow or blue corn tortilla chips (or crackers)

1. **MAKE THE SALSA** In a medium bowl, toss together the tomatoes, onion, cilantro, jalapeño, lime juice, olive oil, and salt until well combined.

2. **MAKE THE GUACAMOLE** In a small bowl, combine the avocado, lemon juice, garlic, and salt. Mash together using a fork. You don't want the avocado to be completely smooth, so make sure to leave some chunks.

3. **ASSEMBLE THE DIP** In a large, deep serving bowl, spread the refried pinto beans on the bottom, followed by the guacamole, sour cream, nacho cheese sauce, lettuce, salsa, and green onions. Serve immediately with tortilla chips or crackers.

South of the Border Jalapeño Poppers

I love to spice things up with fresh, bright, bold flavours, and these crispy jalapeño poppers are all that and more. The divine contrast between the crunchy surface and the oozing, gooey cheese filling will send you to heaven with each bite. You might want to make a couple of batches, and you definitely should try them with Ranch Dressing (page 233).

MAKES 8 POPPERS

Prep ahead

Almond Milk Cheese Curds (page 217)

Ranch Dressing (page 233)

Ingredients

8 jalapeño peppers (see Tip)

1 cup (250 mL) Almond Milk Cheese Curds (see Tip)

1 cup (250 mL) unsweetened almond milk

½ cup (125 mL) Dijon mustard

½ teaspoon (2 mL) sea salt, divided

½ cup (125 mL) all-purpose flour

½ cup (125 mL) fine cornmeal

2 tablespoons (30 mL) lemon zest

1 tablespoon (15 mL) garlic powder

1 tablespoon (15 mL) cornstarch

1 teaspoon (5 mL) smoked paprika

8 to 10 cups (2 to 2.5 L) vegetable oil, for frying

½ batch Ranch Dressing, for dipping

1. Using a small knife, cut the tops (stem ends) off the jalapeños and discard. Insert a small spoon into each jalapeño, gently scrape out the seeds and ribs, and discard. Carefully spoon 2 to 3 tablespoons (30 to 45 mL) of almond milk cheese curds into each jalapeño, filling it to the top. Set aside.

2. In a small bowl, whisk together the almond milk, mustard, and ¼ teaspoon (1 mL) of the salt. Set aside.

3. In another small bowl, whisk together the flour, cornmeal, lemon zest, garlic powder, cornstarch, paprika, and the remaining ¼ teaspoon (1 mL) salt.

4. Dip each stuffed jalapeño in the almond milk mixture, shake off excess liquid, then roll it in the flour mixture until completely coated. Transfer the stuffed jalapeños to a baking sheet lined with parchment paper and place in the freezer until firm, at least 2 hours or overnight.

5. Heat the vegetable oil in a large pot or small deep fryer to a temperature of 400°F (200°C).

6. Remove the stuffed jalapeños from the freezer. Dip in the hot oil and fry until golden brown, crisp, and hot in the middle, using metal tongs to turn the jalapeños as necessary, 5 to 6 minutes. Remove the peppers from the oil using the metal tongs. Serve with ranch dressing for dipping.

TIP

1. Substitute your favourite meltable vegan cheese (see page 12) for the almond milk cheese curds. **2.** Most of the heat in jalapeño peppers comes from the membranes and seeds. Make sure you wear gloves when removing these, and don't touch the skin on your face until after you wash your hands thoroughly.

Blooming Onion

Make any day feel more festive by re-creating this fair and festival favourite at home. You'll need to make precise cuts into the onion, so I have created specific instructions below. Learning how to create this unique recipe may take some time at first, but your future self will thank you when you're loving life, ripping this dish apart, and savouring every tasty piece. Smother it in Tartar Sauce (page 225), Ranch Dressing (page 233), or even Nacho Cheese Sauce (page 224) for a real treat.

SERVES 2

Ingredients

2 cups (500 mL) unsweetened almond milk or soy milk

3 tablespoons (45 mL) Dijon mustard

2 teaspoons (10 mL) sea salt, divided

2 cups (500 mL) medium or coarse grind cornmeal (see Tip)

2 cups (500 mL) all-purpose flour (see Tip)

½ tsp (2 mL) smoked paprika

½ tsp (2 mL) garlic powder

¼ tsp (1 mL) cane sugar or coconut sugar

¼ tsp (1 mL) finely ground black pepper

¼ tsp (1 mL) chili powder

¼ tsp (1 mL) onion powder

1 large Vidalia onion (see Tip)

——

8 to 10 cups (2 to 2.5 L) vegetable oil, for frying

1. In a medium bowl, whisk together the almond milk, mustard, and 1 teaspoon (5 mL) of the salt.

2. In a separate medium bowl, whisk together the cornmeal, flour, and remaining 1 teaspoon (5 mL) salt, paprika, garlic powder, sugar, black pepper, chili powder, and onion powder.

3. On a work surface, trim ½ inch (1 cm) from the root end of the onion and peel the outer skin off. Using a sharp knife, make a series of cuts into the onion. You want the cuts to slice almost directly through the onion but not all the way, so that the onion holds together.

4. Place the onion cut side down on a cutting board. Starting ½ inch (1 cm) from the root end, using the tip of a sharp knife, make a downward cut all the way through to the board, taking care not to cut right through the onion. You want the root end to hold the onion together. Repeat to make 4 evenly spaced cuts around the onion, so that you have 4 equal sections. Make 4 more slices in the middle of each section of the onion, until you have 16 evenly spaced cuts. You want the onion to hold together at the root end, but you want the slices to go all the way through.

5. Turn the onion over and, using your fingers, gently separate the outer pieces. At this point the onion should be open and all of the pieces should be exposed; it will look a bit like a flower. Dip the onion in the almond milk mixture, then in the cornmeal mixture. You want to make sure the entire onion is well coated. Any areas that do not have coating will burn.

6. Heat the vegetable oil in a large pot or small deep fryer to a temperature of 375°F (190°C).

7. Gently lay the onion, upside down, in the pot or fryer and fry until golden brown, 3 to 5 minutes. Using metal tongs, flip the onion to cook on the other side, until golden brown and soft in the middle and crispy on the outside, 3 to 5 minutes. Remove from the oil using metal tongs. Serve immediately with your favourite sauce or dressing.

TIP

1. Fine grind cornmeal will not give you a nice crunchy texture for this recipe. Make sure to use medium or coarse grind. **2.** To make this recipe gluten-free, substitute an equal amount of brown rice flour for the all-purpose flour. **3.** Vidalia onion is ideal for this recipe, as it has a higher sugar content than most onions. It will get soft and sweet after you cook it. If you cannot find a Vidalia onion, any standard white or yellow onion will work.

Creamy Tomato Bisque

This bisque perfectly balances a light silky-smooth texture with deeply rich and satisfying flavours. Traditional bisques get their texture from ground seashells and rice, but this hearty dish gets the same signature mouthfeel from blended sweet potato and olive oil, so there's no need for any exoskeletons. The subtle sweetness of the tomatoes is brought out by the tamari and balsamic vinegar. And of course, it couldn't be called classic if it wasn't served with my mouth-watering Stuffed Grilled Cheese Sandwiches (page 149).

SERVES 4 TO 5

Ingredients

3 tablespoons (45 mL) vegetable oil

1 cup (250 mL) thinly sliced white onion

½ cup (125 mL) peeled chopped carrot

½ teaspoon (2 mL) sea salt

12 cloves garlic, minced

3 cups (750 mL) peeled chopped sweet potatoes

1 cup (250 mL) peeled chopped yellow potatoes, such as Yukon Gold

1 cup (250 mL) water

½ cup (125 mL) raw cashews

3 cans (28 ounces/796 mL each) diced tomatoes

3 tablespoons (45 mL) tamari or soy sauce

½ cup (125 mL) balsamic vinegar

¾ cup (175 mL) extra-virgin olive oil

1. In a large pot, heat the vegetable oil over medium heat. Add the onion, carrot, and salt and cook, stirring frequently, until the vegetables are softened, 7 to 8 minutes. Stir in the garlic and cook until fragrant, 2 to 3 minutes. Add the sweet potatoes, yellow potatoes, water, cashews, tomatoes, tamari, and balsamic vinegar, then stir to combine. Bring to a boil, reduce the heat, and simmer, stirring frequently, until the potatoes are fork-tender, about 30 minutes.

2. Remove the soup from the heat. Using an immersion blender, blend the soup, adding the olive oil in a slow, steady stream. Blend until the oil is emulsified and there are no visible oil droplets.

3. Using a high-speed blender, fill the blender jar halfway with the soup. Blend on high speed until smooth and creamy. Transfer the puréed soup to a medium pot. Purée the remaining soup and add it to the pot. Place the pot over medium heat and bring the soup to a simmer. Serve immediately or let cool, transfer to an air-tight container, and store in the fridge for up to 1 week.

Appetizers

Creamiest Cream of Mushroom Soup

Whenever I eat cream of mushroom soup, it's like my taste buds go through a time machine back to those blissful childhood days at the dinner table, happily slurping up a big, warm bowl of Campbell's canned comfort. Now that I'm vegan, mushrooms might as well be their own food group, so the idea of re-creating this iconic recipe had me excited! Portobello mushrooms provide that wholesome, earthy flavour, and I throw in some button mushrooms for good measure.

SERVES 4 TO 5

Ingredients

3 tablespoons (45 mL) vegetable oil

1 cup (250 mL) thinly sliced white onion

¼ teaspoon (1 mL) sea salt

10 cloves garlic, minced

12 cups (3 L) thinly sliced button mushrooms, stems on

4 whole portobello mushrooms, stems on and thinly sliced

¼ cup (60 mL) loosely packed chopped fresh thyme leaves

10 cups (2.5 L) water

½ cup (125 mL) nutritional yeast

⅓ cup (75 mL) tamari or soy sauce

½ cup (125 mL) dried red lentils

1. In a large pot, heat the vegetable oil over medium-high heat. Add the onions and salt and cook, stirring frequently, until the onions are soft and starting to brown, 5 to 6 minutes. Add the garlic and cook, stirring frequently, until fragrant, 2 to 3 minutes. Add the button and portobello mushrooms. Increase the heat to high and cook, stirring occasionally, until the mushrooms are soft and some of the liquid has started to release, 8 to 10 minutes.

2. Add the thyme, water, nutritional yeast, tamari, and lentils. Place a lid on the pot and bring to a boil. Remove the lid, reduce to a simmer, and cook until the lentils are soft, 12 to 15 minutes. Remove from the heat.

3. Using a ladle, transfer the mushroom mixture to a high-speed blender, filling the blender jar a little less than halfway. Blend on medium speed to start. You want to start low so that the steam does not escape and blow the top off the blender. Increase the speed to high and blend until the soup is smooth and creamy. Transfer the blended soup to a medium pot. Blend the remaining mushroom mixture in batches, taking care to fill the blender jar only a little less than halfway each time. Serve immediately or cool and store in an airtight container in the fridge for up to 1 week.

TIP

You can substitute any strong-flavoured mushroom, such as cremini, oyster, or shiitake, for the portobellos. Or even use wild mushrooms like lobster or chanterelle. You want to make sure to use a strong-flavoured mushroom like portobello if you are substituting them so that you do not take away from the flavour of the soup.

VARIATION

If you want an even creamier soup, substitute an equal amount of soaked raw cashews for the red lentils. To soak the cashews, place them in a small bowl and cover with 2 cups (500 mL) hot water for at least 1 hour or overnight, covered and stored in the fridge. Drain and rinse the cashews, discarding the soaking liquid.

Un-Chicken Noodle Soup

One of the best kitchen tricks passed on to me years ago was the brilliant notion of substituting nutritional yeast for that fluorescent yellow chicken stock powder. I remember rushing home to try it out right away and being shocked at how similar the flavour was! My version uses lots of fresh herbs to re-create the same home-style chicken noodle soup taste that's helped us all through stuffy noses and sore tummies for so long. This soup will feed not only your belly and your soul, but your conscience!

SERVES 5 TO 6

Ingredients

2 tablespoons (30 mL) vegetable oil

1 cup (250 mL) diced white onion

1 cup (250 mL) diced celery

1 cup (250 mL) diced peeled carrot

2 cloves garlic, minced

1½ cups (375 mL) nutritional yeast, divided

2 tablespoons (30 mL) chopped fresh thyme leaves, divided

4 quarts (4 L) water

4 ounces (115 g) dried spaghetti

½ cup (125 mL) tightly packed roughly chopped fresh flat-leaf parsley leaves

1. In a large pot, heat the vegetable oil over medium heat. Add the onion, celery, and carrot and cook, stirring frequently, until the vegetables are soft, 4 to 5 minutes.

2. Add the garlic, 1 cup (250 mL) of the nutritional yeast, and 1 tablespoon (15 mL) of the thyme. Cook, stirring constantly, until the garlic is fragrant, 2 to 3 minutes.

3. Add the water and bring to a boil uncovered. Reduce the heat to medium-low and cook, uncovered, for 20 minutes.

4. In a small pot of salted water, cook the spaghetti according to package directions. Drain and rinse in cold water to stop the pasta from cooking further.

5. Remove the soup from the heat and stir in the parsley, the remaining ½ cup (125 mL) nutritional yeast, the remaining 1 tablespoon (15 mL) thyme, and the pasta. Serve immediately or cool and store in an airtight container in the fridge for up to 1 week.

Crispy Corn and Squash Hush Puppies

You'll want to break out the barbecue for a good ole Southern-style cookout when you try one of these hush puppies. Each deep-fried morsel is crispy on the outside and soft in the middle, sending your mouth down South for a few blissful moments. You'll want to chew slowly to savour the experience. I added corn kernels to the batter for some extra texture. Serve these with a side of Sour Cream (page 231), Tartar Sauce (page 225), or Russian Dressing (page 234) for a satisfying snack or side.

MAKES 20 HUSH PUPPIES; SERVES 5 AS AN APPETIZER

Ingredients

3 cups (750 mL) peeled cubed butternut squash

1 cup (250 mL) frozen corn kernels

½ cup (125 mL) cooked white quinoa (see Tip)

3 tablespoons (45 mL) all-purpose flour

2 tablespoons (30 mL) ground golden flaxseed

½ teaspoon (2 mL) garlic powder

½ teaspoon (2 mL) sea salt

¼ teaspoon (1 mL) ground cumin

8 to 10 cups (2 to 2.5 L) vegetable oil, for frying

1. In a medium pot, add the squash, cover with water, and cook over medium-high heat until the squash is fork-tender, 10 to 12 minutes. Drain, discarding the liquid.

2. In a medium bowl, combine the cooked squash, corn kernels, cooked quinoa, flour, flaxseed, garlic powder, salt, and cumin. Using a potato masher or whisk, mash the mixture until well combined. It is okay and desirable to have some larger pieces of squash, but they should not be too big. Allow the mixture to sit for 5 to 10 minutes so that the flaxseed can swell and start to bind.

3. Heat the vegetable oil in a large pot or small deep fryer to a temperature of 375°F (190°C).

4. Using a spoon, drop 20 equal portions of the mixture onto a baking sheet lined with parchment paper. Using your hands, roll and shape them into round balls. Dip the balls in the hot oil and fry until golden brown and crisp, using metal tongs to turn them as necessary, 5 to 6 minutes. Remove the hush puppies from the oil using the metal tongs and place on a plate lined with paper towel to absorb any excess oil. Serve with your favourite dipping sauce.

TIP

To cook the quinoa for this recipe, place ¼ cup (60 mL) dry white quinoa in a pot. Cover with ½ cup (125 mL) water and add a pinch of sea salt. Bring to a boil uncovered. Cook until most of the liquid has evaporated. When most of the liquid has cooked out, place the lid on the pot and remove from the heat. Allow the quinoa to sit for 10 minutes so that the steam can finish the cooking.

51

Caprese Stacks

Italian food is beloved for its simplicity and refreshing ingredients. Sometimes a dish needs only a few vibrant staple ingredients to make something tantalizing to all the senses. This recipe marries the luscious flavours of ripe and juicy tomatoes with soft and decadent cheese, and comes together with a salty olive dressing. This dish is best made using fresh tomatoes picked right off the vine or bought at a local farmers market. When possible, use heirloom tomatoes at the height of the season. If you feel the need for even more creamy deliciousness, pair this dish with my Baked Crab Dip (page 58).

MAKES 4 STACKS

Prep ahead
Almond Milk Cheese Curds
   (page 217)

Ingredients
¼ cup (60 mL) pitted and
   chopped Kalamata olives

¼ cup (60 mL) extra-virgin
   olive oil, more for serving

2 teaspoons (10 mL) balsamic
   vinegar

3 medium tomatoes, each cut
   into four 1½-inch (4 cm)
   thick slices (see Tip)

½ teaspoon (2 mL) sea salt

½ teaspoon (2 mL) freshly
   cracked black pepper

12 slices Almond Milk Cheese
   Curds, each ¼ inch (5 mm)
   thick

1 cup (250 mL) tightly packed
   fresh basil leaves

1. In a small bowl, whisk together the olives, olive oil, and balsamic vinegar.
2. Lay the tomato slices on a work surface. Sprinkle lightly with the salt and pepper. Top each tomato slice with a slice of the almond milk cheese curds, then 1 or 2 fresh basil leaves, depending on size.
3. Assemble a caprese stack by layering 3 loaded tomato slices on top of one another. Repeat to create the remaining 3 stacks. Place the stacks on a serving platter or individual plates and drizzle with the olive oil dressing. Serve immediately.

TIP

1. Tomatoes vary in size, so it may be necessary to adjust the number of tomatoes. If using large heirloom tomatoes, you might need only 2. If using smaller tomatoes, you might need as many as 6. **2.** Fresh basil leaves vary in size, so use your judgment when making this dish. You want to make sure that with every bite of this salad, you get a little bit of fresh basil.

Killer Crispy Latkes with Sour Cream and Chives

Everyone loves potatoes, and everyone loves pancakes, so these "potato pancakes" are perhaps one of life's true joys! Potato pancakes are so diversely delicious that many cultures have their own savoury or sweet versions, from these Jewish holiday staples called latkes, to a Korean version called *gamja-jeon*, to the traditional Irish boxty. The trick to making the perfect latke is removing as much of the starch as possible and making the potato as dry as possible before cooking. Serve them hot with my Sour Cream (page 231) and feel free to get creative with toppings, though I suggest a classic sprinkling of chives.

MAKES 24 LATKES

Prep ahead
Sour Cream (page 231)

Ingredients
2½ pounds (1.125 kg) russet potatoes, skin on

2 tablespoons (30 mL) ground golden flaxseed

6 tablespoons (90 mL) hot water (see Tip)

2 tablespoons (30 mL) vegetable oil

½ cup (125 mL) finely diced white onion

2 teaspoons (10 mL) chopped fresh thyme leaves

½ cup (125 mL) all-purpose flour (see Tip)

1 tablespoon (15 mL) sea salt

———
Vegetable oil, for frying

Garnish
¼ cup (60 mL) chopped fresh chives

½ cup (125 mL) Sour Cream

1. Using a food processor fitted with the shredding attachment or a box grater, grate the potatoes. If using a food processor, cut the potatoes first to fit through the feed tube.

2. Fill a deep large bowl with cold water. Add the grated potatoes to the water. This will help remove starch from the potatoes.

3. In a small bowl, whisk together the flaxseed and hot water until well combined. Set aside to soak for 10 minutes so that the flaxseed can swell and absorb the liquid.

4. In a medium frying pan, heat the vegetable oil over medium-high heat. Add the onion and sauté, stirring frequently, until soft and translucent, 5 to 6 minutes. Add the thyme and cook, stirring frequently, 1 to 2 minutes. Set aside to cool.

5. Using your hands, squeeze the water from the potatoes until they are completely dry. You want to remove as much water as you can so that your cooked latkes will be nice and crispy. Place the potatoes in a medium bowl. Add the flaxseed mixture, flour, sautéed onions, and salt. Mix until well combined.

6. Preheat the oven to 400°F (200°C). Line a baking sheet with parchment paper (you may need 2 prepared baking sheets).

7. Using a ¼-cup (60 mL) measuring cup, divide the mixture into 24 equal portions. Using your hands, shape each latke so it is roughly 3 inches (8 cm) in diameter. In a large frying pan, add enough vegetable oil so that the bottom is covered and the oil comes about ¼ inch (5 mm) up the sides of the pan. Heat the oil over medium-high heat. Taking care not to crowd the pan, fry the latkes in batches until golden brown, 4 to 5 minutes per side. Add more oil between batches as necessary. Remove the latkes from the pan and place them on the prepared baking sheet. Bake until cooked in the middle, 4 to 5 minutes.

8. Serve garnished with chopped chives and sour cream.

Continued

TIP

1. Use hot water when making a flax egg, as it is best to help speed up the process of gelling the flax. **2.** Store the latkes in an airtight container for up to 2 days in the fridge. To reheat them, remove them from the fridge and reheat in the oven at 400°F (200°C) on a baking sheet lined with parchment paper for 8 to 10 minutes. **3.** Substitute an equal amount of brown rice flour for the all-purpose flour for a gluten-free version.

VARIATION

To make sweet potato latkes, substitute an equal amount of peeled and grated sweet potato for the russet potato. You will not need to soak the sweet potato in water prior to mixing; simply squeeze out any excess water. Sweet potato latkes will not be as crispy as traditional latkes, but they are still delicious.

The Classics Veganized

Classic Poutine

Canadians take their poutine seriously, and like the true patriot that I am, two of my favourite food groups are gravy and vegan cheese. I will never forget digging into poutine as a little boy with my dad at hockey games. There's nothing more Canadian than diving into a mound of crispy french fries, savoury gravy, and gooey cheese while cheering on your local team or after a game of shinny. This classic dish is a hat trick of crunchiness, creaminess, and richness. My gravy for this dish uses red wine and tamari for a strong flavour that makes it stand out in a sea of subpar sauces. If you don't have the time to make the cheese curds from scratch, substitute your favourite melty, dairy-free cheese. See page 12 for vegan cheeses that work well in this recipe.

SERVES 4

Prep ahead

Almond Milk Cheese Curds
   (page 217)

Anytime Gravy (page 228)

Perfect French Fries and
   Seasoning Salt (page 64)

Ingredients

1 cup (250 mL) Almond Milk
   Cheese Curds

8 cups (2 L) Perfect French
   Fries and Seasoning Salt

2 cups (500 mL) Anytime Gravy

1. Remove the almond milk cheese curds from the brine and gently pat dry with a kitchen towel or paper towel. Cut the curds into ½-inch (1 cm) pieces.

2. Once fried, place the hot french fries in a large bowl. While they are still hot, toss them with the seasoning salt and cheese curds.

3. Divide the fries among 4 serving bowls and top each bowl with ½ cup (125 mL) anytime gravy so that they are well coated. Serve immediately.

Baked Crab Dip

One of my favourite foods in my pre-vegan days was seafood, especially crab! There is something so satisfying about biting into their delicately sweet meat sprinkled with a few drops of lemon. Luckily for us and crabs everywhere, I've done the hard work for you and come up with this ridiculously yummy recipe made from shredded hearts of palm! Hearts of palm have the same mildly sweet flavour and delicate texture, so they are a perfect replacement for crab meat. Plus, there's no need to crack open any exoskeletons. Bake this dip and serve it with toasted baguette slices or your favourite crackers. A great choice for entertaining, this dish is sure to be the hit of the dinner party.

SERVES 4

Prep ahead
Cream Cheese (page 222)
Creamy Mayo (page 232)

Ingredients
1 can (14 ounces/398 mL) hearts of palm

½ cup (125 mL) Cream Cheese

3 tablespoons (45 mL) Creamy Mayo

¼ cup (60 mL) finely diced red sweet pepper

¼ cup (60 mL) roughly chopped fresh dill

3 tablespoons (45 mL) finely diced celery

3 tablespoons (45 mL) finely diced red onion

3 tablespoons (45 mL) finely chopped flat-leaf parsley

1 tablespoon (15 mL) thinly sliced fresh chives

1 tablespoon (15 mL) thinly sliced green onion (white and light green parts only)

1 tablespoon (15 mL) nutritional yeast

1 teaspoon (5 mL) lemon zest

1 tablespoon (15 mL) freshly squeezed lemon juice

1 teaspoon (5 mL) hot sauce (optional)

1 teaspoon (5 mL) sweet paprika

¾ teaspoon (4 mL) garlic powder

½ teaspoon (2 mL) vegan Worcestershire sauce (see Tip)

¼ teaspoon (1 mL) freshly cracked black pepper

¼ teaspoon (1 mL) ground mustard powder

¼ cup (60 mL) panko crumbs

1. Preheat the oven to 400°C (200°C). Lightly grease a 6-inch (15 cm) cast-iron skillet with vegetable oil.

2. On a cutting board, using 2 forks, shred the hearts of palm by pulling the forks apart and tearing the hearts of palm lengthwise, like pulled pork. There should not be many large pieces left. Place in a large bowl.

3. Add the cream cheese, creamy mayo, red pepper, dill, celery, red onion, parsley, chives, green onion, nutritional yeast, lemon zest, lemon juice, hot sauce (if using), paprika, garlic powder, Worcestershire sauce, black pepper, and mustard powder. Using the back of a spatula, combine well, until no large pieces remain.

4. Transfer the mixture to the prepared baking dish and top with the panko, spread evenly over the mixture. Bake until hot in the middle and the panko is browned on top, 12 to 15 minutes. Serve immediately or allow to cool and store in an airtight container in the fridge for up to 5 days.

TIP

If you do not have vegan Worcestershire sauce, you can substitute a dash each of fancy molasses and tamari or soy sauce.

Sides and Salads

Twice Baked Vegan Taters

Potatoes are basically just carby, starchy, conveniently packaged little miracles. Don't try to convince me otherwise. They are one of those magical foods that can be made in an endless number of ways and are the star of the meal each and every time! These heaven-sent ovals of goodness are loaded with a trifecta of my favourite recipes: my creamy Almond Milk Cheddar Cheese (page 216), Cream Cheese (page 222), and Sour Cream (page 231). On second thought, these are so sinfully delicious, I'm not sure if they could be sent from heaven after all. Bake them until they're as hot as you-know-where and golden brown and serve them whenever you're feeling particularly gluttonous.

SERVES 6

Prep ahead

Cream Cheese (page 222)

Almond Milk Cheddar Cheese (page 216)

Sour Cream (page 231)

Seitan Bacon (page 105)

Ingredients

3 large russet potatoes (see Tip)

1 cup (250 mL) Cream Cheese

¾ cup (175 mL) unsweetened almond milk (see Tip)

½ cup (125 mL) nutritional yeast

1 teaspoon (5 mL) sea salt

1 cup (250 mL) thinly sliced green onions (white and light green parts only; about 2 bunches)

1 cup (250 mL) Almond Milk Cheddar Cheese

For serving

½ cup (125 mL) Sour Cream

½ cup (125 mL) Seitan Bacon, broken into bits

1. Preheat the oven to 400°F (200°C). Line a baking sheet with parchment paper.

2. On the prepared baking sheet, bake the potatoes until soft in the middle, 45 to 60 minutes. You will know they are done when a fork easily pushes into the middle of the largest potato. Remove from the oven and set aside until the potatoes are cool enough to handle, about 1 hour.

3. Cut the potatoes in half lengthwise. Using a spoon, remove the flesh from the potato, leaving the skin behind. Place the flesh into a food processor fitted with a metal blade. Add the cream cheese, almond milk, nutritional yeast, and salt. Blend until smooth. You may need to stop the machine and use a rubber spatula to scrape down the sides of the bowl. Stir in the green onion, taste, and add more salt, if necessary.

4. Spoon the blended filling into the potato skins. Top with almond milk cheddar cheese. Place the skins back in the preheated oven and bake until golden brown and crispy, 15 to 20 minutes. Serve with sour cream and seitan bacon bits.

TIP

1. I highly recommend using russet potatoes. They are higher in starch and turn out nice and fluffy when cooked. You can also use Yukon Gold potatoes if you don't have russets on hand. **2.** Using a higher fat non-dairy milk for this recipe is ideal. If you do not have almond milk, you can substitute an equal amount of unsweetened cashew milk or canned full-fat coconut milk.

Perfect French Fries and Seasoning Salt

There's a secret science to making the perfect french fries, and it involves cooking them twice. The first time, you're softening and breaking down the starch in the potatoes without burning the sugars. The second time gives them that characteristic crispiness we all know and love. To me, (and probably to the rest of the world, too) there's simply no better side dish than impeccably baked french fries. These fries pair superbly with so many dishes, but some favourites are my Bacon Double Cheeseburgers (page 137), The NY Strip (page 129), Hickory Smoked Ribs (page 167), and Chickpea Pot Pie (page 133).

SERVES 4 TO 6

Prep ahead

Creamy Mayo (page 232)

French Fries

4 to 6 cups (1 to 1.5 L) vegetable oil, for frying

2 pounds (900 g) russet potatoes, unpeeled

Seasoning Salt

½ cup (125 mL) sea salt

3 tablespoons (45 mL) smoked paprika

3 tablespoons (45 mL) sugar

2 tablespoons (30 mL) onion powder

2 tablespoons (30 mL) garlic powder

1 tablespoon (15 mL) freshly cracked black pepper

1 tablespoon (15 mL) chili powder

1 tablespoon (15 mL) hickory smoked salt (optional; see Tip)

For serving

½ cup (125 mL) Creamy Mayo

Ketchup (optional)

1. **MAKE THE FRIES** Heat the vegetable oil in a large pot or small deep fryer to a temperature of 300°F (150°C). If using a pot, heat the vegetable oil over medium-low heat. A candy thermometer will work well to gauge the temperature.

2. Lay the potatoes on a work surface and cut them into flat strips, about ¼ inch (5 mm) thick. Stack the strips of potatoes on top of each other and cut into the shape of french fries, about ¼ inch (5 mm) thick. Alternatively, if you have a mandoline, use it to cut the potatoes to the same size.

3. Place the fries in a large bowl of cold water and soak for about 5 minutes. This helps remove excess starch. Drain the fries, shaking off any excess water, and pat dry.

4. **MAKE THE SEASONING SALT** In a small bowl, whisk together the salt, paprika, sugar, onion powder, garlic powder, black pepper, chili powder, and smoked salt (if using) until well combined and no lumps remain.

5. **COOK THE FRIES** In small batches, carefully dip the fries in the hot oil. Using metal tongs, turn the fries and cook until soft in the middle, 3 to 5 minutes. Using metal tongs, remove the fries from the oil and place them on paper towel or a clean kitchen cloth to drain any excess oil. You do not want to crowd the pot or the deep fryer basket, or the temperature of the oil will lower and the fries will absorb more oil. You may need to cook the fries in a few batches.

6. If using a deep fryer, increase the temperature to 400°F (200°C). If using a pot, increase the temperature to medium-high and wait about 10 minutes for the temperature of the oil to increase to 400°F (200°C). Use a candy thermometer to gauge the temperature. Carefully dip the fries in the hot oil. Using metal tongs, turn the fries and cook until golden brown and crisp, about 4 to 5 minutes, working in batches as necessary so as not to crowd the pot or the deep fryer basket. Using metal tongs, remove the fries from the oil and toss them in a large bowl with a good amount of seasoning salt. Serve immediately with creamy mayo and ketchup (if using) for dipping.

TIP

Hickory smoked salt is available in most large grocery stores, in specialty stores, or online. The seasoning salt will still be great without it, but it does add an extra layer of flavour, so I recommend using it if you can. If you are not using the hickory smoked salt, add an additional 1 tablespoon (15 mL) sea salt to the blend.

Smashed Taters

Smashed potatoes are so simple and versatile—they're easy to make and work with so many different dishes. Personally, I love pairing this carbolicious dish with a good source of protein like The NY Strip (page 129), Home-Style Meatloaf (page 130) or Bacon Double Cheeseburgers (page 137). They are tender and creamy on the inside, yet buttery and crispy on the outside. Get ready to catch yourself, because you're about to fall in love with the seductively delicious flavours of fresh butter, thyme, garlic, and paprika.

SERVES 2 TO 3

Ingredients

1 pound (450 g) fingerling potatoes (see Tip)

1½ teaspoons (7 mL) sea salt, divided

⅓ cup (75 mL) melted vegan butter or Whipped Butter (page 229)

2 tablespoons (30 mL) chopped fresh thyme leaves

2 tablespoons (30 mL) nutritional yeast

½ teaspoon (2 mL) garlic powder

¼ teaspoon (1 mL) sweet paprika

1. In a medium pot, combine the potatoes, 1 teaspoon (5 mL) of the salt, and enough water to cover the potatoes and bring to a boil uncovered. Cook the potatoes until they are soft in the middle, about 20 minutes for smaller potatoes or 30 minutes for larger ones. It's okay if the skins split a little bit. Drain and allow the potatoes to cool slightly. This will help remove some of the moisture. Transfer the potatoes to a baking sheet lined with parchment paper.

2. Preheat the oven to 350°F (180°C).

3. Using a potato masher, the back of a heavy-bottomed pot, or a fork, press into the potatoes and gently flatten them. They should be about ½ inch (1 cm) thick.

4. In a small bowl, whisk together the butter, thyme, nutritional yeast, garlic powder, paprika, and the remaining ½ teaspoon (2 mL) salt until well combined. Drizzle the butter mixture over the smashed potatoes. Bake until the potatoes are crisp, 30 to 40 minutes. Do not flip the potatoes during the cooking process. Serve immediately or allow to cool completely and store in an airtight container in the fridge for up to 1 week.

TIP

Any yellow-flesh potatoes, such as Yukon Gold, will work well in this recipe. If the potatoes are big, cut them in half lengthwise before boiling.

Maple Baked Beans

Baked beans are one of those easy recipes that are great as a side or topping on virtually any type of meal. Growing up, my dad wasn't much of a cook, so it was baked beans and wieners on most nights when my mom wasn't cooking! Even though I've upgraded my meals considerably from those nights filled with wieners and beans, I'm still fond of the savoury and sweet flavours, so I tried my best to re-create this childhood classic, with a Canadian twist. These go great with my Stuffed Grilled Cheese Sandwiches (page 149), Dirty South Sausages and Biscuits with Gravy (page 120), or Home-Style Meatloaf (page 130).

SERVES 4

Ingredients

2 tablespoons (30 mL) vegetable oil

½ cup (125 mL) finely diced white onion

1 tablespoon (15 mL) ground ginger

½ teaspoon (2 mL) sea salt

1 tablespoon (15 mL) Dijon mustard

2 cans (19 ounces/540 mL each) tomato purée

1 cup (250 mL) maple syrup

½ cup (125 mL) ketchup

¼ cup (60 mL) blackstrap molasses (see Tip)

2 cans (14 ounces/398 mL each) navy beans

1. Preheat the oven to 350°F (180°C).

2. In a medium oven-proof pot with a tight-fitting lid, heat the vegetable oil over medium heat. Add the onion, ginger, and salt and cook, stirring occasionally, until slightly browned, 5 to 6 minutes. Stir in the mustard and cook for 1 to 2 minutes. Add the tomato purée, maple syrup, ketchup, and molasses, then bring to a boil. Add the beans and stir to combine.

3. Reduce the heat to simmer and cover with the tight-fitting lid. Transfer to the oven and bake until the mixture has thickened, about 30 minutes. Serve immediately or allow to cool and store in an airtight container in the fridge for up to 1 week.

TIP

Blackstrap molasses has always been loved in the vegan world for its high levels of vitamin B_{12}. I like it for the rich, dark flavour it gives these baked beans.

Herbed Holiday Stuffing

When I was younger, I visited Farm Sanctuary in Upstate New York for Thanksgiving. We got to feed the turkeys instead of the other way around, and boy, did this help cement my love for these intelligent birds! Usually stuffing is made using stale bread tossed with various seasonings and liquid, bound together with eggs. My version uses a flax egg for binding, which is simply ground flaxseed and hot water mixed together. I prefer golden flaxseed to keep the colour light. Double or triple the recipe as necessary and serve with my Home-Style Meatloaf (page 130), Meatball Sub (page 139), or Maple Baked Beans (page 68).

SERVES 4 TO 6

Ingredients

- 1 tablespoon (15 mL) ground golden flaxseed
- 3 tablespoons (45 mL) hot water (see Tip)
- 3 tablespoons (45 mL) vegetable oil, more for baking dish
- 2 cups (500 mL) finely diced white onion
- 2 cups (500 mL) finely diced celery
- 2 cups (500 mL) finely diced peeled carrots
- 1 teaspoon (5 mL) sea salt
- 3 to 4 cloves garlic, finely minced
- 1 loaf of day-old bread, cut in cubes
- 2 cups (500 mL) pure apple juice (see Tip)
- ½ cup (125 mL) roughly chopped fresh sage leaves
- 2 tablespoons (30 mL) chopped fresh thyme leaves
- 2 tablespoons (30 mL) chopped fresh rosemary leaves

1. In a small bowl, whisk together the flaxseed and hot water until well combined. Set aside to soak for 10 minutes so that the flaxseed can swell and absorb the liquid.

2. In a large frying pan, heat the vegetable oil over medium heat. Add the onions, celery, carrots, and salt and cook, stirring frequently, until the vegetables are soft and the onions are translucent, 5 to 6 minutes. Add the garlic and cook, stirring constantly, until soft and fragrant, about 2 minutes. Set aside to completely cool the vegetables, 15 to 20 minutes.

3. Preheat the oven to 350°F (180°C). Lightly grease an 8-inch (2 L) square baking dish with vegetable oil.

4. In a large bowl, combine the cubed bread with the cooked vegetables, apple juice, sage, thyme, rosemary, and flaxseed mixture. Using your hands, mix all the ingredients together until very well combined. The mixture should be slightly wet and stick together when pressed between 2 fingers.

5. Transfer the stuffing to the prepared baking dish and bake until golden brown on top and the middle is piping hot, 30 to 35 minutes. Remove from the oven and allow to cool slightly before serving, about 10 minutes. This will allow the bread to firm up a bit. Serve or allow to cool completely and store in an airtight container in the fridge for up to 1 week.

TIP

1. Use hot water when making a flax egg, as it is best to help speed up the process of gelling the flax. **2.** If you do not have any apple juice on hand, place about 3 cups (750 mL) of roughly chopped apples (peel on is fine) in a blender with ½ cup (125 mL) water. Blend until the mixture is smooth. Strain the juice through a fine mesh strainer, discarding the pulp.

Creamy Risotto

Creamy, hearty, and rich are the three words I think of when describing risotto. Traditionally, risotto is finished with a ton of cheese and butter. In my equally creamy, hearty, and rich version, nutritional yeast, tahini, and miso make up for the lack of Parmesan cheese, while my Whipped Butter (page 229) or your favourite vegan butter substitute can easily stand in for the dairy. I promise, you're not going to notice the difference. And don't worry, no one will judge you for drinking a little Chardonnay while you're whipping this up; just make sure to save some for the recipe.

SERVES 4 TO 6 AS A SIDE

Prep ahead
Whipped Butter (page 229)

Ingredients
4 quarts (4 L) vegetable stock
2 tablespoons (30 mL) vegetable oil
½ cup (125 mL) finely diced white onion
2 cups (500 mL) arborio or carnaroli rice (see Tip)
½ cup (125 mL) dry white wine, such as Chardonnay (see Tip)
⅓ cup (75 mL) nutritional yeast
3 tablespoons (45 mL) Whipped Butter or vegan butter
2 tablespoons (30 mL) tahini (see Tip)
2 tablespoons (30 mL) tamari or soy sauce
½ teaspoon (2 mL) white miso
¼ teaspoon (1 mL) Dijon mustard
Freshly cracked black pepper
Fresh lemon wedges, for garnish

1. In a large pot, bring the vegetable stock to a simmer over medium heat. Reduce the heat to low and cover until ready to use.

2. In a medium pot, heat the vegetable oil over medium heat. Add the onion and rice and cook, stirring constantly, until the onion is golden, 4 to 5 minutes. Add the white wine and cook until the liquid is completely absorbed by the rice.

3. Using a ladle, add 1 or 2 ladleful of warm stock to the rice mixture at a time, stirring constantly until the liquid is absorbed. You always want liquid simmering in the pot while cooking the rice. Be careful not to let the mixture cook until no liquid remains, which is why gradually adding a few ladleful at a time is important when making risotto. Repeat until all the stock has been used and the rice is creamy and tender but firm, about 20 minutes. Remove from the heat.

4. Stir in the nutritional yeast, whipped butter, tahini, tamari, miso, and mustard. Divide the risotto among serving bowls and serve sprinkled with some cracked black pepper and with a fresh lemon wedge for squeezing.

TIP

1. Arborio rice is short, plump rice that absorbs liquid well, and its starch breaks down to create a creamy texture. Some people prefer the texture and flavour of carnaroli rice, but either type of rice will work well. **2.** Substitute 2 tablespoons (30 mL) white wine vinegar for the white wine if you do not consume alcohol. **3.** Some varieties of tahini can be very thick. If the tahini is thick and difficult to scoop out of the container, reduce the amount to 1 tablespoon (15 mL). If the tahini is thin and pours easily, use 2 tablespoons (30 mL).

Creamed Garlic Spinach

If you're looking for a healthier side dish, look no further than this vitamin and nutrient-packed delicacy. Add it as a counterbalance to heartier dishes like The NY Strip (page 129), or toss it with freshly cooked pasta topped with a sprinkle of nutritional yeast. Your taste buds and metabolism will thank you. Popeye would be proud of this dish!

SERVES 4

Ingredients

3 tablespoons (45 mL) vegetable oil

½ cup (125 mL) finely diced white onion

¾ teaspoon (4 mL) sea salt, divided

⅓ cup (75 mL) minced garlic

8 cups (2 L) packed baby spinach leaves (see Tip)

1 cup (250 mL) raw cashews, soaked and drained (see Tip)

1 cup (250 mL) unsweetened almond milk

1. In a large sauté pan or medium pot, heat the vegetable oil over medium heat. Add the onion and ¼ teaspoon (1 mL) of the salt. Cook, stirring frequently, until the onion is soft and translucent, 3 to 4 minutes. Add the garlic and cook, stirring constantly, until fragrant, 1 to 2 minutes

2. Add the spinach and cook, stirring constantly, until soft and wilted, 3 to 4 minutes. Remove from the heat.

3. In a high-speed blender, combine the cashews, almond milk, and the remaining ½ teaspoon (2 mL) salt. Blend on high speed until smooth and creamy.

4. In a food processor fitted with a metal blade, combine the cashew cream and cooked spinach. Process until broken down but not completely smooth; you want a bit of texture to remain from the spinach. Serve immediately or allow to cool and store in an airtight container in the fridge for up to 3 days.

TIP

1. Substitute 4 cups (1 L) of tightly packed chopped bunch spinach for the baby spinach. This is the spinach that comes wrapped in individual bunches. **2.** To soak the cashews, place them in a large bowl and cover with 4 cups (1 L) hot water for at least 1 hour or overnight, covered, and stored in the fridge. Drain and rinse, discarding the soaking liquid.

Crispy Dillies with Ranch Dressing

Some of my favourite memories of being a kid involve going to outdoor carnivals and festivals with my family and enjoying crunchy deep-fried dill pickles on a stick. Actually, nothing is more fun to a kid than eating something, anything really, off a stick. Still, without a doubt this is one of the all-time best comfort foods. I highly recommend serving these pickles hot with a nice big portion of my creamy Ranch Dressing (page 233), which tastily offsets that dill pickle tang. And of course, no cages are needed here to satisfy your craving!

SERVES 4 TO 6

Prep ahead
Ranch Dressing (page 233)

Ingredients

1 cup (250 mL) beer (see Tip; any type will work well)

1 cup (250 mL) all-purpose flour

2 tablespoons (30 mL) roughly chopped fresh dill

1 tablespoon (15 mL) nutritional yeast

1¼ teaspoons (6 mL) sea salt, divided

¼ teaspoon (1 mL) sugar

¼ teaspoon (1 mL) chili powder

¼ teaspoon (1 mL) + 1 tablespoon (15 mL) sweet paprika, divided

4 cups (1 L) panko crumbs

1 teaspoon (5 mL) garlic powder

½ teaspoon (2 mL) dried thyme

8 large whole dill pickles, cut in quarters (for smaller pickles, cut in half)

—

4 to 6 cups (1 to 1.5 L) vegetable oil, for frying

1 batch Ranch Dressing, for serving

1. In a medium bowl, combine the beer, flour, dill, nutritional yeast, ¼ teaspoon (1 mL) of the salt, sugar, chili powder, and ¼ teaspoon (1 mL) of the paprika. Whisk until well combined and no lumps remain.

2. In a large bowl, whisk together the panko, remaining 1 teaspoon (5 mL) salt, remaining 1 tablespoon (15 mL) paprika, garlic powder, and thyme.

3. Dredge the pickle spears in the beer batter and then in the seasoned panko. Roll each pickle in the panko until coated on all sides; you do not want to see any pickle, only crumb. Place the pickles in a single layer on a baking sheet lined with parchment paper, then place in the freezer for 15 to 20 minutes to help them firm up.

4. Heat the vegetable oil in a large pot or small deep fryer to a temperature of 375°F (190°C).

5. Remove the pickles from the freezer. Dip in the hot oil and fry until golden brown and crisp, using metal tongs to turn the pickles as necessary, 4 to 5 minutes. Remove from the oil using metal tongs. Serve immediately with ranch dressing.

TIP

Not all beer is considered vegan. Some use animal products like isinglass or gelatin in the refining or clarification process. Make sure to look for beers that have no animal products.

Slow-Cooked Southern-Style Collard Greens

Collard greens can seem intimidating, and many people don't know how to cook them. Don't let their giant, leafy greenness scare you off from trying them. The key to mastering collard greens is to cook them slowly with a little bit of vinegar and other seasonings. That's when they start to fall apart, becoming so tender and tasty they would please the palate of even the most carnivorous among us.

SERVES 4

Prep ahead
Seitan Bacon (page 105)

Ingredients
¼ cup (60 mL) deodorized coconut oil

¼ cup (60 mL) thinly sliced jalapeño peppers (see Tip)

¼ cup (60 mL) thinly sliced garlic

½ cup (125 mL) finely diced white onion

4 strips Seitan Bacon, thinly sliced

½ teaspoon (2 mL) sea salt

2 bunches of collard greens, stems removed and cut into 1-inch (2.5 cm) pieces

½ cup (125 mL) water

¼ cup (60 mL) unpasteurized apple cider vinegar

2 tablespoons (30 mL) tamari or soy sauce

2 tablespoons (30 mL) nutritional yeast

1 teaspoon (5 mL) smoked paprika

1 teaspoon (5 mL) vegan Worcestershire sauce

1. In a large pot, heat the coconut oil over medium-high heat. Add the jalapeño and garlic and cook, stirring frequently, until the peppers are light golden brown and softened, 6 to 8 minutes. Add the onions, seitan bacon, and salt and cook, stirring occasionally, until the onions are light golden brown, 5 to 6 minutes.

2. Add the collard greens, water, and apple cider vinegar. Cover and cook, stirring occasionally, over low heat for 30 minutes or until the collard greens are soft and falling apart. Stir in the tamari, nutritional yeast, paprika, and Worcestershire sauce. Serve immediately or let cool and store in an airtight container in the fridge for up to 1 week.

TIP

Most of the heat in jalapeño peppers is in the seeds and ribs. If you like heat, leave the seeds and ribs in the jalapeños. If you like the flavour of the jalapeños but not as much heat, remove the seeds and ribs.

Buttermilk Onion Rings

Traditional buttermilk is made by adding something acidic with naturally produced bacteria to dairy. The added acids help to soften the onions, giving them an awesome texture after they're cooked. In my version, I add unpasteurized apple cider vinegar to soy milk, giving it the same properties as buttermilk. Like their classic counterparts, these onion rings are just the right amount of chewy in the middle, crispy on the outside, and sweet and salty all around, making them the perfect side dish for my Bacon Double Cheeseburgers (page 137), Hickory Smoked Ribs (page 167), or The NY Strip (page 129).

SERVES 4 TO 6 AS A SIDE

Prep ahead
Creamy Mayo (page 232) or Ranch Dressing (page 233)

Ingredients
2 large Vidalia onions, peeled and left whole (see Tip)

4 cups (1 L) unsweetened soy milk

⅔ cup (150 mL) unpasteurized apple cider vinegar

¼ cup (60 mL) Dijon mustard

2 tablespoons (30 mL) brown sugar

½ teaspoon (2 mL) sea salt

1 cup (250 mL) all-purpose flour

1 cup (250 mL) panko crumbs

½ cup (125 mL) cornstarch

3 tablespoons (45 mL) nutritional yeast

1 tablespoon (15 mL) garlic powder

1 teaspoon (5 mL) sweet paprika

1 teaspoon (5 mL) onion powder

½ teaspoon (2 mL) freshly cracked black pepper

---

4 to 6 cups (1 to 1.5 L) vegetable oil, for frying

1 batch Creamy Mayo or Ranch Dressing, for serving

1. Slice the onions into 1-inch (2.5 cm) thick rounds. Using your fingers, separate the rounds into rings and transfer to a large bowl.

2. In another large bowl, whisk together the soy milk, apple cider vinegar, mustard, brown sugar, and salt. Add the onion rounds and submerge them in the liquid. Marinate for 30 minutes to 1 hour.

3. In a medium bowl, whisk together the flour, panko, cornstarch, nutritional yeast, garlic powder, paprika, onion powder, and black pepper.

4. Heat the vegetable oil in a large pot or small deep fryer to a temperature of 375°F (190°C).

5. Remove the onions from the marinade. Keep the marinade for breading the onions. Dip the onion rounds in the flour mixture, then the marinade, and then in the flour again. Gently drop the onion rings into the hot oil and fry until golden brown, and crispy, and the onion is soft in the middle, using metal tongs to turn the onions as necessary, 5 to 6 minutes. Using metal tongs, remove from the oil and season with salt while still hot. Serve immediately with creamy mayo or ranch dressing for dipping.

TIP

Vidalia onions are best for onion rings. They are sweeter and have a softer, milder onion flavour than regular cooking onions.

Deviled Eggs

Deviled eggs have always been a popular dish served at dinner parties, during cocktail hour, or on top of a hearty salad. This base recipe is a great way to add some protein and substance to salads like my Waldorf Salad (page 87) or Cobb Salad (page 82). In traditional deviled eggs, the cholesterol-laden yolks are used as the filling, but in my healthier version, I use cooked mashed potatoes mixed with Creamy Mayo (page 232) and add turmeric for a bright yellow colour. They're so sinfully delicious, the devil himself would approve, despite this recipe being cruelty-free! You will need specialty egg moulds to set the eggs in this recipe. They can be found in specialty stores or online and come in various shapes and sizes, but I prefer one that has space for six egg halves.

MAKES 8 HALVES

Prep ahead
Creamy Mayo (page 232)

Egg white
1 block (12 ounces/340 g) firm silken tofu (see Tip)
2 tablespoons (30 mL) agar powder
1 teaspoon (5 mL) black salt

Egg Yolk
1 large whole russet potato, peeled
⅓ cup (75 mL) Creamy Mayo
2 tablespoons (30 mL) prepared yellow mustard
1 tablespoon (15 mL) prepared sweet relish
½ teaspoon (2 mL) black salt
¼ teaspoon (1 mL) ground turmeric

———

Sweet paprika, for garnish

1. **MAKE THE EGG WHITE** In a high-speed blender, combine the tofu, agar powder, and black salt. Blend until smooth and creamy, scraping down the sides of the bowl with a rubber spatula as required.

2. Transfer the mixture to a small saucepan and bring to a simmer. Cook, stirring constantly, for 3 to 4 minutes. You do not want the mixture to boil, only simmer. Transfer the mixture to the egg moulds, levelling off any excess with a knife. Refrigerate until cooled completely and set, about 1 hour. The mixture should be firm to the touch. One hour is usually enough, but longer is fine.

3. **MAKE THE EGG YOLK** Place the potato in a small pot, cover with at least 2 inches (5 cm) of water and bring to a boil. Reduce the heat to a simmer and cook until the potato is soft in the middle, 30 to 35 minutes. Remove the potato from the water and set aside until it is cool enough to handle, about 30 minutes.

4. Chop the potato flesh into small pieces and transfer to a medium bowl. Add the creamy mayo, mustard, relish, black salt, and turmeric. Using a potato masher, mash until well combined.

5. **ASSEMBLE THE DEVILED EGGS** Remove the egg whites from the fridge. Using a 1-teaspoon (5 mL) measuring spoon, gently scoop out the centre of each egg white. This is where the egg yolk filling will go.

6. You can either use a piping bag with a star tip to pipe the filling into the centre of each egg white or use a spoon to scoop in the filling. I like to use a piping bag. Serve garnished with a sprinkle of sweet paprika. Serve immediately or cover and store in the fridge for up to 3 days.

TIP

For this recipe, you will need to use firm silken tofu. Medium or soft tofu is too soft, and extra-firm tofu is too firm.

Cobb Salad

Cobb salad is undoubtedly one of the most iconic salads in the world. Even though some of the ingredients are interchangeable, no matter what, it's always an awesome medley of textures and flavours. Traditional Cobb salads contain iceberg lettuce, cherry tomatoes, blue cheese, red wine vinegar dressing, hard boiled eggs, avocado, and bacon. My version uses all of the same ingredients, only they're made with a lot of plants instead—and a little bit of vegan magic!

MAKES 1 LARGE OR 2 SIDE SALADS

Prep ahead

Deviled Eggs (page 81)

Blue Cheese (page 220)

Coconut Bacon (see page 85)

Dressing

¼ cup (60 mL) olive oil

¼ cup (60 mL) vegetable oil

3 tablespoons + 1 teaspoon (50 mL) red wine vinegar

2 tablespoons (30 mL) Dijon mustard

1½ teaspoons (7 mL) agave nectar

¼ teaspoon (1 mL) garlic powder

¼ teaspoon (1 mL) sea salt

⅛ teaspoon (0.5 mL) dried oregano

Cheesy Chickpeas

3 tablespoons (45 mL) vegetable oil

½ cup (125 mL) cooked chickpeas

2 tablespoons (30 mL) nutritional yeast

¼ teaspoon (1 mL) sea salt

Salad

½ head iceberg lettuce, cut into bite-size cubes

6 cherry tomatoes, cut in half

¼ avocado, peeled, pitted, and cut into bite-size cubes

¼ cup (60 mL) thinly sliced green onion (white and light green parts only)

For serving

4 Deviled Egg halves

½ cup (125 mL) crumbled Blue Cheese

½ cup (125 mL) Coconut Bacon

1. **MAKE THE DRESSING** In a blender, combine the olive oil, vegetable oil, red wine vinegar, mustard, agave, garlic powder, salt, and oregano. Blend until smooth and creamy.

2. **MAKE THE CHEESY CHICKPEAS** In a small frying pan, heat the vegetable oil over medium-high heat. Add the chickpeas and cook, stirring constantly, until they start to turn golden brown, 8 to 10 minutes. Remove from the heat, add the nutritional yeast and salt, toss to combine, and set aside to cool completely.

3. **ASSEMBLE THE SALAD** Divide the lettuce, cherry tomatoes, avocado cubes, green onion, and cheesy chickpeas between 2 serving bowls. Top with the deviled eggs, blue cheese, coconut bacon, and drizzle each salad with 3 to 4 tablespoons (45 to 60 mL) of the dressing. Serve immediately.

Creamy Caesar Salad

For decades, people have enjoyed this creamy salad as a side, appetizer, or in many cases, their main dish. Perfectly balanced despite the seemingly random combination of ingredients, the dressing these days usually gets its salty richness from anchovy fillets and Parmesan cheese, although the original version just used Worcestershire sauce. My version more closely resembles the original recipe, replacing the fish with vegan Worcestershire sauce, tamari, or soy sauce and the cheese with nutrient-packed nutritional yeast.

MAKES 1 LARGE OR 4 SIDE SALADS

Prep ahead
Creamy Mayo (page 232)

Croutons (makes 2 cups/500 mL)
2 cups (500 mL) day-old bread cut into ½-inch (1 cm) cubes (see Tip)
¼ cup (60 mL) vegetable oil
2 tablespoons (30 mL) nutritional yeast
¼ teaspoon (1 mL) sweet paprika
¼ teaspoon (1 mL) garlic powder
¼ teaspoon (1 mL) sea salt
⅛ teaspoon (0.5 mL) freshly cracked black pepper

Caesar Dressing (makes 2 cups/500 mL)
1½ cups (375 mL) Creamy Mayo
¼ cup (60 mL) freshly squeezed lemon juice

¼ cup (60 mL) nutritional yeast
1 tablespoon (15 mL) minced garlic
2 teaspoons (10 mL) vegan Worcestershire sauce
1 tablespoon (15 mL) + 1½ teaspoons (7 mL) Dijon mustard
1 teaspoon (5 mL) garlic powder
½ teaspoon (2 mL) freshly cracked black pepper
¼ teaspoon (1 mL) celery salt
1 tablespoon (15 mL) hot sauce (optional)

Almond Parmesan Cheese (makes 1 cup/250 mL)
1 cup (250 mL) blanched almond flour
½ cup (125 mL) nutritional yeast
½ teaspoon (2 mL) garlic powder
¼ teaspoon (1 mL) celery salt

¼ teaspoon (1 mL) sea salt
¼ teaspoon (1 mL) vegan lactic acid (optional)

Coconut Bacon (makes 2 cups/500 mL)
2 cups (500 mL) sliced raw coconut (see Tip)
2 tablespoons (30 mL) vegetable oil
1 tablespoon (15 mL) maple syrup
1 teaspoon (5 mL) sea salt
½ teaspoon (2 mL) liquid smoke

For assembly
2 heads romaine lettuce (hearts preferably), cut in 2-inch (5 cm) squares
¼ cup (60 mL) soaked sun-dried tomatoes (see Tip)
4 lemon wedges

1. **MAKE THE CROUTONS** Preheat the oven to 400°F (200°C). Line a baking sheet with parchment paper.

2. In a medium bowl, combine the bread cubes, vegetable oil, nutritional yeast, paprika, garlic powder, salt, and pepper. Toss until well combined. Transfer to the prepared baking sheet and bake until golden brown and crisp, 4 to 5 minutes. Remove from the oven and allow to cool completely. Reduce the temperature of the oven to 375°F (190°C) and keep the lined baking sheet to use again for the coconut bacon.

3. **MAKE THE CAESAR DRESSING** In a medium bowl, whisk together the creamy mayo, lemon juice, nutritional yeast, garlic, Worcestershire sauce, mustard, garlic powder, pepper, celery salt, and hot sauce, if using. Store leftover dressing in an airtight container in the fridge for up to 1 week.

4. **MAKE THE ALMOND PARMESAN CHEESE** In a food processor fitted with a metal blade, combine the almond flour, nutritional yeast, garlic powder, celery salt, sea salt, and vegan lactic acid, if using. Process until the almonds have a powder-like consistency. You do not want any large to medium pieces of almond left, but you also do not want to overprocess or you will start to make almond butter. Store leftover cheese in an airtight container at room temperature for up to 2 weeks.

5. **MAKE THE COCONUT BACON** In a medium bowl, combine the coconut, vegetable oil, maple syrup, salt, and liquid smoke. Toss until well combined. Transfer to the prepared baking sheet and bake until the coconut is golden brown and fragrant, 12 to 15 minutes. Store leftover coconut bacon in an airtight container at room temperature for up to 2 weeks.

Sides and Salads

Continued

6. **ASSEMBLE THE SALAD** In a large bowl, combine the romaine lettuce, 1 cup (250 mL) of the Caesar dressing, 1 cup (250 mL) of the croutons, ½ cup (125 mL) of the almond Parmesan cheese, ½ cup (125 mL) of the coconut bacon, and the sun-dried tomatoes. Toss well to combine. Serve in a large bowl or 4 small serving bowls and top the salad with a bit more almond Parmesan cheese, coconut bacon, and a few croutons. Serve with lemon wedges.

TIP

1. I like using sourdough bread to make the croutons, but you can use any type of bread. If gluten-free bread is required, use your favourite type; just be careful to make sure that you cook the croutons long enough so that all of the moisture has been removed. Some gluten-free bread can have more moisture in it. **2.** When making coconut bacon, it is best to use sliced coconut that looks like chips, not shredded coconut, which is much more common. Most grocery stores carry sliced coconut, or it can be purchased online. **3.** To soak the sun-dried tomatoes, place them in a small bowl and cover with 1 cup (250 mL) hot water. Cover and set aside to soak for 30 minutes. Drain, discarding the soaking water.

Waldorf Salad

Created in the famously regal Waldorf Astoria hotel in New York City during the 1800s, this salad is truly a classic as well as being one of the easier dishes in this book to veganize. In my version, I use Creamy Mayo (page 232) as the base and top it with a mix of crunchy, sweet, and fresh ingredients. This is great on its own as a refreshing and healthy meal or as a summery side dish.

MAKES 1 LARGE OR 4 SIDE SALADS

Prep ahead

Creamy Mayo (page 232)

Dressing

½ cup (125 mL) Creamy Mayo

2 tablespoons (30 mL) freshly squeezed lemon juice

1 tablespoon (15 mL) sugar

Salad

1 cup (250 mL) red seedless grapes, cut in half

1 Granny Smith apple, peeled and cut in cubes

3 stalks celery, thinly sliced

1 head Boston lettuce, trimmed, washed, and dried (see Tip)

1 cup (250 mL) lightly toasted raw walnuts, whole or halves (see Tip)

1. **MAKE THE DRESSING** In a small bowl, whisk together the creamy mayo, lemon juice, and sugar.

2. **ASSEMBLE THE SALAD** In a medium bowl, toss together the dressing, grapes, apple, and celery until well combined.

3. Lay the lettuce leaves on a serving dish. Top with the dressing-coated mixture and top with the toasted walnuts. Serve immediately.

TIP

1. Boston lettuce is also called butter lettuce or bibb lettuce. It is a soft green lettuce that has a mellow flavour and is great in salads that have a creamy dressing. You can substitute a head of green leaf lettuce for this recipe if you do not have any Boston lettuce. 2. To toast walnuts, heat a pan over medium heat with no oil. Add the walnuts and gently shake the pan until they start to turn golden brown and become fragrant, about 3 to 4 minutes. Remove the walnuts from the heat right away and place in a cold bowl or on a cold baking sheet. Nuts and seeds continue to cook if kept on the heat; removing them from the heat prevents overcooking or burning.

Greek Salad

Probably the only kind of salad I would willingly eat as a child was a crunchy, salty, flavourful Greek salad. Before I knew any better, I would happily top it with as much feta as I could get my hands on, unaware that the cheese was made from the milk of a friendly sheep or sassy goat. The good news is that we don't need to miss out on the creamy and crumbly texture of feta, because my version uses tofu, which falls apart on your tongue in the same way!

MAKES 1 LARGE OR 4 SIDE SALADS

Prep ahead

Feta Cheese (page 221)

Dressing (makes about 1½ cups/375 mL)

1 cup (250 mL) extra-virgin olive oil

¼ cup (60 mL) freshly squeezed lemon juice

2 tablespoons (30 mL) olive brine (see Tip)

2 tablespoons (30 mL) chopped fresh flat-leaf parsley (see Tip)

1 tablespoon (15 mL) nutritional yeast

1 tablespoon (15 mL) Dijon mustard

2 teaspoons (10 mL) minced garlic

1 teaspoon (5 mL) dried basil

¾ teaspoon (4 mL) dried oregano

½ teaspoon (2 mL) sea salt

Salad

2 heads romaine lettuce (hearts preferably), cut in 2-inch (5 cm) squares

1 cup (250 mL) cubed English cucumbers, seeds removed

1 cup (250 mL) Feta Cheese, more for serving

½ cup (125 mL) cubed red sweet pepper

½ cup (125 mL) pitted Kalamata olives, more for serving

¼ cup (60 mL) thinly sliced red onion

———

Fresh oregano leaves, for garnish (optional)

1. **MAKE THE DRESSING** In a blender, combine the olive oil, lemon juice, olive brine, parsley, nutritional yeast, mustard, garlic, basil, oregano, and salt. Blend until smooth and creamy. Store in an airtight container in the fridge for up to 1 week.

2. **ASSEMBLE THE SALAD** In a large bowl, combine the romaine lettuce, 1 cup (250 mL) of the dressing, cucumbers, feta cheese, red pepper, olives, and red onion. Toss well to combine. Serve in a large bowl or 4 small serving bowls and top the salad with a bit more feta cheese, a few olives, and oregano leaves, if using. Serve immediately.

TIP

1. Olives are usually sold packed either in a brine made from salt and water or in olive oil. The brine has a lot of flavour and works really well for this recipe. If you do not have any brine, add another 2 tablespoons (30 mL) lemon juice. **2.** Parsley comes in either flat-leaf or curly varieties. Flat-leaf parsley is desirable for this recipe for its flavour, but either variety will do.

Chopped Salad

To me, there is no point to eating a salad if it's not filled with a mix of great textures and flavours (okay, besides the whole being-really-good-for-you thing). For this reason, chopped salad is always a winner because all the components come together to create an overall awesome experience in the mouth—or as I like to call it, my gullet! You'll be so focused on how yummy it is that you won't even notice how healthy it is. The key to making a great chopped salad is making sure that all of the ingredients are fresh and preferably picked at the height of the season. For extra protein, try adding the seitan meat from my Boneless Wings (page 24) or even top it with my Deviled Eggs (page 81).

MAKES 1 LARGE OR 4 SIDE SALADS

Prep ahead

Classic Vinaigrette (page 233) or Russian Dressing (page 234)

Roasted Sweet Potato

1 cup (250 mL) peeled, cubed sweet potato

2 tablespoons (30 mL) vegetable oil

¼ teaspoon (1 mL) chili powder

¼ teaspoon (1 mL) sea salt

Salad

1 head romaine lettuce (hearts preferably), cut in 2-inch (5 cm) squares

½ cup (125 mL) cubed red sweet pepper

½ cup (125 mL) cooked black beans or chickpeas

¼ cup (60 mL) peeled, pitted, and cubed avocado

¼ cup (60 mL) fresh corn kernels

¼ cup (60 mL) sliced cherry tomatoes

¼ cup (60 mL) lightly toasted raw sunflower seeds (see Tip)

2 tablespoons (30 mL) thinly sliced green onion (white and light green parts only)

⅓ cup (75 mL) Classic Vinaigrette or Russian Dressing

1. **ROAST THE SWEET POTATOES** Preheat the oven to 425°F (220°C). Line a baking sheet with parchment paper.

2. In a small bowl, toss together the sweet potato, vegetable oil, chili powder, and salt. Place on the prepared baking sheet and bake until soft in the middle and golden brown, 10 to 12 minutes. Remove from the oven and allow to cool completely.

3. **ASSEMBLE THE SALAD** Lay the lettuce on the bottom of a serving plate. One at a time, arrange a neat, even strip of each of the following ingredients over the lettuce: roasted sweet potatoes, red pepper, black beans, avocado, corn, tomatoes, sunflower seeds, and green onion. You want this salad to be visually appealing, so each ingredient gets its own space. Drizzle the classic vinaigrette or Russian dressing over the salad and serve immediately.

TIP

To toast sunflower seeds, heat a pan over medium heat with no oil. Add the sunflower seeds and gently shake the pan until they start to turn golden brown and become fragrant, about 3 to 4 minutes. Remove the sunflower seeds from the heat right away and place in a cold bowl or on a cold baking sheet. Nuts and seeds continue to cook if kept on the heat; removing them from the heat prevents overcooking or burning.

Brunch

Buttermilk Blueberry Pancakes

For most people, nothing is more idyllic or familiar on a slow, lazy weekend than a giant stack of light and fluffy pancakes, spotted with many sweet bursts of purple blueberries. Even though most pancake recipes use eggs, you might be shocked to learn that they aren't necessary at all. I know I was—I almost felt like my whole childhood had been a lie! There are so many egg substitutes for baking. My version uses baking powder and baking soda to leaven, doing the exact same job that eggs would have done. Make sure to smother your stack with pure Canadian maple syrup.

MAKES 8 TO 10 PANCAKES

Ingredients

2¼ cups (550 mL) unsweetened almond milk

½ cup (125 mL) fresh blueberries

¼ cup (60 mL) melted deodorized coconut oil or virgin coconut oil

2 tablespoons (30 mL) unpasteurized apple cider vinegar

1 tablespoon (15 mL) freshly squeezed lemon juice

1½ teaspoons (7 mL) pure vanilla extract

1 cup (250 mL) all-purpose flour

1 cup (250 mL) whole wheat flour

½ cup (125 mL) quick rolled oats

2 tablespoons (30 mL) sugar

1¼ teaspoons (6 mL) baking powder

¾ teaspoon (4 mL) baking soda

¼ teaspoon (1 mL) sea salt

———

Vegetable oil, for cooking

Maple syrup, for serving

1. Preheat the oven to 200°F (100°C). Line a baking sheet with parchment paper.
2. In a medium bowl, whisk together the almond milk, blueberries, coconut oil, apple cider vinegar, lemon juice, and vanilla. Set aside so the vinegar and lemon can slightly curdle the milk, about 5 minutes. Using the whisk or the back of a wooden spoon, gently mash some of the blueberries to release their flavour.
3. In another medium bowl, whisk together the all-purpose flour, whole wheat flour, oats, sugar, baking powder, baking soda, and salt.
4. Add the almond milk mixture to the flour mixture and stir to combine. You do not want to overmix the batter, or the pancakes will be tough. A few lumps in the batter is okay.
5. In a medium frying pan, heat just enough vegetable oil to coat the bottom of the pan over medium heat. Add ¼ cup (60 mL) of batter for each pancake to the pan. Cook the pancakes until bubbles form around the outside and they are golden brown on the bottom, 4 to 5 minutes. Flip and continue to cook until golden brown on the other side, 4 to 5 minutes. Transfer to the prepared baking sheet and keep warm in the oven while you cook the remaining pancakes. Serve with maple syrup.

Peanut Butter Fudge and Chocolate Waffles

Chocolate. Peanut butter. Waffles. It's hard to imagine more delicious words on their own, but together they make for a sinfully scrumptious combination. Is it breakfast? Is it dessert? It doesn't matter, because you deserve it any time of the day. The chocolate is rich and sweet, the peanut butter is smooth and salty, and even if you consider yourself team flapjack, you can't deny that waffles are pretty much one of the most fun foods out there. Enjoy straight off the waffle maker and don't be afraid to drizzle your heart out.

MAKES 4 WAFFLES

Peanut Butter Fudge

1 cup (250 mL) smooth natural peanut butter

¼ cup (60 mL) maple syrup

¼ cup (60 mL) melted deodorized coconut oil

½ teaspoon (2 mL) pure vanilla extract

Pinch of sea salt

Chocolate Sauce

½ cup (125 mL) cocoa powder

¼ cup (60 mL) melted deodorized coconut oil

¼ cup (60 mL) maple syrup

¼ teaspoon (1 mL) pure vanilla extract

2 teaspoons (10 mL) cold water

Pinch of sea salt

Waffles

1½ cups (375 mL) unsweetened almond milk

¼ cup (60 mL) melted deodorized coconut oil

2 teaspoons (10 mL) pure vanilla extract

2 cups (500 mL) all-purpose flour

1 tablespoon (15 mL) baking powder

1 tablespoon (15 mL) sugar

⅛ teaspoon (0.5 mL) sea salt

For serving

Vegan vanilla ice cream (optional)

Dairy-free chocolate chips

Fresh berries

1. Preheat the oven to 200°F (100°C). Line a baking sheet with parchment paper.

2. **MAKE THE PEANUT BUTTER FUDGE** In a medium bowl, combine the peanut butter, maple syrup, coconut oil, vanilla, and salt. Using a spatula, mix until well combined. Transfer the mixture to a small container, cover, and refrigerate until completely firm, at least 2 hours or overnight. Remove the fudge from the fridge and transfer it to a cutting board. Cut the fudge into bite-size pieces, return to the container, and refrigerate until ready to use.

3. **MAKE THE CHOCOLATE SAUCE** In a blender, combine the cocoa powder, coconut oil, maple syrup, vanilla, water, and salt. Blend until smooth and creamy.

4. **MAKE THE WAFFLES** In a medium bowl, whisk together the almond milk, coconut oil, and vanilla.

5. In another medium bowl, combine the flour, baking powder, sugar, and salt. Whisk until well combined and no lumps remain.

6. Add the almond milk mixture to the flour mixture and mix until well combined. There should be no lumps remaining.

7. Preheat the waffle maker to medium-high. Lightly oil the base of the waffle maker with a little vegetable oil. Ladle about ½ cup (125 mL) of batter into the middle of the waffle maker. Close the lid and cook according to the waffle maker's directions. Transfer to the prepared baking sheet and keep warm in the oven while you cook the remaining waffles. Serve with chunks of peanut butter fudge, drizzled with chocolate sauce, and with a scoop of ice cream (if using), chocolate chips, and fresh berries.

Stuffed and Stacked French Toast

When I first went vegan, I thought I would have to say goodbye to my beloved French toast breakfasts. Egg and milk-soaked bread fried in butter is not necessarily the first thing you think of when you think of vegan cuisine. Thankfully, I came up with the perfect recipe to replace this decadent breakfast staple. In my version, I substitute the eggs with a little bit of soft tofu and flour, giving this dish the same body and texture as traditional French toast. Bon appetit!

MAKES 9 SLICES FRENCH TOAST; SERVES 3

Mascarpone

2 cups (500 mL) water

1 tablespoon (15 mL) agar powder

2 cups (500 mL) raw cashews, soaked and drained (see Tip)

¼ cup (60 mL) deodorized coconut oil

3 tablespoons (45 mL) maple syrup

1 teaspoon (5 mL) finely grated lemon zest

2 tablespoons (30 mL) freshly squeezed lemon juice

1 tablespoon (15 mL) pure vanilla extract

¼ teaspoon (1 mL) sea salt

Strawberry Compote

1 cup (250 mL) frozen strawberries

3 tablespoons (45 mL) sugar

1 tablespoon (15 mL) pure vanilla extract

1 teaspoon (5 mL) freshly squeezed lemon juice

¼ teaspoon (1 mL) cinnamon

French Toast

1 cup (250 mL) unsweetened almond milk

⅓ cup (75 mL) chopped firm vacuum-packed tofu

¼ cup (60 mL) all-purpose flour

1 tablespoon (15 mL) agave nectar

½ teaspoon (2 mL) cinnamon

½ teaspoon (2 mL) pure vanilla extract

¼ teaspoon (1 mL) black salt

9 slices of your favourite bread

Vegetable oil, for cooking

For serving

Maple syrup

Fresh berries (optional)

1. Preheat the oven to 200°F (100°C). Line a baking sheet with parchment paper.
2. **MAKE THE MASCARPONE** In a small pot, combine the water and agar powder. Bring to a boil, uncovered, then reduce the heat to a simmer and cook, stirring constantly, 1 to 2 minutes.
3. In a high-speed blender, combine the agar mixture with the drained cashews, coconut oil, maple syrup, lemon zest, lemon juice, vanilla, and salt. Blend until smooth and creamy. Transfer to a container and refrigerate until cold, about 3 hours. Remove from the fridge and place in a food processor fitted with a metal blade. Process until smooth and creamy.
4. **MAKE THE STRAWBERRY COMPOTE** In a small saucepan, combine the strawberries, sugar, vanilla, lemon juice, and cinnamon and bring to boil, uncovered. Reduce the heat to a simmer and cook, stirring occasionally, until the mixture thickens, about 15 minutes.
5. **MAKE THE FRENCH TOAST** In a blender, combine the almond milk, tofu, flour, agave, cinnamon, vanilla, and black salt. Blend until smooth and creamy. Transfer the batter to a medium bowl.
6. In a large frying pan, preferably nonstick, heat just enough vegetable oil to coat the bottom of the pan over medium-high heat. Dip a slice of bread in the batter. Turn and dip the bread in the batter again so that all sides are coated evenly. You want the bread to be completely covered in batter. Cook the bread until golden brown on the bottom, 3 to 4 minutes. Flip and continue cooking until the other side is golden brown, 3 to 4 more minutes. You may need to add a little oil to the pan when you flip the bread. Transfer to the prepared baking sheet and keep warm in the oven while you cook the remaining slices of French toast.
7. To serve, place 6 slices of the French toast on a work surface. Generously spread the mascarpone over each slice, followed by a layer of strawberry compote. For each serving, stack 2 slices of French toast, slathered with the mascarpone and strawberry compote, on top of one another. Top each stack with a plain slice of French toast. Serve immediately with maple syrup and fresh berries, if using.

TIP

To soak the cashews, place them in a large bowl with 4 cups (1 L) of hot water for at least 1 hour or overnight, covered, and stored in the fridge. Drain and rinse the cashews, discarding the soaking liquid.

Muesli and Cashew Yogurt Parfait

Don't let the seeming simplicity of this dish fool you—it's packed with flavours and textures that are sure to wake up your senses and please your palate. The silky-smooth yogurt is made with creamy cashews and pairs perfectly with the nutty homemade muesli. Top with fresh berries for extra bursts of flavour and a sweet morning meal that will definitely put a smile on your face as you start the day.

MAKES 2 OR 3 PARFAITS

Muesli

2 cups (500 mL) old-fashioned rolled oats

½ cup (125 mL) raisins

¼ cup (60 mL) raw walnut halves

¼ cup (60 mL) raw pumpkin seeds

¼ cup (60 mL) raw sunflower seeds

¼ cup (60 mL) raw pecan halves

1 teaspoon (5 mL) cinnamon

¼ teaspoon (1 mL) sea salt

Cashew Yogurt

1 cup (250 mL) raw cashews

2½ cups (625 mL) water, divided

¼ cup (60 mL) maple syrup

1½ teaspoons (7 mL) finely grated lemon zest

¼ cup (60 mL) freshly squeezed lemon juice

1 tablespoon (15 mL) pure vanilla extract

1 probiotic capsule (optional; see Tip)

Softened Berries

½ cup (125 mL) frozen or fresh strawberries

½ cup (125 mL) frozen blueberries

2 teaspoons (10 mL) maple syrup

1 teaspoon (5 mL) freshly squeezed lemon juice

½ teaspoon (2 mL) pure vanilla extract

1. **MAKE THE MUESLI** In a medium bowl, combine the oats, raisins, walnuts, pumpkin seeds, sunflower seeds, pecans, cinnamon, and salt. Mix until well combined.

2. **MAKE THE CASHEW YOGURT** In a small pot, combine the cashews and 2 cups (500 mL) of the water. Bring to a boil, then reduce the heat to a simmer and cook for 1 to 2 minutes. Remove from the heat and allow to cool slightly, about 5 minutes. Drain the cooking water and discard.

3. In a high-speed blender, combine the cooked cashews with the remaining ½ cup (125 mL) water, maple syrup, lemon zest, lemon juice, vanilla, and the contents of the probiotic capsule, if using. Blend on high speed until smooth and creamy.

4. **MAKE THE SOFTENED BERRIES** In a small bowl, mix together the strawberries, blueberries, maple syrup, lemon juice, and vanilla. Set aside in a warm place so that the berries can defrost, about 30 minutes. Using the back of a fork, gently press on the berries so they release some of their juices.

5. **ASSEMBLE THE PARFAITS** In parfait dishes or glasses, start by filling each dish one-third full with the yogurt. Add about ¼ cup (60 mL) of the berries, followed by about ⅓ cup (75 mL) of the muesli. Repeat until the dishes are full and serve immediately. Store leftover muesli in an airtight container at room temperature for up to 2 weeks. Store leftover yogurt and berries separately in airtight containers in the fridge for up to 1 week.

TIP

Adding a probiotic capsule (make sure it's vegan!) to the mixture adds some of the beneficial bacteria that traditional yogurt has. If you want to take this a step further, leave the bowl of yogurt, covered with a kitchen towel, on the counter in a warm place for 24 hours so that the bacteria can grow. Store in an airtight container in the fridge for up to 2 weeks.

Cage-Free Cheesy Omelette

One of the most interesting and perhaps most surprising characteristics of tofu is its ability to stand in for eggs in so many recipes. Although most people think you need eggs to make an omelette, this vegan version will convince you otherwise! This recipe is versatile, so you can fill the omelettes with whatever you have on hand, from mushrooms to spinach to sweet peppers. Bonus: No cages needed!

MAKES 4 OMELETTES

Prep ahead

Mac and Cheese Sauce
  (page 223)

Ingredients

1 block (12 ounces/340 g)
  firm or extra-firm silken
  tofu

¾ cup (175 mL) unsweetened
  almond milk

½ cup (125 mL) corn flour
  (see Tip)

3 tablespoons (45 mL)
  vegetable oil

3 tablespoons (45 mL)
  nutritional yeast

2 tablespoons (30 mL) all-
  purpose flour

2 tablespoons (30 mL) ground
  golden flaxseed

1 tablespoon (15 mL) +
  1½ teaspoons (7 mL)
  cornstarch

1 teaspoon (5 mL) black salt

½ teaspoon (2 mL) ground
  turmeric

1 cup (250 mL) Mac and Cheese
  Sauce

———

Vegetable oil, for cooking

1. Preheat the oven to 200°F (100°C). Line a baking sheet with parchment paper.

2. In a blender, combine the tofu, almond milk, corn flour, vegetable oil, nutritional yeast, flour, flaxseed, cornstarch, black salt, and turmeric. Blend until smooth.

3. In a large nonstick frying pan, heat enough vegetable oil to coat the bottom of the pan. Using a ladle, pour about ½ cup (125 mL) of the batter into the pan. Cook until the omelette is firm around the edges and golden brown on the bottom, 4 to 5 minutes. Flip and cook until golden brown on the other side, 3 to 4 minutes. Transfer to the prepared baking sheet and keep warm in the oven while you cook the remaining omelettes.

4. Remove the omelettes from the oven and place them on serving plates. Pour about ¼ cup (60 mL) of the mac and cheese sauce into the middle of each omelette, then fold the top half over the bottom half for a half-moon omelette. Serve immediately.

TIP

If you do not have corn flour, you can substitute ½ cup (125 mL) cornmeal processed in a blender until it has a flour-like consistency.

Breakfast in Bed Scones

Feel like something light yet filling at the same time? Then you'll want to whip up a batch of these scones! These fluffy scones use coconut cream in place of the heavy cream that's traditionally used in this British staple. If you don't like the taste of coconut, or if you don't have any coconut cream on hand, feel free to use unsweetened almond milk instead. Serve these warm, and you'll probably want to slather them with jam and peanut butter!

MAKES 12 SCONES

Scones

2 cups (500 mL) all-purpose flour, more for dusting

⅓ cup (75 mL) sugar

1½ teaspoons (7 mL) baking powder

½ teaspoon (2 mL) sea salt

½ cup (125 mL) cold chopped vegan butter

½ cup (125 mL) cold coconut cream (see Tip)

Vegan Egg Wash

¼ cup (60 mL) unsweetened almond milk

2 tablespoons (30 mL) maple syrup

1 tablespoon (15 mL) melted deodorized coconut oil

1. Preheat the oven to 375°F (190°C). Line a baking sheet with parchment paper.

2. **MAKE THE SCONES** In a medium bowl, whisk together the flour, sugar, baking powder, and salt. Add the butter and, using a pastry cutter or a fork, mix to combine. Using your hands, combine until the mixture is dry and crumbly. Add the coconut cream and mix with your hands until the dough comes together into a ball. Transfer to a lightly floured work surface. Knead the dough 3 to 4 times only; you want the dough to only barely come together.

3. Divide the dough into 2 equal portions and transfer to a lightly floured work surface. Using a rolling pin, roll each portion of the dough so it is about 1½ inches (4 cm) thick. Using a knife, score each portion of dough into 6 triangles, then gently separate the triangles from each other. Transfer to the prepared baking sheet. You want to leave about ¼ to ½ inch (5 mm to 1 cm) between each scone.

4. **MAKE THE VEGAN EGG WASH** In a small bowl, whisk together the almond milk, maple syrup, and coconut oil until well combined.

5. Brush the tops of the scones with the egg wash and make sure there is about ¼ to ½ inch (5 mm to 1 cm) between them. Bake for 15 to 18 minutes, or until the centres are no longer raw and the bottoms are golden brown. Serve immediately or allow to cool and store in an airtight container at room temperature for 3 days or in the fridge for up to 2 weeks.

TIP

Coconut cream is similar to coconut milk, but it has a higher fat content. It is available in most well-stocked grocery stores, in Indian grocery stores, or online. You can use an equal amount of unsweetened almond milk in this recipe, but the scones will not be as decadent.

Seitan Bacon

I think that society's obsession with bacon mainly stems from its crisp texture and a balance of sweet, salty, and smoky flavours that makes us salivate. Trick your taste buds and soothe your soul with my version of plant-based bacon made with vital wheat gluten flour. Use this recipe whenever bacon is needed. It is awesome in my Quiche Lorraine (page 107), Bacon Double Cheeseburgers (page 137), and Stuffed to the Rim Skins (page 36).

MAKES 25 TO 30 BACON SLICES

Seitan (Bacon) Dough

2 cups (500 mL) vital wheat gluten flour

2 teaspoons (10 mL) garlic powder

1 teaspoon (5 mL) smoked paprika

1 teaspoon (5 mL) sea salt

½ teaspoon (2 mL) onion powder

1 cup (250 mL) water

⅓ cup (75 mL) nutritional yeast

¼ cup (60 mL) chopped firm or extra-firm vacuum-packed tofu

¼ cup (60 mL) vegetable oil

¼ cup (60 mL) maple syrup

2 tablespoons (30 mL) tamari or soy sauce

1 tablespoon (15 mL) liquid smoke

1 tablespoon (15 mL) tomato paste

Smoky Broth

1 cup (250 mL) water

¼ cup (60 mL) maple syrup

¼ cup (60 mL) tamari or soy sauce

¼ cup (60 mL) vegetable oil

2 teaspoons (10 mL) liquid smoke

Marinade

¼ cup (60 mL) tamari or soy sauce

2 tablespoons (30 mL) maple syrup or agave nectar

2 tablespoons (30 mL) vegetable oil

2 tablespoons (30 mL) water

1 teaspoon (5 mL) liquid smoke

———

Vegetable oil, for cooking

1. **MAKE THE SEITAN DOUGH** In a large bowl, whisk together the wheat gluten flour, garlic powder, paprika, salt, and onion powder.

2. In a blender, combine the water, nutritional yeast, tofu, vegetable oil, maple syrup, tamari, liquid smoke, and tomato paste. Blend until smooth.

3. Make a well in the centre of the flour mixture. Pour the water mixture into the well of the flour mixture. Using your hands, mix together until well combined and it comes together as a dough. You do not want to see any dry patches of the flour left. Transfer the dough to a work surface and knead it for 3 to 4 minutes to give it a firmer consistency. By kneading it, you are working to develop the gluten and make the dough firm enough that it holds together while cooking.

4. Shape the dough so it is about 6 inches (15 cm) long, 3 inches (8 cm) wide, and 1 inch (2.5 cm) thick.

5. Preheat the oven to 350°F (180°C). Line an 11- × 7-inch (2 L) baking dish with foil, leaving an extra 3 inches (8 cm) of foil on each side. You will be cooking the seitan in a foil package and you do not want the steam to escape, so it is important to have enough foil to close all sides tightly.

6. **MAKE THE SMOKY BROTH** In a blender, combine the water, maple syrup, tamari, vegetable oil, and liquid smoke. Blend until smooth.

7. Place the seitan in the middle of the foil and gather the sides to create a pouch. Pour the smoky broth over the seitan, making sure not to let any of the liquid spill out of the foil. Gather the foil and make an airtight package. Bake until the seitan is firm to the touch, about 60 minutes. You do not want it to be soft or have the texture of dough at this point. If it is a little soft, tighten the foil again and continue baking for another 10 to 15 minutes. Remove from the oven and allow it to cool enough to handle, about 1 hour.

8. **MEANWHILE, MAKE THE MARINADE** In a blender, combine the tamari, maple syrup, vegetable oil, water, and liquid smoke. Blend until smooth.

9. Using a sharp knife, slice the bacon into 25 to 30 thin strips. Pour the marinade over the bacon, turning it to coat all sides.

10. In a large frying pan, preferably nonstick, heat enough vegetable oil to coat the bottom of the pan over medium heat. Cook the bacon until golden brown and crisp on the bottom, 4 to 5 minutes. Turn and cook until golden brown on the other side, 3 to 4 minutes. Serve immediately or allow to cool and store in an airtight container in the fridge for up to 1 week.

Quiche Lorraine

Need to make a good impression, or just want to prove how classy you are? Whip up this dish! It's based on the classic dish Quiche Lorraine and stuffed to the brim with vegan bacon and cheese—who wouldn't love this combo? It's perfect for a buffet or when you're entertaining guests for lunch or brunch. Complete this hearty meal with a simple green salad. Leftovers can be refrigerated and make a great meal-on-the-go. Out go the eggs, in goes the tofu!

SERVES 6 TO 8

Prep ahead

Crust of Chickpea Pot Pie (see page 133)

Seitan Bacon (page 105)

Cashew Mozzarella (page 218)

Ingredients

1 batch crust of Chickpea Pot Pie

3 tablespoons (45 mL) vegetable oil

2 cups (500 mL) thinly sliced white onion

¼ teaspoon (1 mL) sea salt

1 cup (250 mL) thinly sliced Seitan Bacon

2 tablespoons (30 mL) tamari or soy sauce

½ cup (125 mL) unsweetened almond milk

2 blocks (12 ounces/340 g each) firm silken tofu

½ cup (125 mL) nutritional yeast

¼ cup (60 mL) all-purpose flour

1 tablespoon (15 mL) freshly squeezed lemon juice

1 teaspoon (5 mL) black salt

½ teaspoon (2 mL) ground turmeric

½ cup (125 mL) shredded Cashew Mozzarella or vegan shredded mozzarella

1. Preheat the oven to 350°F (180°C). Lightly grease a 9-inch (23 cm) pie plate with vegetable oil.

2. Gently press the prepared pie crust into the pie plate, evenly covering the bottom and sides. Using a fork, poke several holes in the dough to allow steam to escape when baking. Bake for 15 minutes or until the crust is golden brown. Remove from the oven and set aside to cool.

3. In a large frying pan, heat the vegetable oil over high heat. Add the onions and salt and cook, stirring frequently, until the onions are lightly golden brown, 5 to 6 minutes. Add the bacon and cook until it is lightly golden brown and fragrant, 8 to 10 minutes. Add the tamari and stir to remove any brown bits from the bottom of the pan. Remove from the heat.

4. In a blender, combine the almond milk, tofu, nutritional yeast, flour, lemon juice, black salt, and turmeric. Blend until smooth. Transfer to a large bowl and stir in the vegetable mixture and cashew mozzarella.

5. Spread the tofu and vegetable mixture evenly in the prebaked pie crust. Bake for 35 to 40 minutes, or until the quiche is firmly set in the middle (it shouldn't jiggle too much when gently shaken). Remove from the oven and let cool for 20 minutes before serving. Store in an airtight container in the fridge for up to 1 week.

VARIATION

HAM AND CHEESE QUICHE Substitute Seitan Ham (see page 109) for the Seitan Bacon and Almond Milk Cheddar Cheese (page 216) for the Cashew Mozzarella.

Count of Monte Cristo

Usually, a Monte Cristo sandwich is stuffed with ham and cheese and dipped in an eggy batter, then fried until golden brown. My version is just as mouth-watering but uses tofu and flour as a replacement for eggs, my masterful Seitan Ham (see page 109) invention, plus my magnificent recipe for Swiss Cheese (page 219) as the filling. Epic, is all I have to say. The Count would truly be proud!

MAKES 4 SANDWICHES

Prep ahead

Swiss Cheese (page 219)

Seitan Ham (see page 109)

Ingredients

2 cups (500 mL) unsweetened almond milk

⅓ cup (75 mL) whole wheat flour

¼ cup (60 mL) chopped soft water-packed tofu, drained and patted dry

¼ teaspoon (1 mL) ground turmeric

¼ teaspoon (1 mL) black salt

Vegetable oil, for cooking

8 slices bread

1 cup (250 mL) Swiss Cheese

2 cups (500 mL) Seitan Ham

1. Preheat the oven to 350°F (180°C). Line a baking sheet with parchment paper.

2. In a high-speed blender, combine the almond milk, whole wheat flour, tofu, turmeric, and black salt. Blend until smooth. Transfer to a medium bowl.

3. In a large frying pan, heat enough vegetable oil to coat the bottom of the pan over medium heat. Dip the slices of bread in the batter, coating them on both sides. Cook the bread in batches, being careful not to crowd the pan, until golden brown on each side, 3 to 4 minutes per side. You will need to add a little more vegetable oil to the pan to cook all of the bread.

4. Place 4 slices of cooked bread on the prepared baking sheet. Spread ¼ cup (60 mL) of the Swiss cheese on each slice, then top each with ½ cup (125 mL) of the seitan ham. Place another slice of cooked bread on top of the ham and gently press down. Bake until the middle of the sandwich is hot and the cheese is soft and bubbling, about 8 to 10 minutes. Serve immediately.

Croque Monsieur

French food made vegan is awesome! If you happened to wake up on the fancy side of the bed this morning, you've got to try this elegant French breakfast sandwich made with my version of creamy Mornay sauce, seitan ham, and Swiss Cheese (page 219). This dish should be the centrepiece for any serious brunch, or lunch, or dinner—or anytime, really!

MAKES 4 SANDWICHES

Prep ahead

Swiss Cheese (page 219)

Mornay Sauce

½ cup (125 mL) roughly chopped white onion

½ cup (125 mL) deodorized coconut oil

½ cup (125 mL) all-purpose flour

2 tablespoons (30 mL) + 1½ teaspoons (7 mL) semi-sweet white wine, such as Riesling

2½ cups (625 mL) unsweetened almond milk

6 tablespoons (90 mL) nutritional yeast

1 teaspoon (5 mL) garlic powder

1 teaspoon (5 mL) sea salt

¼ teaspoon (1 mL) brown rice miso, or any type of miso

2 tablespoons (30 mL) Swiss Cheese

Seitan (Ham) Dough

2 cups (500 mL) vital wheat gluten flour

2 tablespoons (30 mL) nutritional yeast

½ teaspoon (2 mL) sea salt

¾ cup (175 mL) water

½ cup (125 mL) pineapple juice

2 tablespoons (30 mL) tamari or soy sauce

2 tablespoons (30 mL) Dijon mustard

1½ tablespoons (22 mL) vegetable oil

1 tablespoon (15 mL) unpasteurized apple cider vinegar

1 teaspoon (5 mL) liquid smoke

Broth

4 quarts (4 L) water

¼ cup (60 mL) tamari or soy sauce

1 sprig fresh thyme

2 whole cloves

Marinade

½ cup (125 mL) fresh beet juice

1 tablespoon (15 mL) Dijon mustard

2 tablespoons (30 mL) vegetable oil

1 teaspoon (5 mL) sea salt

¼ teaspoon (1 mL) liquid smoke

———

8 slices soft white bread

2 cups (500 mL) Swiss Cheese

1. **MAKE THE MORNAY SAUCE** In a medium pot, over medium heat, combine the onion, coconut oil, and flour. Cook, stirring frequently, for about 6 to 8 minutes.

2. Remove the pot from the heat. Add the white wine, stirring constantly to help remove some of the grittiness from the flour and to make a thick paste. Add the almond milk in a constant, steady stream while whisking at the same time.

3. Return the pot to medium heat and add the nutritional yeast, garlic powder, salt, and miso. Increase the heat to medium-high and bring the mixture to a boil, stirring frequently. Reduce the heat to a simmer and cook for 2 to 3 minutes to help remove some of the raw taste from the flour.

4. Remove the pot from the heat and stir in the Swiss cheese. In batches, taking care not to fill the blender more than halfway with the hot sauce, blend until completely smooth. Transfer the sauce to a clean medium pot.

5. **MAKE THE SEITAN DOUGH** In a medium bowl, whisk together the wheat gluten flour, nutritional yeast, and salt.

6. In a blender, combine the water, pineapple juice, tamari, mustard, vegetable oil, apple cider vinegar, and liquid smoke. Blend until well combined.

7. In a large mixing bowl, add the pineapple juice mixture to the flour mixture and mix until well combined. You want to make sure that no dry lumps remain. Remove the dough from the bowl and transfer it to a work surface. Using your hands, knead the dough for 3 to 4 minutes. You want the dough to be shiny and elastic, with no visible dry patches. It should be the shape of a large ball. Cut the dough into 2 equal pieces.

8. **MAKE THE BROTH AND COOK THE SEITAN DOUGH** In a large, deep pot, combine the water, tamari, thyme, and cloves. Place the dough in the pot. Bring the mixture to a boil, reduce the heat to a simmer, and cook until the centre of each piece of dough no longer has a chewy texture but is firm when pinched between 2 fingers. Once cooked, remove the seitan from the broth and place it, uncovered, on a plate. Allow to cool completely, about 1 hour.

Continued

9. **MAKE THE MARINADE** In a small bowl, whisk together the beet juice, mustard, vegetable oil, salt, and liquid smoke.

10. Cut the seitan ham into thin strips. Toss with the marinade until well combined. Allow to sit for 30 minutes or overnight, covered and stored in the fridge.

11. Preheat the oven to 350°F (180°C) and line a baking sheet with parchment paper.

12. **ASSEMBLE THE SANDWICHES** Lay 4 slices of bread on a work surface. Spread ¼ cup (60 mL) of the Swiss cheese on each slice of bread. Top each slice with about ½ cup (125 mL) of the seitan ham. Place another slice of bread on top of the ham and gently press down. Spread another ¼ cup (60 mL) of the Swiss cheese on top of each sandwich.

13. Place the sandwiches on the prepared baking sheet. Pour about ¾ cup (175 mL) of the Mornay sauce over each sandwich. Bake until hot in the middle and the cheese and Mornay sauce are golden brown on top, 12 to 15 minutes. Serve immediately.

Brunch Club Sandwich

Everyone knows that brunch is just breakfast but taken up a level. So, step up your game from standard breakfast sandwiches and try my scrumptious brunch club sandwich. This one is a perfect balance of sweet, salty, creamy, crunchy, and more. The quick and easy scrambled tofu makes a great replacement for scrambled eggs, offering a better breakfast for the health conscious and for the heart conscious.

MAKES 1 SANDWICH

Prep ahead

Creamy Mayo (page 232)

Tempeh Bacon

½ block (8½ ounces/240 g) tempeh

4 cups (1 L) + 2 tablespoons (30 mL) water, divided

¼ cup (60 mL) tamari or soy sauce, divided

2 tablespoons (30 mL) maple syrup

2 tablespoons (30 mL) vegetable oil

1 tablespoon (15 mL) nutritional yeast

1 teaspoon (5 mL) liquid smoke

Club Sandwich

2 tablespoons (30 mL) vegan butter or vegetable oil

½ cup (125 mL) crumbled medium-firm vacuum-packed tofu

¼ cup (60 mL) nutritional yeast

½ teaspoon (2 mL) black salt

½ teaspoon (2 mL) Dijon mustard

⅛ teaspoon (0.5 mL) ground turmeric

Dash of tamari or soy sauce

For assembly

3 slices thick-cut sourdough bread, toasted

¼ cup (60 mL) Creamy Mayo, divided

4 leaves romaine lettuce

½ avocado, peeled, pitted, and thinly sliced

2 slices tomato

1. **MAKE THE TEMPEH BACON** In a medium pot, bring to a boil the tempeh, 4 cups (1 L) of the water, and 2 tablespoons (30 mL) of the tamari. Reduce the heat and simmer for 15 minutes. Transfer the tempeh to a bowl and set aside.

2. In a small bowl, whisk together the remaining 2 tablespoons (30 mL) water, the remaining 2 tablespoons (30 mL) tamari, maple syrup, vegetable oil, nutritional yeast, and liquid smoke.

3. Slice the cooled tempeh into strips about ⅓ inch (8 mm) thick (you should have about 26 strips). Layer the slices in a large bowl and pour the tamari mixture over top. Cover and set aside for at least 30 minutes or refrigerate overnight.

4. Preheat the oven to 400°F (200°C). Line a baking sheet with parchment paper.

5. Remove the tempeh from the marinade. Place the tempeh strips in a single layer on the prepared baking sheet and bake until no liquid remains and the tempeh is slightly crisp, about 15 minutes. Discard the marinade.

6. **MAKE THE CLUB SANDWICH** In a large frying pan, heat the butter over medium-high heat. Add the tofu and cook, stirring constantly, until most of the liquid has been absorbed and the tofu begins to brown, 4 to 5 minutes. Remove from the heat and add the nutritional yeast, black salt, mustard, turmeric, and tamari. Stir to combine, picking up any brown bits from the bottom of the pan. Set aside until ready to use.

7. To assemble, spread 2 tablespoons (30 mL) of the creamy mayo on 1 piece of toast. Top with 2 lettuce leaves, avocado, and tofu. On a second piece of toast, spread the remaining 2 tablespoons (30 mL) creamy mayo and top with 2 slices of tomato, tempeh bacon, and the remaining lettuce. Place the remaining piece of toast on top and cut in half. Serve immediately.

Sunny Side Up Vegan Eggs with Yolks

Step into the role of scientist for a while with this recipe! Science and experimentation are always involved in the cooking and baking processes. However, I've got to pat myself on the back for this one, because I was able to create the exact texture and flavour of sunny side up eggs, complete with runny yolks, using a technique called spherification that is taken from molecular gastronomy. So, strap on your apron and let this delectable science experiment begin!

MAKES 15 TO 16 EGGS

Egg Whites

4 blocks (12 ounces/340 g each) firm or extra-firm silken tofu (see Tip)

Pinch of black salt

Egg Yolks

¾ cup (175 mL) nutritional yeast

1 teaspoon (5 mL) sodium alginate (see Tip)

1 teaspoon (5 mL) black salt

2¼ cups (550 mL) cold water, divided

2 teaspoons (10 mL) calcium chloride (see Tip)

———

Cold water, to rinse the egg yolks (about 2 cups/500 mL)

Vegetable oil, for frying

TIP

1. Be sure to use firm or extra-firm silken tofu for this recipe. Soft or medium tofu will break.

2. Sodium alginate is available in specialty stores or online. It is a common ingredient in molecular cuisine.

3. Calcium chloride is available in most health food stores, in specialty stores, or online. Make sure to buy food-grade calcium chloride.

1. **MAKE THE EGG WHITES** Carefully open each pack of tofu, taking care not to damage its shape. Using a thin, sharp knife, cut each block of tofu into 4 slices through the middle. Lay each slice on a work surface. Using a cookie cutter, cut a circle out of each slice of tofu; this will be your egg white. If you do not have a cookie cutter, use a sharp knife to cut the shape of a circle. Save the trimmings for a later use. Using a 1-teaspoon (5 mL) measuring spoon, carefully scoop out a bit of the middle of each piece of tofu. You do not want to cut through to the back of the tofu but only remove a little bit.

2. **MAKE THE EGG YOLKS** In a blender, combine the nutritional yeast, sodium alginate, and black salt. Blend until well combined and the nutritional yeast has broken down into a fine powder, about 30 seconds. Add 1¼ cup (300 mL) of the cold water. Blend until completely smooth, about 1 minute. You should not see any large pieces of nutritional yeast or any lumps of black salt. Transfer to a small bowl.

3. In a medium bowl, combine the remaining 1 cup (250 mL) water and the calcium chloride. Mix until the calcium chloride is completely dissolved.

4. Place the cold water in a separate medium bowl. You will use this to rinse the egg yolks after you remove them from the calcium chloride solution.

5. Drop about 1 tablespoon (15 mL) of the yolk mixture into the calcium chloride solution. (I like using a tablespoon ice cream scoop.) Drop the yolk mixture as close to the calcium chloride solution as possible to make a sphere. It is okay if a small tail forms; simply pinch this off after the yolk has set and is in the cold rinse water. Repeat with the remaining yolk mixture. Allow the egg yolks to sit in the solution for about 5 minutes, or until a skin forms around the outside of the yolk but the middle is still soft. Transfer the yolks to the bowl of cold water to rinse off any excess solution. Use the egg yolks right away or store in the rinse water, covered, in the fridge for up to 2 days.

6. **COOK THE EGG WHITES** In a large frying pan, preferably nonstick, heat enough vegetable oil to coat the bottom of the pan over medium-high heat. Season the egg whites with a pinch of black salt and cook until they are golden brown and crisp on the outside, 4 to 5 minutes per side.

7. **ASSEMBLE THE EGGS** In a small pot, bring about ½ cup (125 mL) water to a low simmer. Drop the egg yolks into the simmering water and cook until warm in the center, about 30 seconds only. Do not overcook the eggs. Remove the yolks from the water with a slotted spoon and place one yolk in the middle of each cooked egg white. Serve immediately.

Perfect Vegan Scramble

Scrambled eggs are the most iconic breakfast dish known to the Western Hemisphere, served at almost any table. Soft, silky, and moist, they're perfect served with toast and a host of other side dishes. The secret to my vegan scrambled eggs is that it's made using medium-firm tofu that's pressed overnight. This method gives you the closest texture to eggs, so even your most egg-loving friends will think it's the real thing. Nutritional yeast gives it the cheesy quality of conventional scrambled eggs, while the sauce helps make it creamy and oh so good!

SERVES 4

Creamy Sauce
- ¼ cup (60 mL) extra-virgin olive oil
- ¼ cup (60 mL) nutritional yeast
- ¼ cup (60 mL) water
- 1 tablespoon (15 mL) tamari or soy sauce
- 2 teaspoons (10 mL) Dijon mustard
- ¼ teaspoon (1 mL) black salt

Scrambled Eggs
- 1 block (1 pound/450 g) medium-firm water-packed tofu, pressed overnight (see Tip)
- 1 tablespoon (15 mL) nutritional yeast
- 1 teaspoon (5 mL) black salt
- ¼ teaspoon (1 mL) ground turmeric
- ¼ teaspoon (1 mL) garlic powder
- 3 tablespoons (45 mL) vegetable oil, for cooking

1. **MAKE THE CREAMY SAUCE** In a blender, combine the olive oil, nutritional yeast, water, tamari, mustard, and black salt. Blend until smooth.

2. **MAKE THE SCRAMBLED EGGS** In a medium bowl, crumble the tofu using your hands. Add the nutritional yeast, black salt, turmeric, and garlic powder. Using a wooden spoon or spatula, mix until well combined.

3. In a large frying pan, preferably nonstick, heat the vegetable oil over medium-high heat. Cook the tofu, stirring frequently, for 5 to 6 minutes. Remove from the heat and add the sauce while stirring constantly. Serve immediately or allow to cool and store in a covered container in the fridge for up to 1 week.

TIP

Pressing water-packed tofu overnight releases some of the water and gives it a great texture. To do this, place a kitchen towel on a plate. Place the tofu in the middle of the towel. Place another plate on top of the tofu and then a weight on top of the plate. Store in the fridge overnight so that the water can slowly drain away from the tofu.

Downhome Fries

Home fries for breakfast are always appetizing and appropriate (especially after a night of drinking a little too much, or so I hear). By far one of the simplest yet most satisfying ways to start the day, these perfectly seasoned potatoes will undoubtedly soak up any alcohol (or feelings of regret) left in your system from the night before so that you can face the day hangover- and hangry-free. If you're feeling up to it, serve these with my Cage-Free Eggs Florentine (page 118), Buttermilk Blueberry Pancakes (page 95), or Croque Monsieur (page 109).

SERVES 6 TO 8

Ingredients

2 pounds (900 g) medium red-skin potatoes, cut in halves or quarters (see Tip)

4 quarts (4 L) water

1½ teaspoons (7 mL) sea salt, divided

¼ cup (60 mL) vegetable oil

1 tablespoon (15 mL) nutritional yeast

¼ teaspoon (1 mL) smoked paprika

¼ teaspoon (1 mL) garlic powder

1 tablespoon (15 mL) chopped fresh thyme leaves

1. In a medium pot, combine the potatoes, water, and 1 teaspoon (5 mL) of the salt. Bring to a boil, uncovered, and reduce the heat to a simmer. Cook the potatoes until fork-tender, about 15 minutes. Drain, discarding the water.

2. In a large frying pan, preferably nonstick, heat the vegetable oil over medium-high heat. Add the potatoes and cook, stirring frequently, until golden brown, 10 to 12 minutes. During the last couple of minutes of cooking, add the nutritional yeast, remaining ½ teaspoon (2 mL) salt, paprika, garlic powder, and thyme. Cook, stirring constantly, for 1 to 2 minutes. Serve immediately.

TIP

I like to use red-skin potatoes because they are considered a waxy potato, and they hold their shape well when cooked. Yukon Gold potatoes will also work well for this recipe.

The Classics Veganized

Buttermilk Fried Chicken

I don't know who came up with the wild idea to combine salty fried chicken with sweet maple syrup and waffles, but I would like to personally thank them for making the world a tastier place. My bird-friendly version of fried chicken is made using vital wheat gluten flour, the perfect assortment of spices and seasonings, and nutritional yeast to give it that savoury flavour!

SERVES 4

Seitan (Chicken) Dough

2 cups (500 mL) vital wheat gluten flour

⅓ cup (75 mL) nutritional yeast

2 teaspoons (10 mL) sweet paprika

2 teaspoons (10 mL) garlic powder

2 teaspoons (10 mL) onion powder

1 teaspoon (5 mL) sea salt

½ teaspoon (2 mL) celery salt

½ teaspoon (2 mL) freshly cracked black pepper

¼ teaspoon (1 mL) dried ground thyme

¼ teaspoon (1 mL) ground ginger

¼ teaspoon (1 mL) dried oregano

2 cups (500 mL) water

2 tablespoons + 2 teaspoons (40 mL) vegetable oil

2 teaspoons (10 mL) unpasteurized apple cider vinegar

1 tablespoon (15 mL) vegan Worcestershire sauce

1 teaspoon (5 mL) Dijon mustard

Broth

4 quarts (4 L) water

4 to 6 cloves garlic

½ teaspoon (2 mL) sea salt

Breading

1 cup (250 mL) all-purpose flour

1 cup (250 mL) cornstarch

2 tablespoons (30 mL) nutritional yeast

1 tablespoon (15 mL) + 1½ teaspoons (7 mL) sweet paprika

1 tablespoon (15 mL) garlic powder

1 tablespoon (15 mL) onion powder

½ teaspoon (2 mL) celery salt

½ tablespoon (7 mL) sea salt

4 cups (1 L) unsweetened soy milk

⅓ cup (75 mL) unpasteurized apple cider vinegar

2 tablespoons (30 mL) Dijon mustard

1 tablespoon (15 mL) brown sugar

———

4 to 6 cups (1 to 1.5 L) vegetable oil, for frying

1. **MAKE THE SEITAN DOUGH** In a medium bowl, combine the wheat gluten flour, nutritional yeast, paprika, garlic powder, onion powder, sea salt, celery salt, pepper, thyme, ginger, and oregano. Whisk until well combined and no lumps remain.

2. In a blender, combine the water, vegetable oil, apple cider vinegar, Worcestershire sauce, and mustard. Blend until smooth.

3. Make a well in the centre of the flour mixture. Pour the water mixture into the well of the flour mixture. Using your hands, mix until just combined; do not overmix, or it can become tough.

4. **MAKE THE BROTH** In a large pot, combine the water, garlic, and salt.

5. **COOK THE SEITAN DOUGH** Using your hands, tear the dough into pieces the size of a golf ball. Place the dough in the pot with the broth. Bring to a boil, then reduce the heat to a simmer and cook until the middle of the seitan is no longer soft and gooey (the mixture should be firm and easy to cut with a knife), about 45 minutes. Remove the seitan from the broth and set aside until cool enough to handle, about 1½ hours.

6. **MAKE THE BREADING** In a medium bowl, whisk together the flour, cornstarch, nutritional yeast, paprika, garlic powder, onion powder, celery salt, and sea salt.

7. In a large bowl, whisk together the soy milk, apple cider vinegar, mustard, and sugar.

8. Heat the vegetable oil in a large pot or small deep fryer to a temperature of 375°F (190°C).

9. **FRY THE CHICKEN** Using one hand only, keeping the other hand clean, roll each piece of seitan in the flour mixture until coated on all sides. Remove from the dry mix and coat in the wet mix, then coat in the dry mix again. Dip in the hot oil and fry until golden brown and crisp, using metal tongs to turn the seitan as necessary, about 5 to 6 minutes. Serve immediately.

Cage-Free Eggs Florentine

You work hard. You've got it all taken care of. So, you deserve to indulge in a brunch fit for royalty this weekend. If you don't happen to have a fairy godmother to magically whip this up for you, follow my easy recipe for eggs Florentine glazed with my plant-based Hollandaise Sauce (226). The sauce is so lush and creamy, you'll wonder how you ever functioned without it.

SERVES 2

Prep ahead

Hollandaise Sauce (page 226)

Tofu

3 tablespoons (45 mL) nutritional yeast

2 tablespoons (30 mL) all-purpose flour

1 teaspoon (5 mL) black salt, more for serving

½ teaspoon (2 mL) onion powder

½ teaspoon (2 mL) garlic powder

¼ teaspoon (1 mL) ground turmeric

⅛ teaspoon (0.5 mL) freshly cracked black pepper

½ pound (225 g) medium-firm tofu, sliced lengthwise into 4 pieces

3 tablespoons (45 mL) vegetable oil

Spinach

2 tablespoons (30 mL) vegetable oil

4 cups (1 L) tightly packed chopped spinach

1 teaspoon (5 mL) garlic powder

1 teaspoon (5 mL) chopped fresh thyme leaves

¼ teaspoon (1 mL) sea salt

For assembly

2 English muffins, toasted

1 hothouse or beefsteak tomato, cut in 4 slices

1 cup (250 mL) Hollandaise Sauce

1. **COOK THE TOFU** In a small bowl, whisk together the nutritional yeast, flour, black salt, onion powder, garlic powder, turmeric, and pepper. Coat the tofu well in the mixture.

2. In a large frying pan, preferably nonstick, heat the vegetable oil over medium-high heat. Cook the tofu until golden brown, 3 to 4 minutes per side. Transfer to a plate and wipe the pan clean.

3. **COOK THE SPINACH** In the same pan, heat the vegetable oil over medium-high heat. Add the spinach and cook until most of the liquid has evaporated. Add the garlic powder, thyme, and sea salt. Cook, stirring constantly, for 2 to 3 minutes. Remove from the heat.

4. To assemble, place 2 halves of the English muffin on each of 2 plates. Place one-quarter of the spinach mixture on top of each muffin half. Top each with a slice of tomato, a sprinkle of black salt, and a piece of cooked tofu. Pour about ½ cup (125 mL) of the hollandaise sauce over the tofu on each plate. Serve immediately.

Dirty South Sausages and Biscuits with Gravy

Honestly, the cooking from the Deep South has it right. After all, who doesn't want comfort food around the clock? Soft, fluffy biscuits are paired with juicy breakfast sausage patties and rich savoury gravy in this take on home-style cooking from the southern United States. My breakfast sausage recipe uses vital wheat gluten flour as the base and poultry seasoning to mock that classic breakfast sausage flavour. Sounds amazing, doesn't it? Also, don't worry—it's easier to make than you might think.

SERVES 6 TO 7

Prep ahead

Anytime Gravy (page 228)

Seitan (Sausage) Dough

2 cups (500 mL) vital wheat gluten flour

2 tablespoons (30 mL) poultry seasoning

1 tablespoon (15 mL) sugar

1 tablespoon (15 mL) garlic powder

1½ teaspoons (7 mL) sea salt, divided

1 teaspoon (5 mL) ground fennel seeds

1 teaspoon (5 mL) chili powder

⅛ teaspoon (0.5 mL) ground nutmeg

1 cup (250 mL) water

¼ cup (60 mL) dry white wine

¼ cup (60 mL) vegetable oil, more for frying

2 tablespoons (30 mL) nutritional yeast

1 tablespoon (15 mL) Dijon mustard

Broth

8 cups (2 L) water

¼ cup (60 mL) tamari or soy sauce

3 to 4 cloves garlic

Biscuits

1 cup (250 mL) all-purpose flour, more for dusting

1½ teaspoons (7 mL) baking powder

¼ teaspoon (1 mL) sea salt

¼ cup (60 mL) cold vegan butter

6 tablespoons (90 mL) unsweetened soy milk

1½ cups (375 mL) Anytime Gravy

1. **MAKE THE SEITAN DOUGH** In a medium bowl, whisk together the wheat gluten flour, poultry seasoning, sugar, garlic powder, 1 teaspoon (5 mL) of the salt, fennel, chili powder, and nutmeg.

2. In a blender, combine the water, white wine, vegetable oil, nutritional yeast, mustard, and the remaining ½ teaspoon (2 mL) salt. Blend until smooth.

3. Add the water mixture to the flour mixture. Using your hands, mix until well combined and the mixture has formed into a dough. You do not want to see any dry patches of flour. Transfer the dough to a work surface and knead for 2 to 3 minutes. Cut the dough into 10 to 12 equal pieces and lightly flatten each piece with the bottom of your hands. You want the sausages to resemble flat patties.

4. **PREPARE THE BROTH AND COOK THE SEITAN DOUGH** In a pot, combine the water, tamari, and garlic. Add the pieces of dough and bring to a boil uncovered, stirring frequently. Reduce the heat to a simmer and cook the seitan until firm to the touch, about 45 minutes. Remove the seitan from the broth and set aside until cool enough to handle, about 1 hour. Discard the broth.

5. **MEANWHILE, MAKE THE BISCUITS** Preheat the oven to 400°F (200°C). Line a baking sheet with parchment paper.

6. In a medium bowl, whisk together the all-purpose flour, baking powder, and salt. Add the cold butter. Using a fork, gently combine until the mixture is crumbly; do not overmix. Make a well in the middle and add the soy milk. Using a fork, combine the mixture until a dough begins to form; do not overmix.

7. Transfer the dough to a lightly floured work surface. Gently dust the top of the dough with flour. Knead the dough 10 to 12 times only. Using a rolling pin, roll out the dough so that it is about ½ inch (1 cm) thick. Cut out circles using a 1½-inch (4 cm) round cookie cutter or a glass. You should have at least 6 biscuits. You can reroll the dough scraps, if needed, to make 1 or 2 more biscuits. Place the biscuits on the prepared baking sheet and bake until the bottoms of the biscuits are golden brown, 10 to 12 minutes.

8. **FRY THE SAUSAGES** In a large frying pan, preferably nonstick, heat enough vegetable oil to coat the bottom of the pan over medium-high heat. Pat the sausages dry with a clean kitchen towel or paper towel. Add the sausages to the pan and cook until golden brown, about 4 to 5 minutes per side.

9. To serve, divide the sausages and biscuits between serving plates and ladle both with plenty of anytime gravy.

No Bull Breakfast Links

Growing up, one of my favourite breakfast foods were those little sausage links you buy frozen and pop in the micro-wave or oven. My vegan sausage links use a similar variety of spices and seasonings to replicate those little links of deliciousness. Serve them with my Buttermilk Blueberry Pancakes (page 95), Stuffed and Stacked French Toast (page 99), or Peanut Butter Fudge and Chocolate Waffles (page 96) for an unbeatable breakfast.

MAKES 8 SAUSAGES

Ingredients

1 tablespoon (15 mL) vegetable oil

½ cup (125 mL) roughly chopped white onion

1 teaspoon (5 mL) sea salt, divided

1 teaspoon (5 mL) minced garlic

1 cup (250 mL) vital wheat gluten flour

½ cup (125 mL) chopped firm tofu

¼ cup (60 mL) extra-virgin olive oil

2 tablespoons (30 mL) nutritional yeast

2 tablespoons (30 mL) tamari or soy sauce

1 tablespoon (15 mL) Dijon mustard

2 teaspoons (10 mL) poultry seasoning

1 teaspoon (5 mL) brown sugar

½ teaspoon (2 mL) dried thyme

½ teaspoon (2 mL) freshly cracked black pepper

½ teaspoon (2 mL) sweet paprika

¼ teaspoon (1 mL) ground nutmeg

¼ teaspoon (1 mL) red chili flakes

1. In a medium frying pan, heat the vegetable oil over medium-high heat. Add the onions and ½ teaspoon (2 mL) of the salt. Cook, stirring frequently, until the onions are soft and start to turn golden brown, about 3 minutes. Add the garlic and cook, stirring frequently, until the garlic is fragrant and soft, about 2 minutes. Remove from the heat.

2. Preheat the oven to 350°F (180°C). Cut eight 9- × 6-inch (23 × 15 cm) pieces of foil.

3. In a food processor fitted with a metal blade, combine the wheat gluten flour, tofu, olive oil, nutritional yeast, tamari, mustard, poultry seasoning, brown sugar, the remaining ½ teaspoon (2 mL) salt, thyme, pepper, paprika, nutmeg, and chili flakes. Process until all of the ingredients have come together and no dry patches of flour remain. Transfer the dough to a work surface.

4. Using your hands, knead the dough for a few minutes until it is the shape of a ball. You want to knead it as you would a traditional bread dough. This helps make the sausages firmer.

5. Divide the dough into 8 equal portions. To do this, cut the dough in half, then in half two more times to get 8 equal portions. Roll each portion of dough into the shape of a log so that it looks like a sausage link, about 4 inches (10 cm) long and ½ inch (1 cm) wide. Place a sausage in the centre of each piece of foil and roll the foil around it so that it fits tightly inside. Twist the ends of the foil to secure. Place the foil packages on a baking sheet and bake for 30 minutes. Remove from the oven and press down on the foil packages. The sausages should be firm to the touch. If they're not firm, bake for 5 to 10 more minutes. Allow the sausages to cool completely before removing them from the foil, about 1 hour. Store in an air-tight container in the fridge for up to 1 week or in the freezer for up to 2 months. To reheat the sausages, heat a large sautée pan with a little vegetable oil and cook the sausges on all sides until hot in the middle.

Cheesy Scramble Biscuits

These fully loaded biscuits are a fantastic treat any day of the week, but I especially like to make them on lazy Sunday mornings. Ooey gooey, soft in the middle, and filled to the brim with melted cheese mixed with my famous tofu scramble, they'll definitely impress you and your friends. Share over breakfast while swapping stories about last night's shenanigans.

MAKES 12 BISCUITS

Prep ahead

Perfect Vegan Scramble
(page 115)

Almond Milk Cheese Curds
(page 217)

Ingredients

2¼ cups (550 mL) all-purpose
flour, more for dusting

¼ cup (60 mL) nutritional
yeast

1 tablespoon (15 mL) baking
powder

½ teaspoon (2 mL) black salt

½ teaspoon (2 mL) ground
mustard powder

1 cup (250 mL) chopped cold
vegan butter

¾ cup (175 mL) unsweetened
soy milk

⅓ cup (75 mL) Perfect Vegan
Scramble

⅓ cup (75 mL) Almond Milk
Cheese Curds or vegan
cheese that melts well

1. Preheat the oven to 400°F (200°C). Line a baking sheet with parchment paper.

2. In a medium bowl, whisk together the flour, nutritional yeast, baking powder, black salt, and mustard powder. Add the cold butter. Using a fork, gently combine until the mixture is crumbly; do not overmix. Make a well in the middle and add the soy milk. Using a fork, combine the mixture until a dough begins to form; do not overmix.

3. Add the perfect vegan scramble and almond milk cheese curds to the dough. Using a spatula, mix only 1 to 2 times to combine. You want the biscuits light and fluffy, so do not overmix. Mixing them more than this amount can make the dough tough.

4. Transfer the dough to a lightly floured work surface and gently dust the dough with flour. Knead the dough 10 to 12 times only. The biscuits will be quite soft at this point; you do not want to overmix, or they can become tough. Using a rolling pin, roll out the dough so it is about ½ inch (1 cm) thick. Cut out circles using a 1½-inch (4 cm) round cookie cutter or a glass. You can reroll the dough scraps, if needed, to make 12 biscuits total. Place the biscuits on the prepared baking sheet and bake until the bottoms are golden brown, 10 to 12 minutes. Serve immediately.

Shakshuka

This Middle Eastern-style meal is rich in spices and chilies and is designed for dipping your favourite crusty bread into. Traditionally, shakshuka is made with poached eggs that you dip harder breads into, as the savoury sauce soaks into it, turning the bread into one tasty vehicle for a mixture of delectable flavours. The traditional recipe is easily turned into a plant-based dish by using my Sunny Side Up Vegan Eggs with Yolks (page 114), which you'll need to prepare ahead of time.

SERVES 4

Prep ahead

Sunny Side Up Vegan Eggs with Yolks (page 114)

Ingredients

2 medium red sweet peppers

1 tablespoon (15 mL) vegetable oil

2 tablespoons (30 mL) extra-virgin olive oil

½ cup (125 mL) finely diced white onion

¼ cup (60 mL) drained capers

2 teaspoons (10 mL) sweet paprika

1½ teaspoons (7 mL) cumin seeds

1½ teaspoons (7 mL) ground cumin

½ teaspoon (2 mL) sea salt

3 tablespoons (45 mL) minced garlic

2 tablespoons (30 mL) tomato paste

2 tablespoons (30 mL) dry white wine

2 cans (14 ounces/398 mL each) diced tomatoes

Pinch of ground cayenne pepper

For serving

8 Sunny Side Up Vegan Eggs with Yolks

1 whole crusty baguette or your favourite bread

1. Preheat the oven to 400°F (200°C). Line a baking sheet with parchment paper.
2. On the prepared baking sheet, toss the red peppers with the vegetable oil to coat well. Bake until slightly shriveled and browned, about 15 minutes. Remove from the oven and transfer to a medium bowl. Cover tightly with plastic wrap and set aside for 10 minutes. The steam will help separate the skin from the flesh, making the peppers easier to peel.
3. Carefully remove the peppers from the bowl and, using your fingers, gently rub the skins off the flesh. Cut the peppers in half and discard the seeds and ribs. Cut the peppers into ½-inch (1 cm) thick strips.
4. In a medium pot, heat the olive oil over medium heat. Add the onions, roasted red pepper slices, capers, paprika, cumin seeds, ground cumin, and salt. Cook, stirring frequently, until the onions are soft and translucent, 5 to 6 minutes. Add the garlic and cook, stirring constantly, until the garlic is soft and fragrant, 2 to 3 minutes.
5. Add the tomato paste and cook, stirring constantly, for 1 to 2 minutes. Add the white wine and cook until most of it has evaporated. Add the diced tomatoes with their juice, and cayenne. Bring to a boil, uncovered, stirring occasionally. Reduce the heat to a simmer and cook, stirring occasionally, until the mixture has thickened, 25 to 35 minutes.
6. To serve, divide the sauce among 4 serving bowls. Top each bowl with 2 sunny side up vegan eggs with yolks. Serve the crusty bread on the side for dipping. Store any leftover sauce in an airtight container in the fridge for up to 2 weeks.

Ultimate Vegan Caesar

Whether you want to call it a Caesar or a Bloody Mary, this iconic drink is perfect to serve with hearty brunches anytime. Essentially a salad in a glass, this delicious and refreshing drink can be made virgin or with vodka. Traditionally, Caesars contain clam juice and Worcestershire sauce. My vegan version uses a mixture of tamari, vegan Worcestershire sauce, and olive brine to replicate the same salty, lip-smacking flavour!

MAKES 4 DRINKS

Ingredients

4 cups (1 L) store-bought tomato cocktail mix (such as V8)

1 tablespoon + 1 teaspoon (20 mL) tamari or soy sauce

2 tablespoons (30 mL) freshly grated horseradish (see Tip)

2 tablespoons (30 mL) freshly squeezed lemon juice

2 tablespoons (30 mL) vegan Worcestershire sauce

1 tablespoon (15 mL) olive brine (see Tip)

¼ teaspoon (1 mL) celery salt

A couple of dashes of your favourite hot sauce, more as needed

4 ounces (115 mL) vodka (optional)

Garnish (see Tip)

4 lemon wheels

Celery salt, for rimming glasses

1 cup (250 mL) crushed ice cubes

4 stalks celery (inner stalk with a few leaves, preferably)

8 cherry tomatoes (optional)

4 pickled green beans (optional)

4 green olives (optional)

4 lime wheels

Pinch of freshly cracked black pepper

1. In a blender, combine the tomato cocktail mix, tamari, horseradish, lemon juice, Worcestershire sauce, olive brine, celery salt, and hot sauce. Blend until completely smooth. Add the vodka (if using) and pulse a couple of times to incorporate.

2. Run the lemon wheels around the rims of 4 tall glasses. Pour the celery salt into a flat dish. Dip the rims of the glasses in the celery salt and roll them around so the edges are completely covered. Divide the ice among the glasses and pour in the Caesar mix. Place a celery stalk in each glass. Add the cherry tomatoes, pickled green beans, and olives, if using. Cut a little slit in the lemon and lime wheels and rest them on the rims of the glasses. Sprinkle the drinks with a bit of cracked pepper and serve immediately.

TIP

1. To grate the horseradish, use a fine-toothed Microplane grater. You can also use the fine blades on the side of a box grater. **2.** Olive brine is the liquid that olives are sold in. If you do not have any, you can omit it from the recipe, but it does impart a flavour unique to this drink. **3.** You can garnish your Caesar with whatever you like. Try using olives, vegan meatballs, vegan chicken wings, and more.

Brunch

The Main Deal

The NY Strip

Before going vegan, I was a huge meat lover. I enjoyed everything about the taste and texture of meat, especially grilled steaks. So, I know what I'm talking about when I say that this dish is a remarkable substitute. My bloodless and cruelty-free steak is made from vital wheat gluten flour and seasonings like red wine, garlic, and Dijon mustard to help give it the desired depth of flavour. Serve this grilled on a barbecue, broiled in the oven, or pan-fried and sliced. I love serving these steaks drizzled with my Garlic Butter (page 230) and sprinkled with some Montreal steak spice.

MAKES 4 TO 5 STEAKS

Seitan (Steak) Dough

- 2 cups (500 mL) vital wheat gluten flour
- 3 tablespoons (45 mL) nutritional yeast
- 1 teaspoon (5 mL) sea salt
- 1 cup (250 mL) water
- 3 tablespoons (45 mL) dry red wine
- 2 tablespoons (30 mL) tamari
- 2 tablespoons (30 mL) vegetable oil
- 1 tablespoon (15 mL) + 1½ teaspoons (7 mL) tomato paste
- 1 tablespoon (15 mL) + 1½ teaspoons (7 mL) Dijon mustard
- 1 tablespoon (15 mL) garlic powder

Broth

- 4 quarts (4 L) water
- ½ cup (125 mL) tamari
- ¼ cup (60 mL) dry red wine
- 4 cloves garlic
- 4 sprigs fresh thyme

Marinade

- ¼ cup (60 mL) dry red wine
- ¼ cup (60 mL) vegetable oil
- 2 tablespoons (30 mL) tamari
- 1 tablespoon (15 mL) Dijon mustard
- 1 tablespoon (15 mL) chopped fresh thyme leaves
- 4 cloves garlic, roughly chopped

1. **MAKE THE SEITAN DOUGH** In a medium bowl, combine the wheat gluten flour, nutritional yeast, and salt. Whisk until well combined and no lumps remain.

2. In a blender, combine the water, red wine, tamari, vegetable oil, tomato paste, mustard, and garlic powder. Blend until completely smooth.

3. Pour the water mixture into the wheat gluten flour mixture. Using your hands, mix until well combined. You do not want to see any dry patches of flour left. Transfer the dough to a work surface and knead to develop the gluten. Shape the mixture into a rectangle about 6 inches (15 cm) long and 1½ inches (4 cm) thick.

4. **PREPARE THE BROTH AND COOK THE SEITAN DOUGH** Place the dough in a wide, large pot and add the water, tamari, red wine, garlic, and thyme. Bring to a boil, uncovered. Reduce the heat to a simmer and cook for 35 to 40 minutes. The seitan is done when the middle is no longer chewy or no longer has the texture of raw dough. It should be slightly spongy but firm to the touch. Remove from the heat and set aside until the seitan is cool enough to handle in the liquid, about 1 hour.

5. **MAKE THE MARINADE** In a medium bowl, whisk together the red wine, vegetable oil, tamari, mustard, thyme, and garlic.

6. Once the seitan is cool enough to handle, remove it from the broth and cut it into 4 or 5 steaks of equal size. Lay the steaks flat in a 13- × 9-inch (3.5 L) baking dish and pour the marinade over top. Flip to make sure that all sides of the steaks are covered with the marinade. Marinate for at least 1 hour or overnight. If marinating overnight, cover with plastic wrap and refrigerate.

7. **COOK THE STEAKS** Remove the steaks from the marinade and pat dry using a clean kitchen towel or paper towel. Discard the marinade. Grill, broil, or pan-fry.

- **TO GRILL THE STEAKS,** preheat a grill to medium-high heat and lightly oil the grill with vegetable oil by adding a little to a kitchen towel. Rub the oil on the grill to help prevent the steaks from sticking. Place the steaks on the grill and do not move them or push down, as this will cause them to burn. Cook until golden brown and sizzling, 4 to 5 minutes per side.

- **TO BROIL THE STEAKS,** turn the broiler on high and place the steaks on a baking sheet. Place under the broiler and cook until golden brown, 4 to 5 minutes per side.

- **TO PAN-FRY THE STEAKS,** heat enough vegetable oil in a sauté pan over medium-high heat. Cook until golden brown and sizzling, 4 to 5 minutes per side.

Home-Style Meatloaf

The best things about meatloaf are the rich, hearty texture and that satisfying feeling you get when you take a big bite of it that leaves you salivating for more! Most meatloaf is fairly simple to make, with ground meat bound together with eggs and breadcrumbs, along with spices and other seasonings, and baked until golden brown. My vegan version is very similar, except I use plant-based counterparts. Instead of eggs I use ground flaxseed and flour to help bind everything together, and for the meaty texture I use soft millet and lentils.

SERVES 6

Ingredients

1 cup (250 mL) millet

8 cups (2 L) water, divided

2 cups (500 mL) dried green lentils

3 tablespoons (45 mL) vegetable oil, more for the loaf pan

½ cup (125 mL) finely diced white onion

½ cup (125 mL) finely diced peeled carrot

½ cup (125 mL) finely diced celery

4 cloves garlic, minced

1 teaspoon (5 mL) ground mustard powder

1 teaspoon (5 mL) dried thyme

½ teaspoon (2 mL) sweet paprika

½ teaspoon (2 mL) dried basil

2 tablespoons (30 mL) chopped fresh thyme leaves

¼ cup (60 mL) tamari or soy sauce

¼ cup (60 mL) nutritional yeast

½ cup (125 mL) all-purpose flour

¼ cup (60 mL) ground golden flaxseed

½ cup (125 mL) ketchup

1. In a small pot, add the millet and 3 cups (750 mL) of the water. Bring to a boil, then reduce the heat to a simmer and cook, uncovered, until soft and tender, 12 to 15 minutes. Set aside to cool.

2. In a medium pot, add the lentils and the remaining 5 cups (1.25 L) water. Bring to a boil, then reduce the heat to a simmer and cook, uncovered, until tender, 10 to 12 minutes. Drain, discarding the cooking water.

3. In a sauté pan, heat the vegetable oil over medium-high heat. Add the onion, carrot, and celery and cook, stirring frequently, until the onions are soft and translucent, 4 to 5 minutes. Add the garlic, mustard powder, thyme, paprika, and basil and cook, stirring constantly, for 2 minutes. Remove the pan from the heat and add the fresh thyme leaves, tamari, and nutritional yeast. Use a wooden spoon to scrape up any bits from the bottom of the pan.

4. In a food processor, add the millet, half of the vegetable mixture, and half of the cooked lentils. Process until smooth. You will need to stop the machine once or twice and use a rubber spatula to scrape down the sides of the bowl.

5. In a medium bowl, combine the processed millet mixture, the remaining vegetable mixture, the remaining lentils, the flour, and flaxseed. Using a spatula, mix until everything is well incorporated.

6. Preheat the oven to 350°F (180°C). Lightly grease a 10- × 6-inch (3 L) loaf pan with vegetable oil.

7. Transfer the mixture to the loaf pan and gently press it into all sides. Bake until the top of the meatloaf is golden brown and the middle is hot, about 30 minutes. Remove from the oven and top evenly with the ketchup. Return to the oven and bake for an additional 15 minutes, or until the ketchup is golden brown and bubbling. Remove from the oven and allow to sit for 20 minutes so that the meatloaf can firm up enough to slice. Serve immediately or cool completely and store in an airtight container in the fridge for up to 1 week.

Chickpea Pot Pie

When I was growing up, my mom made a lot of chicken pot pies. I can still feel the rich and creamy texture from the freshly made, piping hot pies melting in my mouth. Of course, I had to re-create that memory for you! Traditional versions are made with chicken stock, but I use nutritional yeast to help re-create the chicken flavour, as well as fresh rosemary and thyme. Just like mama used to make, except minus the chicken!

MAKES 6 POT PIES

Filling

1 cup (250 mL) deodorized coconut oil

4 cups (1 L) cooked chickpeas

1½ cups (375 mL) finely diced peeled carrots

1½ cups (375 mL) finely diced onions

1 cup (250 mL) finely diced celery

¼ cup (60 mL) minced garlic

1½ cups (375 mL) all-purpose flour

8 cups (2 L) water

4 cups (1 L) unsweetened almond milk

1 tablespoon (15 mL) sea salt

¼ cup (60 mL) finely chopped fresh thyme leaves

¼ cup (60 mL) finely chopped fresh rosemary leaves

1 cup (250 mL) nutritional yeast

2 cups (500 mL) frozen green peas

Crust

2 cups (500 mL) all-purpose flour, more for dusting

1 teaspoon (5 mL) sea salt

½ cup (125 mL) cold vegan butter, cut into ½-inch (1 cm) cubes

¼ cup (60 mL) ice-cold water, more as needed

1 teaspoon (5 mL) white vinegar (see Tip)

Vegan Egg Wash

¼ cup (60 mL) unsweetened almond milk

2 tablespoons (30 mL) maple syrup

1 tablespoon (15 mL) melted deodorized coconut oil

1. **MAKE THE FILLING** In a large pot, heat the coconut oil over medium-high heat. Add the chickpeas, carrots, onions, and celery. Cook, stirring frequently, until the vegetables have softened, 5 to 6 minutes. Add the garlic and cook, stirring constantly, until the garlic is soft and fragrant, about 2 minutes. Add the flour and cook, stirring frequently, for 2 to 3 minutes, to cook out the floury taste.

2. Remove the pot from the heat and add the water. Using a wooden spoon, remove the bits from the bottom of the pan. Add the almond milk, salt, thyme, rosemary, and nutritional yeast. Return to the heat and bring the mixture to a boil, stirring constantly. Once it has come to a full boil, reduce the heat and simmer for 4 to 5 minutes to cook out the floury taste. Remove from the heat and stir in the green peas. Set aside to cool completely, about 1 hour.

3. **MAKE THE CRUST** In a food processor fitted with a metal blade, combine the flour and salt. Process until well combined. Add the butter and pulse a few seconds at a time until the butter is the size of peas. Add the water and vinegar and pulse again until the dough just begins to form. Add more water, 1 tablespoon (15 mL) at a time, if needed.

4. Tip the dough onto a lightly floured work surface. Using your hands, shape the dough into a ball. Cover with plastic wrap and refrigerate for 1 hour.

5. **MAKE THE VEGAN EGG WASH** In a small bowl, whisk together the almond milk, maple syrup, and coconut oil.

6. **ASSEMBLE THE POT PIES** Place the rack in the lowest position in the oven. Preheat the oven to 400°F (200°C). Place six 2-cup (500 mL) ramekins on a baking sheet.

7. Remove the dough from the fridge. Dust a work surface with flour. Using a rolling pin, roll out the dough into a flat disc about ¼-inch (5 mm) thick. Using one of the ramekins, cut out 6 discs of dough for the tops of the pot pies. You can reroll the dough scraps if necessary.

8. Fill each ramekin with about 2 cups (500 mL) of the cooled pot pie filling. Top each dish with a pre-cut crust and brush with the vegan egg wash. Bake until the crusts are golden brown and the mixture is bubbling hot, 45 to 50 minutes. Remove from the oven and allow to cool for 5 minutes before serving.

TIP

1. Adding vinegar to the pie crust mixture prevents gluten from forming, helping to make the crust flakier. **2.** If you do not have a food processor, use a pastry cutter to cut the cold butter into the flour and salt. When adding the cold water, use a knife at first to bring together the water and flour, then mix with your hands to form the dough.

Beer Battered Tempeh and Chips

My first cooking job was at a British pub, and one of the specialties was old school–style fish and chips. Every Wednesday was two-for-one fish and chips, so I became something of an aficionado at making them! My favourite fish to use was cod because of its flaky texture, so my veganized version uses tempeh as a stand-in, because it flakes in the same way when cooked. With everyone talking about the environment lately, why not be truly ocean wise!

SERVES 4

Prep ahead

Perfect French Fries and
    Seasoning Salt (page 64)

Tartar Sauce (page 225)

Tempeh

1 block (12 ounces/340 g)
    tempeh

8 cups (2 L) water

2 tablespoons (30 mL) sea
    salt

2 tablespoons (30 mL) freshly
    squeezed lemon juice

4 cloves garlic

Marinade

1 cup (250 mL) water

⅓ cup (75 mL) roughly
    chopped fresh dill

2 tablespoons (30 mL) freshly
    squeezed lemon juice

1½ teaspoons (7 mL) sea salt

1½ teaspoons (7 mL) Dijon
    mustard

Beer Batter

1½ cups (375 mL) all-purpose
    flour, divided (see Tip)

1½ teaspoons (7 mL) sea
    salt, divided

1 cup (250 mL) dark beer, such
    as IPA or stout (see Tip)

¼ cup (60 mL) cold water

———

4 to 6 cups (1 to 1.5 L)
    vegetable oil, for frying

For serving

1 batch Perfect French Fries
    and Seasoning Salt

1 batch Tartar Sauce

Ketchup

1. **COOK THE TEMPEH** In a large pot, combine the tempeh, water, salt, lemon juice, and garlic. Bring to a boil, uncovered, then reduce the heat to a simmer and cook for 10 minutes. Remove the tempeh from the liquid and set aside until cool enough to handle, 10 to 15 minutes. Discard the cooking liquid.

2. **MAKE THE MARINADE** In a medium bowl, whisk together the water, dill, lemon juice, salt, and mustard. Cut the tempeh lengthwise into 4 equal strips. Toss it in the marinade and allow to sit for at least 30 minutes or overnight. If marinating overnight, transfer to an airtight container and refrigerate.

3. **MAKE THE BEER BATTER** In a medium bowl, combine ½ cup (125 mL) of the flour and ½ teaspoon (2 mL) of the salt. Mix until well combined.

4. In another medium bowl, combine the remaining 1 cup (250 mL) flour, the remaining 1 teaspoon (5 mL) salt, beer, and cold water. Mix until well combined and no lumps remain.

5. Heat the vegetable oil in a large pot or small deep fryer to a temperature of 375°F (190°C).

6. **COOK THE BEER BATTERED TEMPEH** Remove the tempeh from the marinade and pat dry with a clean kitchen towel or paper towel. Discard the marinade. Roll the tempeh in the flour dredge, followed by the beer batter, until well coated. Dip in the hot oil and fry until golden brown and crisp, using metal tongs to turn the tempeh as necessary, 5 to 6 minutes. Remove the tempeh from the oil using metal tongs. Serve immediately with french fries, tartar sauce, and ketchup.

TIP

1. To make this recipe gluten-free, substitute an equal amount of gluten-free flour blend for the all-purpose flour and use your favourite gluten-free beer. **2.** Not all beer is considered vegan. Some use animal products like isinglass or gelatin in the refining or clarification process. Make sure to look for beers that have no animal products.

Bacon Double Cheeseburgers

It just doesn't get more classic than a bacon double cheeseburger. If you can master this staple, you'll have earned the title King or Queen of the Kitchen. When I eat at a new restaurant, the first thing I do is order their veggie burger, which has to have great flavour, but the texture is just as important! I became reigning champ of the barbecue when I came up with a winning tempeh burger. I discovered that when tempeh is finely chopped, it can take on the texture of ordinary ground beef, making it a great addition toward making the perfect veggie burger.

MAKES 8 BURGERS, OR 4 DOUBLE BURGERS

Prep ahead

Seitan Bacon (page 105)

Almond Milk Cheddar Cheese (page 216)

Creamy Mayo (page 232)

Ingredients

1 block (9 ounces/240 g) tempeh (see Tip)

4 cups (1 L) + 2¼ cups (550 mL) water, divided

½ cup (125 mL) millet

¾ teaspoon (4 mL) sea salt, divided

3 tablespoons (45 mL) vegetable oil

½ cup (125 mL) thinly sliced white onion

2 cups (500 mL) diced button mushrooms (see Tip)

2 tablespoons (30 mL) nutritional yeast

¼ cup (60 mL) tamari or soy sauce

¼ cup (60 mL) ketchup

2 teaspoons (10 mL) Dijon mustard

½ cup (125 mL) raw sunflower seeds

½ cup (125 mL) ground golden flaxseed (see Tip)

⅔ cup (150 mL) all-purpose flour

1 cup (250 mL) Almond Milk Cheddar Cheese

8 to 16 slices Seitan Bacon

For serving

4 burger buns, toasted

Ketchup

Mustard

Lettuce

Creamy Mayo

1. Place the tempeh in a medium pot with 4 cups (1 L) of the water. Cover with a tight-fitting lid and bring to a boil. Reduce the heat to a simmer and cook for 10 to 15 minutes. Remove the tempeh from the pot and allow to cool completely before handling, about 15 minutes. Dice the tempeh into small pieces, about ⅛-inch (3 mm) cubes, and place in a large bowl.

2. In a medium pot, combine the millet, the remaining 2¼ cups (550 mL) water, and ½ teaspoon (2 mL) of the salt. Bring to a boil, covered, then reduce the heat to a simmer and cook until the millet is soft and slightly mushy, about 25 minutes. Once cooked, remove from the heat and set aside for 15 minutes so that the millet can swell and absorb any remaining liquid. It is okay to overcook the millet in this step, as it helps bind together the burgers.

3. In another medium pot, heat the vegetable oil over medium-high heat. Add the onions, mushrooms, and the remaining ¼ teaspoon (1 mL) salt. Cook, stirring frequently, until the onions are lightly brown, about 10 minutes. Reduce the heat to medium-low and continue to cook until there is very little liquid left, 10 to 15 minutes. Add the nutritional yeast, tamari, ketchup, and mustard. Bring the mixture to a simmer and cook until the liquid has reduced by half, about 5 minutes.

4. In a food processor fitted with a metal blade, add the cooked millet, sunflower seeds, and half of the onion and mushroom mixture and process until smooth. Transfer to the bowl with the diced tempeh. Stir in the remaining onion and mushroom mixture, flaxseed, and flour. Using a spatula, mix all ingredients until well combined, cover, and set aside for 10 to 15 minutes so that the flaxseed can swell and absorb some of the liquid.

5. Preheat the oven to 400°F (200°C). Line a baking sheet with parchment paper.

6. Using a ½-cup (125 mL) measuring cup, divide the mixture into 8 equal portions. Lightly dampen your palm and flatten each portion into a patty about ½ inch (1 cm) thick. Arrange the patties on the prepared baking sheet and bake for 20 minutes. Flip the patties and spread 2 tablespoons (30 mL) almond milk cheddar cheese over the top of each patty. Then place 2 strips of seitan bacon on half of the patties if making double burgers, or 2 strips on each patty if making single burgers. Return to the oven and cook for another 5 minutes. Remove from the oven and allow to cool completely before handling, 8 to 10 minutes.

7. Place 2 burgers on the bottom of each bun. Top with ketchup, mustard, lettuce, creamy mayo, any other favourite toppings, and the other half of the bun.

Continued

TIP

1. I prefer using unpasteurized tempeh for its texture. I find it is more firm and dense, making it have a meatier texture. It's usually available in the freezer section of your favourite grocery store. However, pasteurized tempeh will work anywhere that tempeh is called for. **2.** To dice a mushroom, turn it on its side and use a knife to cut it lengthwise into mushroom slices. Turn the slices and cut them into thin strips. Turn the strips and cut them into small pieces. **3.** To grind the flax seeds for this recipe, place about 6 tablespoons (90 mL) whole golden flax seeds in a blender or spice grinder. Blend until they have a flourlike consistency. You can also use ground flaxseed; just make sure it is finely ground.

Meatball Sub

For the best meatball sub, I always suggest using a freshly baked bread roll, crispy on the outside and nice and soft in the middle. Marrying this bread with my meatballs and roasted red pepper tomato sauce and topping it off with lots of almond parmesan cheese, you have one heck of a meal! Just a warning: you'll probably want to have napkins on hand. Like, a lot of napkins.

MAKES 4 SANDWICHES

Tomato Sauce

2 medium red sweet peppers

1 tablespoon (15 mL) vegetable oil

2 tablespoons (30 mL) extra-virgin olive oil

½ cup (125 mL) finely diced white onion

½ teaspoon (2 mL) sea salt

3 tablespoons (45 mL) minced garlic

2 teaspoons (10 mL) dried basil

1 can (14 ounces/398 mL) diced tomatoes

Meatballs

2 tablespoons (30 mL) ground golden flaxseed

⅓ cup (75 mL) hot water (see Tip)

1 cup (250 mL) dried green lentils

4 cups (1 L) water

¼ cup (60 mL) raw walnuts

¼ cup (60 mL) raw sunflower seeds

¼ cup (60 mL) nutritional yeast

1½ teaspoons (7 mL) sea salt

2 tablespoons (30 mL) vegetable oil

1 cup (250 mL) finely diced white onion

2 tablespoons (30 mL) minced garlic

1 tablespoon (15 mL) chopped fresh thyme leaves

2 tablespoons (30 mL) dry white wine

½ cup (125 mL) loosely packed finely chopped flat-leaf parsley

Vegetable oil, for cooking

Parmesan Cheese

1 cup (250 mL) blanched almond flour

½ cup (125 mL) nutritional yeast

1 teaspoon (5 mL) dried basil

½ teaspoon (2 mL) garlic powder

½ teaspoon (2 mL) sea salt

¼ teaspoon (1 mL) celery salt

¼ teaspoon (1 mL) vegan lactic acid (optional; see Tip)

––––––––––

4 fresh crusty sub buns or 2 baguettes

1. **MAKE THE TOMATO SAUCE** Preheat the oven to 400°F (200°C). Line a baking sheet with parchment paper.

2. On the prepared baking sheet, toss the red peppers with the vegetable oil to coat well. Bake until slightly shriveled and browned, about 15 minutes. Remove from the oven and transfer to a medium bowl. Cover tightly with plastic wrap and set aside for 10 minutes. The steam will help separate the skin from the flesh, making the peppers easier to peel.

3. Carefully remove the peppers from the bowl and, using your fingers, gently rub the skins off the flesh. Cut the peppers in half and discard the seeds and ribs. Place the peppers in a blender and blend until smooth.

4. In a medium pot, heat the olive oil over medium heat. Add the onion and salt and cook, stirring frequently, until the onions are soft and translucent, 3 to 4 minutes. Add the garlic and basil and cook until the garlic is soft and fragrant, 2 to 3 minutes. Add the puréed red pepper and cook, stirring constantly, for 2 to 3 more minutes. Add the diced tomatoes with their juice and bring to a boil, reduce the heat to a simmer, and cook, uncovered, stirring occasionally, until thick and rich, about 45 minutes.

5. **MAKE THE MEATBALLS** In a small bowl, whisk together the flaxseed and hot water until well combined. Set aside so that the flaxseed can swell and absorb the liquid, about 10 minutes.

6. In a medium pot, combine the green lentils and water. Bring to a boil uncovered, reduce the heat to a simmer, and cook until the lentils are soft, about 15 minutes. Drain, discarding the cooking water.

7. In a food processor fitted with a metal blade, combine the cooked green lentils, walnuts, sunflower seeds, nutritional yeast, and salt. Process until the mixture is mostly smooth, making sure to leave a little bit of texture. Transfer to a medium bowl.

Continued

8. In a medium frying pan, heat the vegetable oil over medium-high heat. Add the onion and cook, stirring frequently, until soft and translucent, 3 to 4 minutes. Add the garlic and thyme and cook, stirring constantly, until the garlic is soft and fragrant, 2 to 3 minutes. Add the white wine and cook until almost all of the liquid has evaporated, about 2 minutes. Allow the onion mixture to cool slightly, then add it to the processed lentils.

9. To the lentils, add the soaked flaxseed mixture and parsley. Mix until well combined. Using an ice cream scoop or your hands, form the mixture into 20 balls. The balls should be the size of small golf balls.

10. In a large, wide frying pan, preferably nonstick, heat enough vegetable oil to coat the bottom of the pan over medium-high heat. Add the meatballs to the pan and cook until browned on all sides, turning with metal tongs as necessary, about 2 to 3 minutes per side, taking care not to crowd the pan. You may have to cook the meatballs in batches.

11. **MAKE THE PARMESAN CHEESE** In a food processor fitted with a metal blade, process the almond flour, nutritional yeast, basil, garlic powder, salt, celery salt, and lactic acid (if using), until broken down into a fine meal. Use immediately or store in an airtight container at room temperature for up to 1 month.

12. **ASSEMBLE THE SUBS** In each bun, place 5 meatballs and top with a good amount of the tomato sauce and about 2 tablespoons (30 mL) Parmesan.

TIP

1. Use hot water when making a flax egg, as it is best to help speed up the process of gelling the flax. **2.** Lactic acid typically comes from animal products. Vegan lactic acid is available in specialty grocery stores or online.

White Widow Mac and Cheese

When someone asks me for a classic dish, I automatically think of mac and cheese. Although most vegan mac and cheese recipes are a play on the standard yellow cheddar variety, how about switching it up? My version is a little more gourmet, because it's made with something more like Swiss cheese. I've used ingredients like miso, tahini, and nutritional yeast to stand in for the traditional Swiss cheese in a Mornay sauce. I call it white widow mac and cheese because it's so good, you'll think you've fallen in love—and then before you know it, you've died and gone to heaven.

SERVES 8

Prep ahead

Swiss Cheese (page 219)

Ingredients

1 cup (250 mL) roughly chopped white onion

1 cup (250 mL) deodorized coconut oil

1 cup (250 mL) all-purpose flour

⅓ cup (75 mL) semi-sweet white wine, such as Riesling

5 cups (1.25 L) unsweetened almond milk

¾ cup (175 mL) nutritional yeast

2 teaspoons (10 mL) garlic powder

2 teaspoons (10 mL) sea salt

½ teaspoon (2 mL) brown rice miso, or any type of miso

¼ cup (60 mL) Swiss Cheese

1 pound (450 g) dried elbow macaroni

½ cup (125 mL) panko crumbs

1. Preheat the oven to 400°F (200°C).
2. In a medium pot, over medium heat, combine the onion, coconut oil, and flour. Cook, stirring frequently, for 6 to 8 minutes. Remove the pot from the heat, add the white wine, and stir constantly for about 2 minutes to help remove some of the grittiness from the flour and to make a thick paste. Add the almond milk in a constant, steady stream while whisking at the same time. Whisk until no lumps remain, 1 to 2 minutes.
3. Return the pot to medium-high heat and add the nutritional yeast, garlic powder, salt, and miso. Bring the mixture to a boil, stirring frequently. Reduce the heat to a simmer and cook for 2 to 3 minutes to help remove some of the raw taste from the flour.
4. Remove the pot from the heat and stir in the Swiss cheese. In batches, transfer the sauce to a blender, taking care not to fill the blender more than halfway with the hot sauce, and blend until completely smooth. Transfer the sauce to a large, clean pot.
5. Bring a large pot of salted water to a rapid boil. Cook the macaroni according to package directions. Drain the pasta in a colander, then rinse with cold running water until the pasta is cold.
6. Add the cooked pasta to the cheese sauce and stir to combine. Transfer the mixture to an 11- × 7-inch (2 L) glass or metal baking dish. Top with the panko and bake until bubbling hot in the middle and golden brown on top, 25 to 30 minutes. Remove from the oven and allow to sit for 10 minutes before serving. Allow leftover mac and cheese to cool completely and store in an airtight container in the fridge for up to 1 week.

Sharp Cheddar Mac and Cheese

Creamy mac and cheese is my personal go-to comfort food. Step up your game from the store-bought, super-processed variety and make this sharp cheddar mac and cheese the next time you need a little consoling or reassurance. Trust me, it will make you feel better. It's basically like getting a hug from the inside out!

SERVES 6

Prep ahead

Mac and Cheese Sauce
    (page 223)

Ingredients

1 pound (450 g) dried elbow
    macaroni

1 batch Mac and Cheese Sauce

½ cup (125 mL) nutritional
    yeast

1 tablespoon (15 mL) dark
    miso

1 tablespoon (15 mL)
    unpasteurized apple cider
    vinegar

1 tablespoon + 1 teaspoon
    (20 mL) ground mustard
    powder

1 teaspoon (5 mL) sea salt

1 teaspoon (5 mL) tamari or
    soy sauce

1 teaspoon (5 mL) freshly
    squeezed lemon juice

1. In a medium pot of boiling salted water, cook the macaroni according to package directions. Drain the pasta in a colander, then rinse with cold running water until the pasta is cold.

2. In a medium pot, add the mac and cheese sauce over medium heat. Bring to a simmer and stir in the nutritional yeast, miso, apple cider vinegar, mustard powder, salt, tamari, and lemon juice. Whisk until well combined. Add the cooked pasta and stir to combine well. Serve immediately or allow to cool completely and store in an airtight container in the fridge for up to 1 week.

Bangers and Mash

My first cooking job was at a British pub, which introduced me to the iconic dish known as bangers and mash. Every day, we deep-fried thick, juicy sausages and placed them lovingly on top of creamy mashed potatoes, then drizzled it all with rich gravy. My plant-based version uses tofu as the base for the meaty texture, along with seasonings that give this recipe its signature sausage-like flavour. It's the next best thing to actually being in Britain. On the bright side, the weather is probably better over here anyway.

SERVES 4

Prep ahead

Anytime Gravy (page 228)

Bangers

1 tablespoon (15 mL) + ¼ cup (60 mL) vegetable oil, divided

½ cup (125 mL) roughly chopped white onion

1 teaspoon (5 mL) sea salt, divided

1 teaspoon (5 mL) minced garlic

1 cup (250 mL) vital wheat gluten flour

½ cup (125 mL) chopped firm vacuum-packed tofu

¼ cup (60 mL) extra-virgin olive oil

2 tablespoons (30 mL) nutritional yeast

2 tablespoons (30 mL) tamari or soy sauce

1 tablespoon (15 mL) Dijon mustard

1 tablespoon (15 mL) tomato paste

2 teaspoons (10 mL) smoked paprika

1 teaspoon (5 mL) fennel seeds

1 teaspoon (5 mL) agave nectar

1 teaspoon (5 mL) dried basil

¼ teaspoon (1 mL) freshly cracked black pepper

Mash

2 pounds (900 g) russet potatoes, peeled and cut into 2-inch (5 cm) cubes

3 tablespoons (45 mL) sea salt, divided

1 cup (250 mL) vegan butter or margarine

1 teaspoon (5 mL) garlic powder

½ cup (125 mL) unsweetened almond milk or soy milk

---

1 cup (250 mL) Anytime Gravy

1. **MAKE THE BANGERS** In a medium frying pan, heat 1 tablespoon (15 mL) of the vegetable oil over medium-high heat. Add the onions and ½ teaspoon (2 mL) of the salt and cook, stirring frequently, until the onions are soft and start to turn golden brown, about 3 minutes. Add the garlic and cook, stirring frequently, until the garlic is fragrant and soft, about 2 minutes. Remove from the heat.

2. In a food processor fitted with a metal blade, combine the cooked onion and garlic mixture, wheat gluten flour, tofu, olive oil, nutritional yeast, tamari, mustard, tomato paste, paprika, fennel seeds, the remaining ½ teaspoon (2 mL) salt, agave, basil, and pepper. Process until all of the ingredients have come together and no dry patches of flour remain. Transfer the dough to a work surface.

3. Using your hands, work the dough for a few minutes, kneading as you would a traditional bread dough. This helps develop the gluten and make the sausages firmer.

4. Preheat the oven to 350°F (180°C). Cut 4 pieces of foil, each about 9 × 6 inches (23 × 15 cm).

5. Cut the dough into 4 equal portions. Roll each portion into a log so that it looks like a sausage, about 4 inches (10 cm) long and ½ inch (1 cm) wide. Place a sausage in the centre of each piece of foil and roll the foil around it so that it fits tightly inside. Twist the ends of the foil to secure. Place the foil packages on a baking sheet and bake for 35 minutes. Remove from the oven and press down on the foil package. The bangers should be firm to the touch. If they're not firm, bake for 10 more minutes. Allow the bangers to cool completely before removing them from the foil, about 1 hour.

6. **MAKE THE MASH** Place the potatoes in a large pot and add cold water to cover by about 1 inch (2.5 cm). Stir in 2 tablespoons (30 mL) of the salt. Bring to a boil, uncovered, over high heat. Reduce the heat to a simmer and cook until the potatoes are soft, 15 to 20 minutes.

7. Drain, discarding the water. Place the potatoes back in the pot and add the butter, the remaining 1 tablespoon (15 mL) salt, garlic powder, and almond milk. Using a potato masher, mash the potatoes until no large pieces remain; it is okay if there are some smaller pieces.

8. **FRY THE BANGERS** In a large frying pan, heat the remaining ¼ cup (60 mL) vegetable oil over medium heat. Add the bangers and cook until heated in the middle, about 5 minutes. Divide the mashed potatoes among 4 serving plates, then top each plate with a banger and about ¼ cup (60 mL) of anytime gravy.

Chickpea Salisbury Steak

When I was developing this recipe, I wanted to make something with the same chew of conventional Salisbury steak, but I didn't want it to feel too heavy in texture. After a lot of experimentation, I came up with the idea to use both chickpeas and some vital wheat gluten flour as the base. The final product has a meaty and slightly crumbly texture. Enjoy with your favourite sauce, potatoes, or rice, and fresh veggies! Double or triple this recipe and freeze the leftovers. Your future self will thank you.

MAKES 4 STEAKS

Ingredients

- 1½ cups (375 mL) cooked chickpeas
- 6 tablespoons (90 mL) vegetable oil, divided
- ½ cup (125 mL) finely diced white onion
- ½ cup (125 mL) thinly sliced button mushrooms
- 1 tablespoon (15 mL) + 1½ teaspoons (7 mL) Dijon mustard
- 1 tablespoon (15 mL) tomato paste
- 1 teaspoon (5 mL) minced garlic
- ¼ cup (60 mL) dry red wine
- 2 tablespoons + 2 teaspoons (40 mL) tamari or soy sauce
- ¼ cup (60 mL) nutritional yeast
- ½ teaspoon (2 mL) sea salt
- ¾ cup (175 mL) + 1 tablespoon (15 mL) vital wheat gluten flour

1. In a food processor fitted with a metal blade, add the chickpeas and process until no large pieces remain. A little bit of texture is good, so do not process until smooth. Transfer to a medium bowl.

2. In a large frying pan, heat 3 tablespoons (45 mL) of the vegetable oil over medium-high heat. Add the onion and mushroom and cook, stirring frequently, until golden brown, 8 to 10 minutes. Add the mustard, tomato paste, and garlic and cook, stirring frequently, until the garlic is fragrant, 2 to 3 minutes.

3. Add the processed chickpeas and red wine and cook, stirring constantly, for 2 minutes. Add the tamari, nutritional yeast, and salt and cook, stirring constantly, for another 2 minutes. Remove from the heat and set aside in a medium bowl.

4. Add the wheat gluten flour to the chickpea mixture and stir to combine using a wooden spoon or spatula. Divide the mixture into 4 equal portions. Flatten each portion into a round steak shape, about 1 inch (2.5 cm) thick.

5. Preheat the oven to 400°F (200°C). Line a baking sheet with parchment paper.

6. In a large frying pan, preferably nonstick, heat the remaining 3 tablespoons (45 mL) vegetable oil over medium-high heat. Cook each steak in the pan until golden brown, 2 to 3 minutes per side. Transfer to the prepared baking sheet and bake until the steaks are cooked in the middle, 12 to 15 minutes. The steak will be a little crumbly but will hold together well. Store in an airtight container in the freezer for up to 2 months.

Lentil Ragout with Cheesy Rice

Hands down, this is one of my all-time favourite dishes. Creamy and rich, red lentils are simmered with sweet potato until the starch breaks down for a stew-like consistency. The key to this recipe is to boil the ragout over high heat at first, then reduce the heat toward the end of the cooking process. Nutritional yeast gives it a cheesiness, adding to the feelings of warmth and comfort it will already give you.

SERVES 4

Ragout

¼ cup (60 mL) vegetable oil, divided

½ cup (125 mL) finely diced peeled carrot

½ cup (125 mL) finely diced celery

½ cup (125 mL) finely diced white onion

½ teaspoon (2 mL) sea salt

1 cup (250 mL) peeled sweet potato cut into 1-inch (2.5 cm) pieces

2 cups (500 mL) dried red lentils

4 cups (1 L) water, divided

2 cups (500 mL) sliced button mushrooms

⅔ cup (150 mL) nutritional yeast

6 tablespoons (90 mL) tamari or soy sauce

2 tablespoons (30 mL) chopped fresh thyme leaves

Cheesy Rice

2 cups (500 mL) short-grain brown rice

4 cups (1 L) water

2 cups (500 mL) nutritional yeast

1½ teaspoons (7 mL) sea salt

1. **MAKE THE RAGOUT** In a medium pot, heat 2 tablespoons (30 mL) of the vegetable oil over medium heat. Add the carrots, celery, onion, and salt and cook, stirring frequently, until the vegetables are soft and translucent, 4 to 5 minutes. Add the sweet potato and lentils and continue to cook, stirring constantly, for 2 to 3 minutes.

2. Add 3 cups (750 mL) of the water and cook over high heat, until most of the water has been absorbed, 10 to 15 minutes. Reduce the heat to low and simmer for 10 minutes.

3. Add the remaining 1 cup (250 mL) water and simmer gently for 10 to 15 minutes or until the lentils have broken down and become thick like a stew. Remove from the heat.

4. In a large frying pan, heat the remaining 2 tablespoons (30 mL) vegetable oil over high heat. Add the mushrooms and cook, stirring frequently, until golden brown, 6 to 7 minutes. Remove from the heat. Stir the mushrooms, nutritional yeast, tamari, and thyme into the cooked lentils.

5. **MAKE THE CHEESY RICE** In a medium pot, combine the rice, water, nutritional yeast, and salt. Bring to a boil uncovered, stir once, then cover with a tight-fitting lid and cook for 45 minutes. Remove from the heat, stir once or twice, cover, and let sit for 5 to 6 minutes so that the rice can fluff.

6. Serve the ragout over the cheesy rice immediately or allow both to cool completely. Store the rice in an airtight container in the fridge for up to 5 days and the ragout in an airtight container in the fridge for up to 1 week.

Stuffed Grilled Cheese Sandwiches

The star of this droolworthy recipe is the tantalizing cheese, oozing deliciously between two pieces of crunchy bread filled with sweet, slowly caramelized onions and crispy seitan bacon. My trick to cooking the perfect grilled cheese is to always keep it on medium heat. That way, by the time the cheese is just the right amount of melted and gooey, the bread will be pristinely browned and toasted.

MAKES 4 SANDWICHES

Prep ahead

Whipped Butter (page 229)

Almond Milk Cheddar Cheese
  (page 216)

Seitan Bacon (page 105)

Ingredients

2 tablespoons (30 mL)
  vegetable oil

2 cups (500 mL) thinly sliced
  white onions

¼ teaspoon (1 mL) sea salt

8 slices artisanal bread,
  such as sourdough or rye

½ cup (125 mL) Whipped
  Butter or vegan butter

1 cup (250 mL) Almond Milk
  Cheddar Cheese or 8 slices
  vegan cheese

8 slices Seitan Bacon

1. In a large frying pan, heat the vegetable oil over high heat. Add the onions and salt and cook, stirring frequently, until the onions start to turn brown. Reduce the heat to low and cook, stirring occasionally, until the onions are golden brown and soft, about 45 minutes.

2. Lay the slices of bread on a work surface. On each slice, spread about 1 tablespoon (15 mL) of the whipped butter. Flip 4 pieces of bread over and spread about ¼ cup (60 mL) almond milk cheddar cheese over each of these slices, then top each with 2 slices of seitan bacon and one quarter of the caramelized onions. Finally, top each with a slice of bread.

3. Heat a large frying pan over medium heat. Cook 2 sandwiches at a time until golden brown on the bottom and the cheese starts to become warm, about 5 minutes. Flip the sandwiches and cook until golden brown on the other side and the cheese is gooey, about 5 more minutes. Transfer to a plate and repeat to cook the remaining sandwiches. Serve immediately.

149

Reuben Sandwiches

The elusive Reuben sandwich haunted my dreams for years after I went vegan, until I decided that I'd had enough! I needed it back in my life, so I came up with this recipe to satiate my midnight cravings for this meaty monster of a sandwich. Stack two slices of rye bread high with my seitan corned beef, Swiss Cheese (page 219), creamy Russian Dressing (page 234), and tangy sauerkraut, and prepare yourself for some serious sensory pleasure.

MAKES 4 SANDWICHES

Prep ahead
Russian Dressing (page 234)
Swiss Cheese (page 219)

Seitan (Corned Beef) Dough
2 cups (500 mL) vital wheat gluten flour
2 tablespoons (30 mL) nutritional yeast
1 teaspoon (5 mL) garlic powder
1 teaspoon (5 mL) sweet paprika
½ teaspoon (2 mL) black pepper
½ teaspoon (2 mL) ground fennel
1 cup (250 mL) water
2 tablespoons (30 mL) dry white wine
2 tablespoons (30 mL) fancy molasses

2 tablespoons (30 mL) tamari or soy sauce
2 tablespoons (30 mL) Dijon mustard
2 tablespoons (30 mL) vegetable oil
1 tablespoon (15 mL) unpasteurized apple cider vinegar

Broth
4 quarts (4 L) water
½ cup (125 mL) tamari or soy sauce
4 cloves garlic
3 to 5 whole cloves
2 sprigs fresh thyme
Pinch of cinnamon

Marinade
1½ cups (375 mL) beet juice
2 tablespoons (30 mL) Dijon mustard
2 tablespoons (30 mL) vegetable oil
2 teaspoons (10 mL) caraway seeds
1 teaspoon (5 mL) sea salt
½ teaspoon (2 mL) freshly cracked black pepper

—
Vegetable oil, for cooking

For assembly
8 slices light rye bread
½ cup (125 mL) Russian Dressing
½ cup (125 mL) Swiss Cheese
1¼ cups (300 mL) sauerkraut

1. **MAKE THE SEITAN DOUGH** In a medium bowl, whisk together the wheat gluten flour, nutritional yeast, garlic powder, paprika, pepper, and fennel.

2. In a blender, combine the water, white wine, molasses, tamari, mustard, vegetable oil, and apple cider vinegar. Blend until well combined. Add to the flour mixture and, using your hands, mix until well combined. You want to make sure that no dry lumps remain.

3. Transfer the dough to a work surface. Using your hands, knead the dough for 3 to 4 minutes. You want the dough to be shiny and elastic, with no visible dry patches. Cut the dough into 2 equal pieces.

4. **MAKE THE BROTH** In a large pot, combine the water, tamari, garlic, cloves, thyme, and cinnamon. Add the dough, bring the mixture to a boil, reduce the heat to a simmer, and cook until the centre of each piece of dough is no longer chewy in texture, but firm when pinched between 2 fingers, about 45 minutes. Remove the seitan from the broth and set aside until cool enough to handle, about 30 minutes. Discard the broth.

5. **MAKE THE MARINADE** In a blender, combine the beet juice, mustard, vegetable oil, caraway seeds, salt, and pepper. Blend until smooth.

6. Using a very sharp knife, cut the corned beef into very thin strips. Transfer to a large bowl and toss with the marinade until well coated. Marinate for 30 minutes or overnight. If marinating overnight, transfer to an airtight container and refrigerate.

7. **ASSEMBLE THE SANDWICHES** In a large frying pan, heat enough vegetable oil to coat the bottom of the pan. Add the thinly sliced corned beef and cook, stirring constantly, until lightly golden, 2 to 3 minutes.

8. Lay the bread on a work surface. Top 1 slice of each sandwich with 2 tablespoons (30 mL) Russian dressing, 2 tablespoons (30 mL) Swiss cheese, and ⅓ cup (75 mL) sauerkraut. Add the corned beef and top with the other slice of bread. Serve immediately.

Philly Cheesesteak Sandwiches

When it comes to the infamous Philly cheesesteak, the debate in the biz has always been peppers and onions, or just onions? Whatever way you enjoy your Philly cheesesteak, make sure that it's messy! Something has gone horribly wrong if there isn't a mountain of used napkins next to your plate after this meal. This version uses a salty marinade to give it that beefy taste!

MAKES 4 SANDWICHES

Prep ahead
Seitan Corned Beef (see page 151)

Mac and Cheese Sauce (page 223)

Ingredients
½ cup (125 mL) + 2 tablespoons (30 mL) vegetable oil, divided

½ cup (125 mL) water

¼ cup (60 mL) tamari or soy sauce

¼ cup (60 mL) Dijon mustard

2 tablespoons (30 mL) black pepper

1 tablespoon (15 mL) garlic powder

2 cups (500 mL) Seitan Corned Beef

2 cups (500 mL) thinly sliced white onions

1 cup (250 mL) thinly sliced green peppers

¼ teaspoon (1 mL) sea salt

4 soft white sub buns

1¼ cups (300 mL) Mac and Cheese Sauce, heated

1. In a blender, combine ½ cup (125 mL) of the vegetable oil, water, tamari, mustard, black pepper, and garlic powder. Blend until smooth. This is the marinade.

2. Using a very sharp knife or deli slicer, cut the seitan corned beef into very thin strips. In a large bowl, toss the seitan corned beef with the marinade until well coated. Marinate for 30 minutes or overnight. If marinating overnight, transfer to an airtight container and refrigerate.

3. In a large frying pan, heat the remaining 2 tablespoons (30 mL) vegetable oil over high heat. Add the onions, green peppers, and salt. Cook, stirring frequently, until the onions and peppers start to turn golden brown. Reduce the heat to low and cook, stirring occasionally, until the onions are soft and golden brown, about 25 minutes. Transfer the mixture to a plate. Wipe the pan clean.

4. In the same pan, heat enough vegetable oil to coat the bottom of the pan over low heat. Add the seitan corned beef to the pan and cook, stirring constantly, until the meat is lightly golden, 2 to 3 minutes.

5. Lay the sub buns on a work surface. Fill each bun with about ½ cup (125 mL) of the seitan corned beef, ⅓ cup (75 mL) of the onion and pepper mixture, and ⅓ cup (75 mL) of the mac and cheese sauce. Serve immediately. If you have any leftover seitan corned beef or peppers and onions, allow them to cool completely and store them separately in airtight containers in the fridge for up to 1 week.

Smoked Carrot Lox Pinwheel Wrap

There is something so satisfying to the senses about the mixture of silky cream cheese and slightly smoked lox, all lovingly crammed together in the middle of a tortilla. My fish-friendly version uses my homemade Cream Cheese (page 222) and lox made from carrots instead of salmon. I love to make these and serve them with a nice big Chopped Salad (page 90).

MAKES 4 WRAPS

Prep ahead

Cream Cheese (page 222)

Ingredients

2 cups (500 mL) peeled roughly chopped carrots

¼ cup (60 mL) extra-virgin olive oil

2 tablespoons (30 mL) freshly squeezed lemon juice

½ cup (125 mL) tightly packed finely chopped flat-leaf parsley

½ cup (125 mL) finely diced red onion

1 teaspoon (5 mL) sea salt

¼ teaspoon (1 mL) liquid smoke

4 large flour tortillas

1¼ cups (300 mL) Cream Cheese

1. In a food processor fitted with a metal blade, process the carrots until broken down into a paste. Transfer to a medium bowl and add the olive oil, lemon juice, parsley, red onion, salt, and liquid smoke. Mix until well combined.

2. Lay the tortillas on a work surface. Place ⅓ cup (75 mL) cream cheese in the centre of each tortilla. Spread the cream cheese through the middle of the wrap so that it almost reaches the edges. Add about 6 tablespoons (90 mL) of the carrot lox mixture to the centre of each wrap. Fold in the sides, then starting from the bottom of the wrap, roll tightly into a cylinder.

3. Cut each wrap into 1½-inch (4 cm) thick round sections. Serve immediately.

TIP

Use hot water when making a flax egg, as it is best to help speed up the process of gelling the flax.

Spaghetti and Meatballs

Whether you're having a romantic candlelit dinner with your spouse or you're a puppy in love slurping it up in an alleyway, nothing is more classic than spaghetti and meatballs! Instead of using animals, my meatballs are made with ground walnuts and sunflower seeds, processed until they take on the texture of ground meat. Mixed with green lentils and diced onions, their texture is eerily similar to traditional meatballs!

SERVES 4

Tomato Sauce

2 tablespoons (30 mL) extra-virgin olive oil

½ cup (125 mL) finely diced white onion

½ teaspoon (2 mL) sea salt

3 tablespoons (45 mL) minced garlic

1 can (14 ounces/398 mL) diced tomatoes

1 cup (250 mL) tightly packed fresh basil leaves

1 tablespoon (15 mL) nutritional yeast

Meatballs

2 tablespoons (30 mL) ground golden flaxseed

6 tablespoons (90 mL) hot water (see Tip)

1 cup (250 mL) dried green lentils

4 cups (1 L) water

¼ cup (60 mL) raw walnuts

¼ cup (60 mL) raw sunflower seeds

¼ cup (60 mL) nutritional yeast

1½ teaspoons (7 mL) sea salt

2 tablespoons (30 mL) vegetable oil

1 cup (250 mL) finely diced white onion

2 tablespoons (30 mL) minced garlic

1 tablespoon (15 mL) chopped fresh thyme leaves

2 tablespoons (30 mL) dry white wine

½ cup (125 mL) tightly packed finely chopped fresh flat-leaf parsley

———

Vegetable oil, for cooking

16 ounces (450 g) dried spaghetti

12 to 15 fresh basil leaves

1. **MAKE THE TOMATO SAUCE** In a medium pot, heat the olive oil over medium heat. Add the onion and salt and cook, stirring frequently, until the onion is soft and translucent, 3 to 4 minutes. Add the garlic and cook, stirring constantly, until the garlic is soft and fragrant, 2 to 3 minutes. Add the tomatoes with their juice, bring to a boil, then reduce the heat to a simmer and cook, stirring occasionally, until the sauce is thick and rich, about 30 minutes. Remove from the heat and stir in the basil and nutritional yeast.

2. **MAKE THE MEATBALLS** In a small bowl, whisk together the flaxseed and hot water until well combined. Set aside so that the flaxseed can swell and absorb the liquid, about 10 minutes.

3. In a medium pot, combine the green lentils and water. Bring to a boil, uncovered, then reduce the heat to a simmer and cook until the lentils are soft, about 15 minutes. Drain, discarding the cooking water.

4. In a food processor fitted with a metal blade, process the cooked green lentils, walnuts, sunflower seeds, nutritional yeast, and salt. Process until the mixture is mostly smooth, making sure to leave a little bit of texture. Transfer to a large bowl.

5. In a large frying pan, heat the vegetable oil over medium-high heat. Add the onion and cook, stirring frequently, until soft and translucent, 3 to 4 minutes. Add the garlic and thyme and cook, stirring constantly, until the garlic is soft and fragrant, 2 to 3 minutes. Add the white wine and cook until almost all of the liquid has evaporated, about 2 minutes. Remove from the heat and allow to cool slightly, then transfer the mixture to the processed lentils.

6. To the lentil mixture, add the soaked flaxseed and parsley. Mix until well combined. Using an ice cream scoop or your hands, form the mixture into 20 balls. The balls should be a little smaller than a golf ball.

7. In a large, wide pan, heat enough vegetable oil to coat the bottom of the pan over medium-high heat. Taking care not to crowd the pan, cook the meatballs until browned on all sides, turning with metal tongs as necessary, 2 to 3 minutes per side.

8. **COOK THE PASTA** In a large pot of boiling salted water, cook the spaghetti according to package directions. Drain, discarding the cooking water.

9. Divide the pasta among plates. Top with hot tomato sauce, 5 or 6 meatballs, and 3 or 4 basil leaves. Serve immediately. Store the tomato sauce, meatballs, and pasta separately in airtight containers in the fridge for up to 1 week.

Fettuccini Alfredo

This popular pasta dish is creamy and rich and has an astounding depth of flavour that will keep you coming back for more. I love to serve it with grilled portobello mushrooms and fresh greens, such as green peas or arugula, then sprinkle the top with a little nutritional yeast and freshly cracked pepper. I also serve it with a lemon wedge for good measure.

SERVES 4

Ingredients

½ cup (125 mL) vegetable oil

1 cup (250 mL) finely diced white onion

10 cloves garlic

¼ cup (60 mL) dry white wine, such as Chardonnay

1 cup (250 mL) raw cashews, soaked and drained (see Tip)

4 cups (1 L) water

1 teaspoon (5 mL) brown rice miso paste (see Tip)

1 tablespoon (15 mL) tamari or soy sauce

½ cup (125 mL) nutritional yeast

2 tablespoons (30 mL) Dijon mustard

2 teaspoons (10 mL) freshly squeezed lemon juice

1 teaspoon (5 mL) sea salt, divided

1 pound (450 g) dried fettucine

1. In a medium pot, heat the vegetable oil over medium-low heat. Add the onion and garlic and cook, stirring frequently with a wooden spoon, until the onion and garlic are browned and golden, 15 to 16 minutes. Add the white wine and cook until most of the liquid has evaporated. Drain the mixture, discarding most of the oil; if there is a little bit left, that is fine.

2. In a high-speed blender, combine the soaked cashews and water. Blend until smooth and creamy. Add the onion and garlic mixture, miso, tamari, nutritional yeast, mustard, lemon juice, and salt. Blend again until smooth and creamy. Pour the cashew mixture into a large pan and set aside until ready to use.

3. In a large pot of boiling salted water, cook the fettucine according to package directions. Drain using a colander, discarding the cooking water. Rinse under cold running water until the pasta is cold.

4. Heat the cashew mixture, your alfredo sauce, over medium heat, taking care not to bring it to a full boil for too long. You do not want to boil cashew-based sauces for very long because the protein and fat can split, giving the sauce the appearance of curdled milk. Stir in the cooked pasta and toss to evenly coat. Cook until the sauce becomes thick and coats the pasta, 2 to 3 minutes only; the texture should not be watery but thick like cream. Divide among 4 bowls and serve immediately.

TIP

1. To soak the cashews, place them in a small bowl with 2 cups (500 mL) hot water for at least 1 hour or overnight, covered and stored in the fridge. Drain and rinse the cashews, discarding the soaking liquid. **2.** Brown rice miso or any dark miso is ideal for this recipe because of its bold flavour. If you do not have brown rice miso, substitute an equal amount of any other miso but keep in mind that the darker the colour, the more flavour it will create in this recipe.

Mushroom and Spinach Lasagna

This ain't yo' mama's lasagna. It's full of mushrooms and spinach, two of my favourite foods! Usually, lasagna is made with a sauce called béchamel and ricotta cheese. Traditional béchamel sauce is made with butter, flour, and milk. My veganized version is made using vegan butter, unsweetened almond milk, and flour, and in this recipe my ricotta is made using firm tofu. This dish is a great way to trick yourself into eating some vegetables!

SERVES 4 TO 6

Prep ahead
Whipped Butter (page 229)

Ingredients
¼ cup (60 mL) Whipped Butter or vegan butter

¼ cup (60 mL) all-purpose flour

2 cups (500 mL) unsweetened almond milk or other non-dairy milk

¾ cup (175 mL) nutritional yeast, divided

2 teaspoons (10 mL) sea salt, divided

3 tablespoons (45 mL) vegetable oil

½ cup (125 mL) finely diced white onion

2 tablespoons (30 mL) minced garlic

8 cups (2 L) tightly packed chopped spinach leaves

2 cups (500 mL) thinly sliced mushrooms

1 cup (250 mL) roughly chopped firm vacuum-packed tofu

2 teaspoons (10 mL) dried basil

1 teaspoon (5 mL) dried thyme

12 dried lasagna noodles

2½ cups (625 mL) tomato sauce

1. **MAKE THE LASAGNA FILLING** In a saucepan, melt the whipped butter over medium heat. Add the flour and cook, stirring constantly, for 6 to 8 minutes, until the raw taste of the flour has cooked out. Remove from the heat and whisk in the almond milk, ¼ cup (60 mL) at a time, until smooth. Bring the mixture to a boil, reduce the heat to low, and simmer for 6 to 8 minutes, until thickened. Remove from the heat and stir in ¼ cup (60 mL) of the nutritional yeast and 1 teaspoon (5 mL) of the salt. Cover and set aside.

2. In a large frying pan, heat the vegetable oil over medium heat. Add the onion and remaining 1 teaspoon (5 mL) salt. Cook, stirring constantly, until the onion is translucent, about 5 minutes. Stir in the garlic and cook until fragrant, about 2 minutes. Add the spinach and mushrooms and cook, stirring constantly, until most of the liquid has evaporated, about 10 minutes. Remove from the heat and transfer to a medium bowl, then allow to cool slightly.

3. In a food processor fitted with a metal blade, process the tofu until no large pieces remain. Place the processed tofu in the bowl with the cooked vegetables. Add ¼ cup (60 mL) of the nutritional yeast, basil, and thyme. Mix until well combined. You want the texture to be like a traditional ricotta cheese, smooth and creamy with a little bit of texture.

4. **COOK THE PASTA** In a large pot of boiling salted water, cook the lasagna according to package directions. Drain using a colander, discarding the cooking water. Rinse under cold running water until the pasta is cold. Cover with a damp kitchen towel and set aside.

5. Preheat the oven to 400°F (200°C).

6. **ASSEMBLE THE LASAGNA** Pour about ¼ cup (60 mL) of the tomato sauce into the bottom of an 11- × 7-inch (2 L) baking dish. Lay 4 lasagna noodles lengthwise across the bottom of the dish, overlapping them slightly. Spread half of the spinach-mushroom-tofu mixture evenly over top. Cover with half of the almond milk sauce, followed by 1 cup (250 mL) of the tomato sauce. Repeat, following the same order, reserving ¼ cup (60 mL) of tomato sauce. Finish with the remaining 4 noodles and top with the remaining ¼ cup (60 mL) tomato sauce. Sprinkle with the remaining ¼ cup (60 mL) nutritional yeast.

7. Bake until the middle is bubbling hot and the top is golden brown, 40 to 45 minutes. Serve immediately or allow to cool and store in an airtight container in the fridge for up to 1 week. The lasagna will also freeze well. Store tightly wrapped in plastic wrap, or with a lid, for up to 2 months.

No-Beef Stroganoff

Beef stroganoff is a rich and hearty dish served over noodles or rice, traditionally made with beef stock and chunks of beef. Sour cream is folded in at the end and served hot. In my veganized version, we've got all the same goodness going on, except no beef! Instead, I use chunks of TVP to stand in for the beef and tamari for the stock and then fold in dairy-free sour cream at the end. It's fantastic served over rice, potatoes, or fettuccini.

SERVES 4

Prep ahead
Sour Cream (page 231)

Ingredients
½ cup (125 mL) dried TVP chunks (see Tip)

2 cups (500 mL) hot water

3 tablespoons (45 mL) vegetable oil

1 cup (250 mL) chopped onion

1 teaspoon (5 mL) ground cumin

½ teaspoon (2 mL) sea salt, divided

6 cloves garlic, minced

4 cups (1 L) sliced cremini mushrooms

¼ cup (60 mL) tamari or soy sauce

¼ cup (60 mL) water, at room temperature

1 cup (250 mL) Sour Cream

—

Cooked rice, potatoes, or fettuccini, for serving

1. In a medium bowl, combine the TVP and hot water. Set aside and allow the TVP to soak and absorb water, about 15 minutes. Drain, discarding any remaining water.

2. In a medium pot, heat the vegetable oil over medium heat. Add the onion, cumin, and salt. Cook, stirring frequently, until the onion begins to brown, about 6 minutes. Add the garlic and cook, stirring constantly, until fragrant, about 2 minutes.

3. Add the soaked TVP and mushrooms. Cook, stirring frequently, until the mushrooms are soft and the TVP has absorbed some of the juices from the mushrooms and onions, about 3 to 4 minutes. It is okay if there is a little liquid from the mushrooms left in the pot. Remove from the heat and stir in the tamari, water, and sour cream. Taste and adjust seasoning, if needed. Serve over rice, potatoes, or fettuccini noodles.

TIP

TVP (textured or texturized vegan protein) comes in various sizes, from small flakes to large chunks. For this recipe, use very large chunks. They can most commonly be found in the bulk section of natural food stores or online.

Shepherd's Pie

Traditionally, shepherd's pie is a mixture of ground meat, spices, and a classic brown sauce from French cuisine called espagnole made from flour, butter, dark stock, and tomatoes. My veganized version uses flour, deodorized coconut oil for the butter, red wine, and tamari for the stock, and tomato paste, plus TVP for the meat. I honestly find the combination of the red wine and tamari to be even tastier than its animal-based counterpart, veal stock. This is a great meal that's easy to make ahead of time. Just pop it in the oven when you're ready for some serious chowing down.

SERVES 5 TO 6

Shepherd's Pie Filling

- 2 cups (500 mL) dried TVP flakes
- 10 cups (2.5 L) hot water, divided
- 3 tablespoons (45 mL) vegetable oil
- 1 cup (250 mL) finely diced white onion
- 1 cup (250 mL) finely diced peeled carrots
- 1 cup (250 mL) finely diced celery
- 1 tablespoon (15 mL) tomato paste
- ½ teaspoon (2 mL) sea salt
- 4 cloves garlic, minced
- 3 tablespoons (45 mL) deodorized coconut oil
- ¼ cup (60 mL) all-purpose flour
- ½ cup (125 mL) dry red wine
- ¼ cup (60 mL) tamari or soy sauce
- 1 tablespoon (15 mL) chopped fresh thyme leaves
- 1 cup (250 mL) frozen corn kernels

Mashed Potato Topping

- 2 pounds (900 g) russet potatoes, peeled and cut into 2-inch (5 cm) cubes
- 3 tablespoons (45 mL) sea salt, divided
- 1 cup (250 mL) vegan butter or margarine
- 1 teaspoon (5 mL) garlic powder
- ½ cup (125 mL) unsweetened almond milk or soy milk
- ¼ teaspoon (1 mL) sweet paprika

1. **MAKE THE SHEPHERD'S PIE FILLING** In a large bowl, combine the TVP and 8 cups (2 L) of the hot water. Cover and set aside so that the TVP can absorb the liquid and swell, 15 to 20 minutes. Drain, discarding any remaining liquid.

2. In a medium pot, heat the vegetable oil over medium heat. Add the onion, carrot, celery, tomato paste, and salt and cook, stirring frequently, until the onion is translucent and lightly browned, 8 to 10 minutes. Stir in the soaked TVP and cook, stirring constantly, for 3 to 4 minutes. Add the garlic and cook, stirring constantly, until fragrant, about 2 minutes. Stir in the coconut oil and flour and cook, stirring constantly, for 5 minutes, until the raw taste of the flour has been cooked out. Add the red wine and cook, stirring constantly, until no liquid remains, 3 to 4 minutes. Add the remaining 2 cups (500 mL) water and tamari. Bring the mixture to a simmer and cook for 10 to 12 minutes. Remove from the heat and stir in the thyme and corn. Transfer the mixture to an 11- × 7-inch (2 L) glass or metal baking dish.

3. Preheat the oven to 375°F (190°C).

4. **MAKE THE MASHED POTATO TOPPING** In a medium pot, add the potatoes and 2 tablespoons (30 mL) of the salt and cover with cold water. Bring to a boil, uncovered. Reduce the heat to a simmer and cook until the potatoes are soft, 15 to 20 minutes.

5. Drain the potatoes, discarding the water. Place the potatoes back in the pot and add the butter, the remaining 1 tablespoon (15 mL) salt, garlic powder, and almond milk. Using a potato masher, mash the potatoes until no large pieces remain; it is okay if there are some smaller pieces. Spread the mashed potatoes evenly over top the shepherd's pie filling. Sprinkle the paprika over the mashed potato topping. Bake until hot and bubbly in the middle and golden brown on top, 25 to 30 minutes. Serve immediately or allow to cool completely and store in an airtight container in the fridge for up to 1 week or in the freezer for up to 2 months.

Holiday Ham

My vegan ham is the perfect substitute for the traditional carved ham that is served around the holidays. I use a mixture of pineapple juice and liquid smoke to help create the classic ham hock flavour. The trick for this recipe is to make the ham and let it rest overnight so that it becomes firm and easy to slice. I like to serve this with tart cranberry sauce, sweet potato mash, and something green like broccoli, kale, or collard greens.

MAKES 1 HAM; SERVES 4 TO 6

Seitan (Ham) Dough

2 cups (500 mL) vital wheat gluten flour

2 tablespoons (30 mL) nutritional yeast

1 teaspoon (5 mL) sea salt

1 cup (250 mL) pineapple juice

¼ cup (60 mL) Dijon mustard

3 tablespoons (45 mL) vegetable oil

2 tablespoons (30 mL) tamari or soy sauce

1 tablespoon (15 mL) agave nectar

1 tablespoon (15 mL) unpasteurized apple cider vinegar

1 tablespoon (15 mL) liquid smoke

Broth

1 cup (250 mL) beet juice

2 tablespoons (30 mL) Dijon mustard

2 tablespoons (30 mL) maple syrup

2 teaspoons (10 mL) sea salt

½ teaspoon (2 mL) liquid smoke

Glaze

⅓ cup (75 mL) Dijon mustard

3 tablespoons (45 mL) brown sugar

1 tablespoon (15 mL) maple syrup

1 tablespoon (15 mL) unpasteurized apple cider vinegar

¼ teaspoon (1 mL) sea salt

⅛ teaspoon (0.5 mL) ground cloves

1. **MAKE THE SEITAN DOUGH** In a medium bowl, combine the wheat gluten flour, nutritional yeast, and salt. Whisk until all ingredients are well combined.

2. In a blender, combine the pineapple juice, mustard, oil, tamari, agave, apple cider vinegar, and liquid smoke. Blend until all ingredients are smooth.

3. Add the wet ingredients to the dry ingredients. Using your hands, mix until well combined and the ingredients come together as a dough. You do not want to see any dry patches of the flour left. Transfer to a work surface and knead the dough for 3 to 4 minutes to develop the gluten. You want the dough to be firm to the touch. Shape it so that it is about 6 inches (15 cm) in diameter. It should be flat on the bottom with a rounded top, like a small ham.

4. Preheat the oven to 350°F (180°C). Line an 11- × 7-inch (2 L) baking dish with aluminum foil, leaving an extra 3 inches (8 cm) of foil on each side. You will be cooking the seitan in a foil package and you do not want the steam to escape, so it is important to have enough foil to close all sides tightly.

5. **MAKE THE BROTH** In a blender, combine the beet juice, mustard, maple syrup, salt, and liquid smoke. Blend until smooth.

6. Place the seitan in the middle of the foil and gather the sides to create a pouch. Pour the cooking liquid over the seitan, making sure not to let any of the liquid spill out of the foil. Gather the foil and make an airtight package. Bake until the seitan is firm to the touch, about 1 hour. You do not want it to be soft or have the texture of a dough at this point. If it is a little soft, tighten the foil again and continue baking for 10 to 15 minutes. Remove from the oven and open the foil package so that the ham can cool completely. Transfer to a container and refrigerate until cold, about 2 hours or overnight.

7. **MAKE THE GLAZE** In a small bowl, combine the mustard, brown sugar, maple syrup, apple cider vinegar, salt, and cloves. Mix until well combined.

8. **BAKE THE SEITAN HAM** Preheat the oven to 350°F (180°C). Place the seitan on a baking sheet lined with parchment paper. Pour the glaze evenly over the seitan; you want to make sure to cover as much of the surface as you can with the glaze. Bake until hot in the middle and the glaze is bubbling hot and golden, 12 to 15 minutes. Serve immediately or cool completely and store in an airtight container in the fridge for up to 1 week.

Hickory Smoked Ribs

When I was an apprentice, I learned the ins and outs of properly cooking a rack of ribs. I loved the way the meat was soft and tender, and how it all fell apart when you took a bite. I created these mouth-watering vegan ribs with quick oats and a lot of diced onion to help replicate the muscle fibres of the meat. Vital wheat gluten flour helps give the ribs a chewy body, and rich barbecue sauce lends a traditional smoky barbecue flavour! This dish gives you all of the flavour and texture, and none of the suffering.

MAKES 2 RACKS OF RIBS; SERVES 4

Ingredients

2 tablespoons (30 mL) vegetable oil

4 cups (1 L) finely diced white onion

1½ cups (375 mL) cooked chickpeas

Dry Mix

2 cups (500 mL) vital wheat gluten four

½ cup (125 mL) quick oats

3 tablespoons (45 mL) nutritional yeast

2 teaspoons (10 mL) smoked paprika

1½ teaspoons (7 mL) garlic powder

1½ teaspoons (7 mL) sea salt

1½ teaspoons (7 mL) Montreal steak spice blend

1 teaspoon (5 mL) onion powder

¼ teaspoon (1 mL) coarsely ground black pepper

Wet Mix

¾ cup (175 mL) + 2 tablespoons (30 mL) water

¼ cup (60 mL) melted deodorized coconut oil

¼ cup (60 mL) diced firm tofu

¼ cup (60 mL) hickory flavoured barbecue sauce (see Tip)

2 tablespoons (30 mL) tamari or soy sauce

2 tablespoons (30 mL) nutritional yeast

1 tablespoon (15 mL) smooth natural peanut butter

1½ teaspoons (7 mL) Dijon mustard

1½ teaspoons (7 mL) tomato paste

Broth

1½ cups (375 mL) water

1¼ cups (300 mL) hickory flavoured barbecue sauce, divided (see Tip)

1½ teaspoons (7 mL) tamari or soy sauce

1. In a large frying pan, heat the vegetable oil over medium-high heat. Add the onions and cook, stirring frequently, until golden brown and lightly caramelized, 6 to 8 minutes. Remove from the heat and set aside to cool completely.

2. In a food processor fitted with a metal blade, process the chickpeas until no large pieces remain.

3. **MAKE THE DRY MIX** In a medium bowl, combine the wheat gluten flour, oats, nutritional yeast, paprika, garlic powder, salt, steak spice blend, onion powder, and pepper until well combined. Add the cooked onions and ground chickpeas, but do not mix yet.

4. **MAKE THE WET MIX** In a blender, combine the water, coconut oil, tofu, barbecue sauce, tamari, nutritional yeast, peanut butter, mustard, and tomato paste. Blend until smooth.

5. **MAKE THE RIBS** Add the wet ingredients to the dry ingredients. Using your hands, mix until well combined. Once the mixture comes together, turn it out onto a work surface and knead until no dry parts remain and the dough is smooth and elastic, 3 to 4 minutes.

6. Position a rack in the top third of the oven. Preheat the oven to 350°F (180°C). Grease an 8- × 4-inch (1.5 L) baking dish with vegetable oil or nonstick cooking spray.

7. Using a rolling pin, roll out the dough so that it will fit into the baking dish. Lay the dough in the baking dish. Using a small knife, cut the dough once through the middle lengthwise, then cut it into thin strips crosswise, each about ½ inch (1 cm) thick. The dough should resemble 2 racks of ribs.

8. **MAKE THE BROTH** In a blender, combine the water, ¼ cup (60 mL) of the barbecue sauce, and tamari. Blend until smooth. Pour the blended broth over the ribs and top with a piece of parchment paper. Bake for 30 to 35 minutes, or until most of the liquid has been absorbed and the dough is no longer soft and mushy. It should have some give when pressed but also be firm to the touch.

Continued

9. Remove the baking dish from the oven, spread the remaining 1 cup (250 mL) barbecue sauce over the ribs, and return to the oven until caramelized and golden, about 15 minutes. Serve immediately or cool completely and store in an airtight container in the fridge for up to 1 week.

TIP

1. Using hickory flavoured barbecue sauce for this recipe is important, as it will impart a traditional rib flavour. You can also use a barbecue sauce labelled as rib flavour, but I prefer hickory. **2.** These ribs are great grilled! Preheat a grill to medium heat. Lay the ribs on the grill and brush with barbecue sauce. Cook until the ribs are hot in the middle and the sauce starts to caramelize, 5 to 6 minutes per side. Do not push down on the ribs or they will burn.

Butter Tofu

Traditionally, this Indian-style recipe is made with heavy cream and an aromatic blend of spices, served with chicken over rice. Instead, I use tofu to replace the chicken and a blend of almond milk and raw cashews to replace the heavy cream. The super-savoury flavours of this dish mainly come from the various spices, so you won't even miss the unethical alternatives.

SERVES 4

Tofu

¼ cup (60 mL) extra-virgin coconut oil

1 pound (450 g) firm tofu

½ teaspoon (5 mL) sea salt

Sauce

¼ cup (60 mL) extra-virgin coconut oil

½ cup (125 mL) finely diced white onion

2 jalapeño peppers, finely chopped and seeds removed

1 tablespoon (15 mL) finely chopped fresh ginger

4 cloves garlic, minced

½ teaspoon (2 mL) sea salt

1 tablespoon (15 mL) garam masala

2 teaspoons (10 mL) chili powder

1 teaspoon (5 mL) ground cumin

½ teaspoon (2 mL) ground coriander

¼ teaspoon (1 mL) cinnamon

3 tablespoons (45 mL) tomato paste

2 cups (500 mL) chopped fresh tomatoes

2 teaspoons (10 mL) maple syrup

¼ cup (60 mL) fresh lime leaves (optional; see Tip)

1 cup (250 mL) raw cashews, soaked and drained (see Tip)

2 cups (500 mL) unsweetened almond milk

2 tablespoons (30 mL) freshly squeezed lime juice

Cooked basmati rice, for serving

1. **PREPARE THE TOFU** In a medium frying pan, preferably nonstick, heat the coconut oil over medium-high heat. Add the tofu and salt and cook, stirring frequently, until the tofu is browned on all sides, 6 to 8 minutes. Transfer to a plate lined with paper towel to drain excess oil.

2. **MAKE THE SAUCE** In the same pan (do not wipe clean), heat the coconut oil over medium heat. Add the onion, jalapeño, ginger, garlic, and salt. Cook, stirring constantly, until the onions are soft and the garlic is fragrant, 2 to 3 minutes. Add the garam masala, chili powder, cumin, coriander, and cinnamon. Cook, stirring constantly, until the spices are toasted and fragrant, about 2 minutes. Add the tomato paste, chopped tomatoes, maple syrup, and lime leaves, if using. Bring the mixture to simmer and cook, stirring frequently, for 8 to 10 minutes.

3. In a high-speed blender, combine the cashews and almond milk. Blend on high speed until smooth and creamy. Stir into the simmering spice blend and add back the cooked tofu. Simmer until the sauce has thickened and coats the back of a spoon. Add the lime juice and cook, stirring frequently, for 1 to 2 minutes. Serve immediately over rice or cool completely and store in an airtight container in the fridge for up to 1 week.

TIP

1. Lime leaves can be found in most Indian specialty markets and well-stocked grocery stores or online. **2.** To soak the cashews, place them in a large bowl and cover with 2 cups (500 mL) hot water for at least 1 hour or overnight, covered and stored in the fridge. Drain and rinse the cashews, discarding the soaking liquid.

General Tso Tofu

In many ways, General Tso sauce is what great cooking is all about. It's the perfect balance of sweet, salty, tangy, and slightly spicy. It's the true embodiment of umami. Usually, crispy chicken is covered in this sauce, then served over fresh, hot rice. Instead, I like to use tofu, made from edamame beans. Maybe it's no coincidence that *edamame* and *umami* rhyme, because tofu is the perfect base to soak up any flavour combination. Like any stir-fry dish, this comes together quickly, so make sure you have all of your ingredients ready before you start!

SERVES 4

Tofu

1 pound (450 g) firm tofu

1 tablespoon + 1 teaspoon (20 mL) cornstarch

Pinch of sea salt

⅓ cup (75 mL) vegetable oil

Sauce

1 tablespoon (15 mL) vegetable oil

2 tablespoons (30 mL) minced fresh ginger

5 cloves garlic, thinly sliced

1 cup (250 mL) green bell peppers cut into 1-inch (2.5 cm) cubes

½ cup (125 mL) green onions (white and light green parts only) cut into 1-inch (2.5 cm) pieces

½ cup (125 mL) tamari or soy sauce

¼ cup (60 mL) rice wine vinegar

¼ cup (60 mL) maple syrup

2 tablespoons (30 mL) toasted sesame oil

1 tablespoon (15 mL) hot sauce (optional)

2 tablespoons (30 mL) cornstarch

2 tablespoons (30 mL) cold water (see Tip)

For serving

Thinly sliced green onion

White sesame seeds

Steamed white or brown rice

1. **PREPARE THE TOFU** Cut the tofu into 1-inch (2.5 cm) cubes. In a medium bowl, toss the tofu with the cornstarch and salt until well combined.

2. In a medium pan, preferably nonstick, heat the vegetable oil over medium-high heat. Using a slotted metal spoon or tongs, carefully add the tofu to the hot oil. Cook until golden brown and crisp, turning as necessary with the metal tongs or slotted spoon, 3 to 4 minutes. Remove the tofu and place on a plate lined with a kitchen towel or paper towel to drain excess oil. Wipe the pan clean.

3. **MAKE THE SAUCE** In the same pan, add the vegetable oil, ginger, and garlic over medium-high heat. Cook, stirring constantly with a wooden spoon, until the ginger and garlic are golden brown and fragrant, taking care not to burn the garlic, 2 to 3 minutes. Add the bell pepper and green onions and cook, stirring frequently, until golden brown, 6 to 7 minutes.

4. Meanwhile, in a small bowl, whisk together the tamari, rice wine vinegar, maple syrup, sesame oil, hot sauce (if using), cornstarch, and cold water, until no lumps remain.

5. Pour the tamari mixture into the pan and add back the fried tofu, stirring to combine. Bring the mixture to a simmer and cook until the sauce is thick and shiny, 4 to 5 minutes. Garnish with a sprinkle of green onion and sesame seeds. Serve immediately over steamed rice.

TIP

A mixture of cornstarch and water is commonly referred to as a slurry and is used to thicken many types of sauces, especially Asian-style sauces. Always use cold water when making a slurry, and if it clumps together, use a whisk to make it smooth before adding it to your sauce.

Drunken Vegan Chicken Stew

Traditionally, this hearty stew is made using the dark meat of chicken and strips of bacon for a smoky flavour and is braised in red wine for a long time until the chicken is soft and tender. In my version, I've used meat's cruelty-free cousins—mock chicken (the same kind used in my Boneless Wings, page 24) and bacon made from seitan—for a similar mouthfeel and flavour. The key to this recipe is allowing everything to brown well in a good, solid Dutch oven, then picking out all the brown bits from the bottom that are saturated with wine.

SERVES 4

Prep ahead
Seitan Wings (see page 24, steps 1 to 4 only)
Seitan Bacon (page 105)

Seitan Chicken
½ cup (125 mL) all-purpose flour
1 tablespoon (15 mL) nutritional yeast
½ teaspoon (2 mL) smoked paprika
¼ teaspoon (5 mL) sea salt
2 cups (500 mL) Seitan Wings or your favourite vegan chicken pieces
2 tablespoons (30 mL) vegetable oil

Stew
2 tablespoons (30 mL) deodorized coconut oil
2 cups (500 mL) finely diced onion
1 cup (250 mL) quartered button mushrooms
1 cup (250 mL) finely diced celery
1 cup (250 mL) finely diced peeled carrot
½ cup (125 mL) finely diced Seitan Bacon
½ cup (125 mL) tomato paste
¼ cup (60 mL) minced garlic
1½ cups (375 mL) dry red wine
¼ cup (60 mL) finely chopped fresh thyme leaves
½ cup (125 mL) tamari
8 cups (2 L) water

Mashed potatoes, rice, or broad pasta noodles such as fettuccini or pappardelle, for serving

1. **MAKE THE SEITAN CHICKEN** In a small bowl, whisk together the flour, nutritional yeast, paprika, and salt until well combined. Coat the seitan wings evenly in the flour mixture.

2. In a Dutch oven or large heavy-bottomed pot, heat the vegetable oil over medium heat. Add the seitan wings and cook until golden brown on all sides, turning the pieces as necessary, about 6 to 8 minutes total. Transfer to a plate lined with paper towel to drain excess oil. Wipe the pot clean.

3. **MAKE THE STEW** In the same pot, over medium heat, add the coconut oil, onions, mushrooms, celery, carrots, and seitan bacon. Cook, stirring frequently, until soft and lightly golden brown, 10 to 12 minutes. Add the tomato paste and garlic. Cook, stirring constantly, until the garlic is fragrant and soft, 2 to 3 minutes. Add the red wine, thyme, tamari, and water. Bring the mixture to a simmer and add back the browned seitan wings. Cover with a tight-fitting lid and reduce the heat to medium-low. Cook, stirring every 10 minutes, for 30 to 35 minutes. You want the broth to be rich and full of body. Uncover and simmer for another 5 to 10 minutes.

4. Serve over mashed potatoes, rice, or pasta. Allow any leftovers to cool completely and store in an airtight container in the fridge for up to 1 week.

Crab Cakes with Remoulade Sauce

Soft and flaky hearts of palm stand in for lump crab meat in my adaptation of this classy dish. If you don't have time to make the remoulade sauce, feel free to serve these crab cakes with whatever dipping sauce you have. Also, you can make smaller cakes for an amazing appetizer at any dinner party or celebration. These will steal the heart of anyone who bites into them, so be sure to make enough to go around—for possibly multiple rounds!

MAKES 4 CRAB CAKES

Prep ahead

Creamy Mayo (page 232)

Crab Cakes

1 can (14 ounces/398 mL) hearts of palm

⅓ cup (75 mL) Creamy Mayo

¼ cup (60 mL) finely chopped celery

¼ cup (60 mL) finely chopped red sweet pepper

2 tablespoons (30 mL) finely diced red onion

2 tablespoons (30 mL) freshly squeezed lemon juice

2 tablespoons (30 mL) Dijon mustard

1 tablespoon (15 mL) dried dill or 3 tablespoons (45 mL) finely chopped fresh dill

1 tablespoon (15 mL) chili powder

2 teaspoons (10 mL) sea salt

2 teaspoons (10 mL) sweet paprika

Breading

½ cup (125 mL) unsweetened almond milk

¼ cup (60 mL) Dijon mustard

¾ teaspoon (4 mL) sea salt, divided

1 cup (250 mL) panko crumbs

1 tablespoon (15 mL) finely grated lemon zest

1 teaspoon (5 mL) dried dill

½ teaspoon (2 mL) sweet paprika

———

Vegetable oil, for frying

Remoulade Sauce

1 cup (250 mL) Creamy Mayo

3 tablespoons (45 mL) thinly sliced green onion, green parts only

2 tablespoons (30 mL) freshly squeezed lemon juice

2 tablespoons (30 mL) finely diced dill pickle

2 tablespoons (30 mL) freshly grated horseradish

1 tablespoon (15 mL) Dijon mustard

2 teaspoons (10 mL) finely chopped drained capers

1 teaspoon (5 mL) smoked paprika

1 teaspoon (5 mL) minced garlic

½ teaspoon (2 mL) chili powder

¼ teaspoon (1 mL) sea salt

Pinch of cayenne pepper

A few dashes of hot sauce, Louisiana style preferably

For serving

¼ cup (60 mL) packed roughly chopped curly parsley

4 lemon wedges

1. **MAKE THE CRAB CAKES** On a cutting board, using 2 forks, shred the hearts of palm by pulling the forks apart and tearing the hearts of palm lengthwise, like pulled pork. There should not be many large pieces left. Place in a medium bowl.

2. To the hearts of palm, add the creamy mayo, celery, red pepper, red onion, lemon juice, mustard, dill, chili powder, salt, and paprika. Mix until all ingredients are well incorporated. Divide the mixture into 4 equal portions. Using your hands, form into puck shapes. Refrigerate.

3. **MAKE THE BREADING** In a medium bowl, combine the almond milk, mustard, and ¼ teaspoon (1 mL) of the salt. Whisk until all ingredients are well combined and no lumps remain.

4. In a separate medium bowl, combine the panko, lemon zest, dill, paprika, and the remaining ½ teaspoon (2 mL) salt. Whisk until all ingredients are well combined.

5. **ASSEMBLE THE CRAB CAKES** Dip the crab cakes, one at a time, in the almond milk mixture and then in the panko mixture, coating completely. Place on a plate lined with parchment paper and refrigerate for about 15 minutes to firm up.

6. **MAKE THE REMOULADE SAUCE** In a medium bowl, combine the creamy mayo, green onion, lemon juice, pickles, horseradish, mustard, capers, paprika, garlic, chili powder, salt, cayenne, and hot sauce. Whisk until all ingredients are well combined.

7. In a large sauté pan, heat enough vegetable oil so it just comes up the sides of the pan. Cook the crab cakes, turning once, until golden brown on each side, about 3 to 4 minutes per side. Serve immediately with the remoulade sauce.

Fiesta Chili

To me, the best way to eat chili is in a big bowl with a dollop of my Sour Cream (page 231) on top and scooped up with some crunchy tortilla chips! The tempeh in this recipe provides some of the meaty texture of traditional chili, so you won't even notice the lack of meat. Make this meal to share with those friends and family who like to think they're carnivores. They won't be able to get over how good it is, and you might even be able to bring someone over to the green side.

SERVES 8

Prep ahead

Sour Cream (page 231)

Tempeh

1 block (9 ounces/240 g) tempeh

4 cups (1 L) water

¼ cup (60 mL) tamari or soy sauce

3 to 4 cloves garlic

½ cup (125 mL) vegetable oil

1 teaspoon (5 mL) ground cumin

¼ teaspoon (1 mL) sea salt

Chili

¼ cup (60 mL) vegetable oil

2 cups (500 mL) finely diced white onion

1 cup (250 mL) finely diced celery

1 cup (250 mL) finely diced red sweet pepper

1 teaspoon (5 mL) sea salt

½ cup (125 mL) chili powder

¼ cup (60 mL) ground cumin

¼ cup (60 mL) minced garlic

¼ cup (60 mL) tamari or soy sauce

¼ cup (60 mL) freshly squeezed orange juice

3 tablespoons (45 mL) freshly squeezed lemon juice

2 tablespoons (30 mL) agave nectar or maple syrup

4 cans (14 ounces/398 mL each) diced tomatoes

1 cup (250 mL) fresh or frozen corn kernels

2 cups (500 mL) cooked black beans

———

Sour Cream, for serving (optional)

1. **PREPARE THE TEMPEH** In a medium pot, combine the tempeh, water, tamari, and garlic. Bring to a boil uncovered, reduce the heat to a simmer, and cook for 15 minutes. Remove the tempeh from the broth and set aside until cool enough to handle, about 10 minutes. Discard the cooking water.

2. Cut the tempeh block in half lengthwise so that the tempeh is half as thick. Cut each half into 3 strips. Turn the strips horizontally and cut into ½-inch (1 cm) cubes. In a medium pot, heat the vegetable oil. Add the tempeh cubes and fry until crispy, turning as necessary with a metal slotted spoon or wooden spoon. Transfer the fried tempeh to a medium bowl and toss with the cumin and salt. Set aside.

3. **MAKE THE CHILI** In a large pot, heat the vegetable oil over medium-high heat. Add the onion, celery, red pepper, and salt and cook, stirring frequently, until the vegetables are soft and translucent, 8 to 10 minutes. Add the chili powder and cumin and cook, stirring constantly, until the spices are toasted and fragrant, 3 to 4 minutes. Add the garlic and cook, stirring constantly, until the garlic is fragrant, 2 minutes.

4. Add the tamari, orange juice, lemon juice, and agave. Using a wooden spoon, scrape up any brown bits from the bottom of the pan. Bring the mixture to a boil, reduce the heat to a simmer, and cook for 2 to 3 minutes. Add the tomatoes with their juice, corn, and black beans. Simmer for 10 to 12 minutes. Remove from the heat.

5. Using a ladle, spoon about one third of the chili mixture into a blender. Pulse a few times to break down some of the black beans and thicken the chili. Stir the blended mixture back into the chili and add the cooked tempeh. Serve immediately topped with sour cream (if using) or allow to cool and store in an airtight container in the fridge for up to 1 week.

Tortilla Bake

This recipe is full of hearty flavours, plant-based protein, and cheesy deliciousness! I love to make this in the colder months to warm up from the inside out, and I pair it with a crisp glass of hoppy beer. This take on a tortilla bake uses nutritional yeast and miso to make a phenomenal cheese sauce that you'll probably want to pour on top of everything you eat for the rest of your life. Which is totally reasonable and acceptable in my book—this is a judgment-free zone.

SERVES 6

Prep ahead
Fiesta Chili (page 179)
Sour Cream (page 231)

Refried pinto beans
½ pound (225 g) dried pinto beans
8½ cups (2.125 L) water, divided
½ cup (125 mL) roughly chopped white onion
½ cup (125 mL) roughly chopped tomato
8 cloves garlic
1 tablespoon (15 mL) tamari or soy sauce
1½ teaspoons (7 mL) chili powder

¼ teaspoon (1 mL) ground cumin
¼ teaspoon (1 mL) smoked paprika
¼ teaspoon (1 mL) ground coriander
¼ teaspoon (1 mL) sea salt
¼ cup (60 mL) olive oil

Cheesy Béchamel
½ cup (125 mL) all-purpose flour
¼ cup (60 mL) deodorized coconut oil
3 tablespoons (45 mL) dry white wine, such as Chardonnay
1½ cups (375 mL) unsweetened almond milk
1½ cups (375 mL) nutritional yeast

1 tablespoon (15 mL) white miso (see Tip)
1 tablespoon (15 mL) freshly squeezed lime juice
1½ teaspoons (7 mL) Dijon mustard
1 teaspoon (5 mL) sea salt
½ teaspoon (2 mL) garlic powder

For assembly
1 Batch Fiesta Chili (provides enough for topping)
12 large corn tortillas
½ cup (125 mL) Sour Cream
Thinly sliced green onion
Smoked paprika or chipotle powder

1. **MAKE THE REFRIED PINTO BEANS** In a large pot, combine the pinto beans, 8 cups (2 L) of the water, onion, tomato, garlic, tamari, chili powder, cumin, paprika, coriander, and salt. Bring to a boil uncovered, reduce the heat to a simmer, and cook until the beans are soft and most of the liquid has evaporated, 45 to 60 minutes.

2. Using an immersion blender, blend the beans while adding the remaining ½ cup (125 mL) water and olive oil in a slow, steady stream. You want the final mixture to be creamy and smooth, but with a little texture from the beans. Taste for seasoning and add salt, if needed.

3. **MAKE THE CHEESY BÉCHAMEL SAUCE** In a small pot, over medium heat, combine the flour and coconut oil. Cook, stirring frequently, for 4 to 5 minutes. Add the white wine and cook, stirring constantly, until most of the liquid has evaporated, 1 to 2 minutes.

4. Remove from the heat and add the almond milk, 1 cup (250 mL) at a time, stirring constantly. You want to add the almond milk in stages to prevent having lumps in the finished sauce. Once all of the almond milk has been added, return the pot to medium heat and bring to a simmer, stirring frequently. Make sure to stir frequently enough so that no lumps form and the sauce is a smooth, homogenous mixture, 4 to 5 minutes total.

5. Add the nutritional yeast, miso, lime juice, mustard, salt, and garlic powder. Cook, stirring constantly, for about 2 minutes. Remove from the heat and blend in small batches in a blender until completely smooth. Transfer the blended sauce back to the pot and keep warm until ready to use.

6. Preheat the oven to 375°F (190°C).

7. **ASSEMBLE THE TORTILLA BAKE** Ladle one third of the chili into an 11- × 7-inch (2 L) casserole dish, covering the bottom completely. Top the chili with 4 corn tortillas; it is okay if they overlap a bit. Top the corn tortillas with one third of the refried pinto beans, then top the beans with one third of the cheesy béchamel sauce. Repeat these steps 2 more times. You want to save enough chili to top the casserole so that the top layer is just covered and no pieces of corn tortilla are exposed. Top with the sour cream, green onions, and a sprinkle of paprika. Bake until hot, bubbly, and oozing, 20 to 25 minutes. Serve immediately or allow to cool and store covered in the fridge for up to 1 week.

TIP

White miso or any light miso is ideal for this recipe because of its cheesier flavour. If you do not have light miso, substitute an equal amount of any other miso, but keep in mind that the lighter the miso is, the cheesier the flavour will be.

Eggplant Parmesan

My recipe for this classic Italian dish layers creamy cashew cheese, garlicky tomato sauce, fresh greens, and crisp eggplant strips that will appeal to *all* self-proclaimed foodies. Traditionally, the eggplant is coated in a mixture of Parmesan cheese and breadcrumbs before being fried. Instead of that basic combination, I use nutritional yeast and lemon zest to stand in for the Parmesan, which makes it so pleasurable to your palate that you won't be able to stop at just one bite.

SERVES 6

Tomato Sauce

2 medium red sweet peppers

1 tablespoon (15 mL) vegetable oil

2 tablespoons (30 mL) extra-virgin olive oil

½ cup (125 mL) finely diced white onion

½ teaspoon (2 mL) sea salt

3 tablespoons (45 mL) minced garlic

2 teaspoons (10 mL) dried basil

1 can (14 ounces/398 mL) diced tomatoes

Herbed Cashew Cheese

2 cups (500 mL) raw cashews, soaked in hot water for at least 1 hour, drained and rinsed

½ cup (125 mL) water

¼ cup (60 mL) freshly squeezed lemon juice

¼ cup (60 mL) nutritional yeast

1 tablespoon (15 mL) chopped fresh thyme leaves

1 teaspoon (5 mL) sea salt

Breaded Eggplant

2 cups (500 mL) medium or coarse grind cornmeal

2 cups (500 mL) all-purpose flour

¾ cup (175 mL) nutritional yeast

2 teaspoons (10 mL) + pinch of sea salt, divided, more for the eggplant

1 tablespoon (15 mL) garlic powder

1 tablespoon (15 mL) roughly chopped fresh flat-leaf parsley

½ teaspoon (2 mL) lemon zest

1⅔ cups (400 mL) unsweetened almond milk

3 tablespoons (45 mL) Dijon mustard

2 Italian eggplants

Vegetable oil, for frying

Sautéed Greens

2 tablespoons (30 mL) extra-virgin olive oil

1 teaspoon (5 mL) minced garlic

2 cups (500 mL) thinly sliced kale

1 cup (250 mL) broccoli florets

⅓ cup (75 mL) dry white wine

¼ teaspoon (1 mL) sea salt

—

⅓ cup (75 mL) nutritional yeast, for topping

1. **MAKE THE TOMATO SAUCE** Preheat the oven to 400°F (200°C). Line a baking sheet with parchment paper.

2. On the prepared baking sheet, toss the red peppers with the vegetable oil to coat well. Bake until slightly shriveled and browned, about 15 minutes. Remove from the oven and transfer to a medium bowl. Cover tightly with plastic wrap and set aside for 10 minutes. The steam will help separate the skin from the flesh, making the peppers easier to peel.

3. Carefully remove the peppers from the bowl and, using your fingers, gently rub the skins off the flesh. Cut the peppers in half and discard the seeds and ribs. Place the peppers in a blender and blend until smooth.

4. In a medium pot, heat the olive oil over medium heat. Add the onion and salt and cook, stirring frequently, until the onion is soft and translucent, 3 to 4 minutes. Add the garlic and basil and cook until the garlic is soft and fragrant, 2 to 3 minutes. Add the puréed peppers and cook for 2 to 3 more minutes. Add the tomatoes with their juice and bring to a boil. Reduce the heat to a simmer and cook, stirring occasionally, until thick and rich, about 45 minutes.

5. **MAKE THE HERBED CASHEW CHEESE** In a food processor fitted with a metal blade, process the cashews, water, lemon juice, nutritional yeast, thyme, and salt until smooth. You will need to stop the machine once or twice and use a rubber spatula to scrape down the sides of the bowl.

6. **PREPARE THE EGGPLANT BREADING** In a large bowl, whisk together the cornmeal, flour, nutritional yeast, 2 teaspoons (10 mL) of the salt, garlic powder, parsley, and lemon zest until well combined.

7. In a medium bowl, whisk together the almond milk, mustard, and pinch of salt until well combined.

Continued

8. **PREPARE THE EGGPLANT** Using a mandoline, slice the eggplants lengthwise, about ¼ inch (5 mm) thick. Lay the eggplant strips in a single flat layer on a baking sheet lined with parchment paper and sprinkle liberally with salt. Lay another layer of eggplant on top and sprinkle again with salt. Repeat until all of the eggplant has been salted. Let the eggplant sit for 30 minutes so that the salt can draw out the moisture as well as the slightly bitter flavour.

9. **MEANWHILE, SAUTÉ THE GREENS** In a large frying pan, heat the olive oil over medium heat. Add the garlic and cook, stirring constantly, just until the garlic is brown, taking care not to burn it, about 1 minute. Add the kale and broccoli and cook, stirring constantly, just until they start to turn bright green, about 2 minutes. You do not want to fully cook them here. Add the white wine and cook, stirring constantly, until no liquid remains, 2 to 3 minutes. Add the salt, remove from the heat, and set aside.

10. **COOK THE EGGPLANT** Dip each slice of eggplant into the almond milk mixture, then dredge through the breading, ensuring that all sides of the eggplant are well coated.

11. In a large frying pan, heat enough vegetable oil so it just comes up the side of the pan. Cook the eggplant slices until golden brown on the bottom, about 3 to 4 minutes. Flip and cook until golden brown on the other side, about 3 to 4 minutes.

12. Preheat the oven to 375°F (190°C).

13. **ASSEMBLE THE EGGPLANT PARMESAN** Ladle one third of the tomato sauce into an 11- × 7-inch (2 L) casserole dish, covering the bottom completely. Cover the sauce with one third of the eggplant strips, one third of the cashew cheese, and one third of the sautéed greens. Repeat these steps 2 more times. You want to save enough tomato sauce to top the casserole, so that the top layer is just covered and no pieces of eggplant are exposed. Top with the ⅓ cup (75 mL) nutritional yeast. Bake until hot, bubbly, and oozing, 20 to 25 minutes. Serve immediately or allow to cool and store covered in the fridge for up to 1 week.

Change Your Life Chana with Tandoori Cauliflower

When I was younger, I worked for a terrific chef who taught me so much about the amazing flavours and textures of Indian cuisine. I fondly remember catering a vegetarian Indian wedding for more than 500 people! The food was remarkable, and the sensory memories have stayed with me to this day. I start to salivate just thinking about it! This traditional dish is delicious for any occasion and is the perfect meal prep recipe because it's easy to make ahead of time and reheat. The cauliflower is veganized using my Sour Cream (page 231) instead of dairy yogurt. For the best results, make sure to use good-quality, fresh spices.

SERVES 4

Prep ahead
Sour Cream (page 231)

Chana Masala
3 tablespoons (45 mL) extra-virgin coconut oil
½ cup (125 mL) finely diced white onion
1 jalapeño pepper, finely diced, seeds and ribs removed
⅓ cup (75 mL) roughly chopped fresh cilantro leaves, more for garnish

2 teaspoons (10 mL) chopped fresh ginger
1 tablespoon (15 mL) minced garlic
1 tablespoon (15 mL) ground cumin
2 teaspoons (10 mL) ground coriander
½ teaspoon (2 mL) ground turmeric
½ teaspoon (2 mL) ground cardamom
¼ teaspoon (1 mL) ground cinnamon
⅛ teaspoon (0.5 mL) ground cloves
1 can (14 ounces/398 mL) diced tomatoes

½ teaspoon (2 mL) sea salt
2 cups (500 mL) cooked chickpeas
2 tablespoons (30 mL) freshly squeezed lime juice

Tandoori Cauliflower
1 cup (250 mL) Sour Cream
2 tablespoons + 1 teaspoon (35 mL) tandoori seasoning
2 tablespoons (30 mL) water
¼ teaspoon (1 mL) sugar
1 head cauliflower, cut into 2-inch (5 cm) pieces

1. **MAKE THE CHANA MASALA** In a medium pot, heat the coconut oil over medium heat. Add the onion and jalapeño and cook, stirring frequently, until the onion is soft and translucent, 3 to 4 minutes. Add the cilantro, ginger, and garlic and cook, stirring constantly, until the garlic is fragrant and the cilantro is just wilted, 2 to 3 minutes. Add the cumin, coriander, turmeric, cardamom, cinnamon, and cloves. Cook, stirring constantly, until the spices are toasted and fragrant, about 2 minutes.

2. Add the tomatoes with their juice, salt, chickpeas, and lime juice, scraping up any brown bits from the bottom of the pot with a wooden spoon. Bring the mixture to a boil and reduce to a simmer. Cook until the tomatoes have released most of their liquid and the mixture has thickened slightly, 10 to 12 minutes.

3. **MAKE THE TANDOORI CAULIFLOWER** Preheat the oven to 500°F (260°C) and line a baking sheet with parchment paper.

4. In a small bowl, whisk together the sour cream, tandoori seasoning, water, and sugar until well combined.

5. Toss the cauliflower in the sour cream mixture until evenly coated. It is important to make sure that all sides are evenly coated and you cannot see the white cauliflower. Place the cauliflower on the prepared baking sheet and cook until soft in the middle and slightly blackened on the outside, 12 to 15 minutes. You can tell the cauliflower is done when a toothpick inserted in the middle of the cauliflower goes in easily. Serve immediately with the chana masala sprinkled with some fresh chopped cilantro leaves for garnish, or cool and store in an airtight container in the fridge for up to 5 days.

Sweet Sinful Desserts

Apple Crisp

What I love most about this recipe is how easy it is to pull it off, despite how impressive it turns out. It is the perfect example of how a classic dish can be the most delicious yet the most simple. This recipe is the epitome of why I love to cook: good-quality ingredients and the right technique come together to make something undeniably scrumptious! Serve it with a big scoop of my Best Banana Soft Serve (page 235) for a perfectly indulgent dessert.

SERVES 4 TO 6

Filling

4 to 5 McIntosh apples, peeled and cored

¼ cup (60 mL) packed light brown sugar or coconut sugar

½ teaspoon (2 mL) freshly squeezed lemon juice

½ teaspoon (2 mL) cinnamon

Topping

1 cup (250 mL) old-fashioned rolled oats

½ cup (125 mL) oat flour (see Tip)

½ cup (125 mL) brown rice flour

½ cup (125 mL) packed light brown sugar or coconut sugar

¼ teaspoon (1 mL) sea salt

¼ teaspoon (1 mL) cinnamon

6 tablespoons (90 mL) melted deodorized or virgin coconut oil

1. Preheat the oven to 375°F (190°C).

2. **MAKE THE FILLING** Cut the apples into ½-inch (1 cm) thick slices. In a large bowl, combine the sliced apples, brown sugar, lemon juice, and cinnamon. Mix until well combined. Transfer to an 8-inch (2 L) square baking dish. Place in the fridge until ready to use.

3. **MAKE THE TOPPING** In a bowl, combine the oats, oat flour, brown rice flour, brown sugar, salt, cinnamon, and coconut oil. Stir until combined.

4. Remove the filling from the fridge and sprinkle the topping evenly over top. Cover the baking dish with a piece of foil big enough to cover the sides completely, so that no air can escape, and bake for 30 minutes. Remove the foil and continue baking until the apples are tender and the topping is golden brown, about 30 more minutes. Set aside and allow the apple crisp to cool slightly before serving, about 30 minutes. Serve or cool completely and store in an airtight container in the fridge for up to 1 week.

TIP

Oat flour can be made by blending rolled oats in a blender until they are a powder. It is best to blend between ½ cup (125 mL) and 1 cup (250 mL) at a time if making your own. You can now also buy ready-made oat flour in most grocery stores and bulk food stores or online.

Crunchy Chocolate Chip Cookies

I think we all have fond memories of dunking homemade chocolate chip cookies into a tall glass of milk when we were kids. These cookies are crunchy on the outside, a little soft in the middle, and so easy to make. Even though most cookie recipes call for eggs, you can easily replace them with a mixture of ground flaxseed and hot water. Just add a little bit of love to them, and they will turn out just like mama used to make! Grab a glass of almond, cashew, or coconut milk and get to dunking.

MAKES ABOUT 36 COOKIES

Ingredients

1 tablespoon (15 mL) ground golden flaxseed

3 tablespoons (45 mL) hot water (see Tip)

½ cup (125 mL) cold vegan butter, cut into cubes

½ cup (125 mL) packed brown sugar

1 teaspoon (5 mL) pure vanilla extract

1½ cups (375 mL) all-purpose flour

½ teaspoon (2 mL) baking soda

¼ teaspoon (1 mL) sea salt

1 cup (250 mL) dairy-free semi-sweet chocolate chips

1. In a small bowl, whisk together the flaxseed and hot water until well combined. Set aside to soak for 10 minutes so that the flaxseed can swell and absorb the liquid.

2. Using an electric mixer with the beater attachment, combine the cold butter and brown sugar in a medium bowl. Start on the lowest setting to combine the ingredients. Gradually increase the speed until it is about half strength. Whipping the butter and sugar together at this stage is commonly referred to as "creaming." Stop the machine and add the soaked flaxseed and vanilla. Mix until well combined.

3. In a medium bowl, combine the flour, baking soda, and salt. Whisk until well combined and no lumps of flour remain.

4. Add the flour mixture to the butter and sugar mixture. Using a spatula, mix until well combined; you should not see any dry patches of flour. Stir in the chocolate chips and mix until just combined. Refrigerate the cookie dough for 1 hour.

5. Preheat the oven to 350°F (180°C). Line 2 baking sheets with parchment paper.

6. Remove the cookie dough from the fridge. Using a 1-tablespoon (15 mL) measuring spoon, drop about 36 heaping tablespoons on the prepared baking sheets. You want to leave at least 1½ inches (4 cm) between each cookie. Bake for 10 minutes or until the edges are golden. If you prefer a crispier cookie, bake them for 12 minutes.

7. Remove from the oven and allow to cool for a few minutes, ideally on a rack. Serve or cool completely and store in an airtight container at room temperature for up to 3 days.

TIP

Use hot water when making a flax egg, as it is best to help speed up the process of gelling the flax.

Pineapple Upside Down Cake

What I love most about this recipe is how beautiful the pineapple slices on the bottom of the cake pan look as they caramelize in the oven while the cake is baking. Adding pineapple juice gives this cake a slightly sweet and tropical flavour that will send your taste buds straight to the Bahamas. This recipe adds apple cider vinegar to baking soda, creating bubbles that help the cake to rise.

MAKES 1 CAKE; SERVES 6 TO 7

Ingredients

- 1½ cups (375 mL) all-purpose flour
- 1¼ cups (300 mL) sugar, divided
- 1 teaspoon (5 mL) baking soda
- ½ teaspoon (2 mL) sea salt
- ¼ teaspoon (1 mL) cinnamon
- ½ cup (125 mL) unsweetened soy milk
- ½ cup (125 mL) pineapple juice
- ⅓ cup (75 mL) vegetable oil
- 1 tablespoon (15 mL) unpasteurized apple cider vinegar
- 1 teaspoon (5 mL) pure vanilla extract
- 1 pineapple, peeled, cored, and sliced into ¼-inch (1 cm) thick rounds

1. Preheat the oven to 350°F (180°C). Line the bottom of an 8-inch (1.2 L) round cake pan with parchment paper.

2. In a medium bowl, combine the flour, 1 cup (250 mL) of the sugar, baking soda, salt, and cinnamon. Whisk until well combined and no lumps remain.

3. In a medium bowl, whisk together the soy milk, pineapple juice, vegetable oil, apple cider vinegar, and vanilla. Add the soy milk mixture to the flour mixture and whisk until no lumps remain, taking care not to overmix or the cake can become tough.

4. Line the prepared cake pan with the pineapple slices. You want the entire bottom of the pan to be covered with the pineapple. Sprinkle with the remaining ¼ cup (60 mL) sugar and set aside.

5. Scrape the batter into the cake pan and, using a spatula, smooth it over the pineapple. Bake until a toothpick inserted in the centre of the cake comes out clean, 30 to 35 minutes. Remove from the oven and allow to cool completely before removing the cake from pan, about 1 hour.

6. To serve the cake, place a serving platter over the cake pan. Invert the platter and cake pan; the pineapple will now be on the top of the cake. Serve immediately or store in an airtight container in the fridge for up to 5 days.

Everyday Pound Cake

Vegan pound cake can be mouth-wateringly moist and provide a lovely snack during tea time or simply whenever you need a treat. Here, I use tofu to replace the eggs that are found in a traditional pound cake, which adds an exquisite richness and helps the cake to rise. Top it off with some fresh vegan whipped cream and berries!

MAKES 1 LOAF; SERVES 6 TO 8

Ingredients

1 cup (250 mL) chopped cold vegan butter

1 cup (250 mL) sugar

½ cup (125 mL) medium water-packed tofu (see Tip)

2 cups (500 mL) cake flour, divided

½ cup (125 mL) unsweetened soy milk

2 teaspoons (10 mL) pure vanilla extract

2 teaspoons (10 mL) baking powder

For serving

Vegan whipped cream

Fresh strawberries, sliced

1. Position a rack in the centre of the oven. Preheat the oven to 350°F (180°C). Lightly grease a 9- × 5-inch (2 L) loaf pan with vegetable oil.
2. Using an electric mixer with the beater attachment, combine the cold butter and sugar in a medium bowl. Start on the lowest setting to combine the ingredients. Gradually increase the speed until it is about half strength. Whipping the butter and sugar together at this stage is commonly referred to as "creaming."
3. In a food processor fitted with a metal blade, process the tofu until smooth. Add the tofu to the butter and sugar mixture and mix until well combined; you should not see any pieces of tofu at this point.
4. Decrease the mixer speed to low and add 1 cup (250 mL) of the cake flour. Mix until the flour is just incorporated. Add the soy milk and vanilla and mix until just combined. Add the remaining 1 cup (250 mL) flour and the baking powder. Increase the mixer speed to medium and beat for 1 to 2 minutes. The mixture should have the consistency of a pancake batter.
5. Scrape the batter into the prepared loaf pan. Tap the pan on the counter a few times to release any air bubbles. Bake until a toothpick inserted in the centre of the cake comes out clean, about 1 hour. Remove from the oven and allow to cool completely before removing from the pan, about 1 hour. Serve with whipped cream and strawberries. Store, without toppings, in an airtight container at room temperature for up to 3 days.

TIP

Soft silken tofu will also work well for this recipe. If you use soft silken tofu, you do not need to process it first.

Molten Lava Chocolate Brownie Cakes

These chocolaty, fudgy cakes will explode in your mouth for a rich and sweet surprise to your senses. These are an epic addition to any special occasion, or just for when you know deep in your heart that you deserve an indulgent dessert. Dairy-free butter makes the texture rich and creamy and helps to develop the rich flavours. Any store-bought vegan butter will do, but this recipe is best made with my Whipped Butter (page 229).

MAKES 4 BROWNIE CAKES

Prep ahead

Whipped Butter (page 229)

Ingredients

2 cups (500 mL) all-purpose flour

2 cups (500 mL) sugar

1 cup (250 mL) cocoa powder

1 teaspoon (5 mL) sea salt

2 teaspoons (10 mL) baking powder

1 teaspoon (5 mL) baking soda

1 cup (250 mL) melted Whipped Butter or store-bought vegan butter

3 cups (750 mL) + 2 teaspoons (10 mL) unsweetened soy milk

1 tablespoon (15 mL) + 1½ teaspoons (7 mL) pure vanilla extract

¾ cup (175 mL) dairy-free chocolate chips, divided

4 pieces (1 to 2 ounces/28 to 55 g each) dark vegan baking chocolate, for melting

1. Preheat the oven to 350°F (180°C). Lightly grease four 6-inch (15 cm) cast-iron skillets with vegetable oil.

2. In a large bowl, combine the flour, sugar, cocoa powder, salt, baking powder, and baking soda. Whisk until well combined and no lumps remain.

3. In a medium bowl, whisk together the melted whipped butter, soy milk, and vanilla until well combined. Add the butter mixture to the flour mixture and whisk until smooth and no lumps remain, taking care not to overmix or the cakes can become tough.

4. Fill a small pot about one-third full of water, bring to a boil uncovered, then reduce the heat to a simmer. Place ½ cup (125 mL) of the chocolate chips in a metal mixing bowl that is larger than the pot of simmering water. The bowl must be able to sit on top of the pot of simmering water without moving or touching the water. This is called a double boiler. Using a rubber spatula, stir the chocolate chips until they begin to melt. Once the chocolate chips are mostly melted, remove from the heat and continue to stir until completely melted, then stir into the cake mixture.

5. Divide the cake mixture between the prepared cast-iron skillets. Drop 1 tablespoon (15 mL) of the remaining chocolate chips over the centre of each cake. Bake for 25 minutes. Remove from the oven, place 1 piece of baking chocolate in the centre of each cake, and bake for 2 to 3 minutes or until the chocolate has melted. Serve immediately.

New York Style Cheesecake

Cheesecake makes my knees quake, it's so tantalizingly tasty. My version of New York style cheesecake is creamy and rich but also light and fluffy. Vegan cream cheese and sour cream easily stand in for the conventional versions. I recommend using the store-bought versions of both because they will help to stabilize the cake a little more. The key is to bake the cheesecake in a hot water bath so that it cooks slowly and doesn't crack.

MAKES 1 CAKE; SERVES 12

Crust

2 cups (500 mL) graham cracker crumbs

2 tablespoons (30 mL) sugar

¼ teaspoon (1 mL) sea salt

⅓ cup (75 mL) melted vegan butter

Filling

6 cups (1.5 L) store-bought vegan cream cheese (see Tip)

1 cup (250 mL) store-bought vegan sour cream (see Tip)

1 cup (250 mL) cane sugar

2 teaspoons (10 mL) lemon zest

2 tablespoons (30 mL) freshly squeezed lemon juice

2 tablespoons (30 mL) pure vanilla extract

1 tablespoon (15 mL) cornstarch

½ teaspoon (2 mL) sea salt

¼ cup (60 mL) all-purpose flour

3 tablespoons (45 mL) melted vegan butter

1. Preheat the oven to 325°F (160°C).

2. **MAKE THE CRUST** In a medium bowl, whisk together the graham cracker crumbs, sugar, and salt. Drizzle in the melted butter and mix until well combined. Place the crust in a 10-inch (3 L) springform pan. Using the back of a measuring cup, press the crust into the pan. Bake for 10 minutes. Remove from the oven and allow to cool completely, about 15 minutes.

3. **MAKE THE FILLING** In a stand mixer fitted with the paddle attachment, combine the cream cheese, sour cream, sugar, lemon zest, lemon juice, vanilla, cornstarch, and salt. Start at the lowest speed and mix for 1 to 2 minutes. Gradually increase the speed every minute or so, until you reach the highest speed and everything is well incorporated. Return the machine to the lowest speed and add the flour and melted butter. Gradually increase the speed again until combined.

4. Pour the filling into the prepared graham cracker crust and tap the pan on a flat surface to remove any air bubbles. Place the springform pan in a deep roasting pan and add enough hot water so it reaches halfway up the cake. Bake for 1 hour and 15 minutes, or until the sides are slightly firm but the cake is still jiggly in the middle. Remove from the oven and allow to cool completely before serving, about 3 hours or overnight. Store covered in the fridge for up to 1 week.

TIP

Store-bought vegan cream cheese and vegan sour cream generally contain stabilizers and/or starches or gums. These help the cheesecake hold its shape and prevent it from cracking during the long cooking time.

VARIATION

STRAWBERRY CHEESECAKE TOPPING In a pot, combine 2 cups (500 mL) sliced fresh strawberries, 2 tablespoons (30 mL) sugar, 1 teaspoon (5 mL) freshly squeezed lemon juice, and a pinch of sea salt. Bring to a boil uncovered, then reduce the heat to a simmer and cook until the mixture is thick, 10 to 12 minutes. Once the cheesecake has been baked and has cooled completely, pour the strawberry mixture over top and refrigerate until set.

Coffee Cake

One of my weaknesses is a giant cup of black coffee made from darkly roasted beans, and every cup of richly flavoured coffee needs a sweet treat to go with it! This recipe is not overly sugary and goes well with a steaming hot mug of your favourite brew. Blended tofu replaces eggs in this recipe, and it not only helps to provide a great mouthfeel, but helps to hold the rise of the cake as well.

MAKES 1 CAKE; SERVES 6 TO 8

Cake

½ cup (125 mL) medium water-packed tofu, drained (see Tip)

½ cup (125 mL) vegetable oil

¼ cup (60 mL) unsweetened apple sauce

¾ cup (175 mL) soy milk

1 teaspoon (5 mL) pure vanilla extract

3 cups (750 mL) all-purpose flour

1 cup (250 mL) sugar

2 teaspoons (10 mL) baking soda

½ teaspoon (2 mL) sea salt

Cinnamon Sugar Filling

1 cup (250 mL) brown sugar

1 teaspoon (5 mL) cinnamon

⸻

½ cup (125 mL) melted vegan butter, for topping the cake

1. Preheat the oven to 350°F (180°C). Line an 8-inch (2 L) square nonstick baking dish with parchment paper.

2. **MAKE THE CAKE** In a food processor fitted with a metal blade, process the tofu until smooth.

3. In a medium bowl, combine the processed tofu, vegetable oil, apple sauce, soy milk, and vanilla. Whisk until well combined.

4. In a large bowl, whisk together the flour, sugar, baking soda, and salt. Add the tofu mixture to the flour mixture. Using a hand mixer on the lowest setting, mix until just combined. You do not want to overmix the batter or it can become tough.

5. **MAKE THE CINNAMON SUGAR FILLING** In a medium bowl, combine the brown sugar and cinnamon. Whisk until well combined.

6. Pour half of the batter into the prepared baking dish. Top with half of the brown sugar and cinnamon filling. Top with the remaining cake batter, then the remaining brown sugar and cinnamon filling. Drizzle the melted vegan butter over the cake. Bake until golden brown and a crust forms on top, or until a toothpick inserted in the centre of the cake comes out clean, about 25 minutes. Remove from the oven and let sit for 10 minutes in the cake pan. Transfer to a rack until cool enough to handle, about 20 minutes.

TIP

Soft silken tofu will also work well for this recipe. If you use soft silken tofu, you do not need to process it first. Whatever tofu you use for this recipe, make sure you drain it.

Chocolate Fudge Cake with Buttercream Frosting

Rich, moist, luscious, and dense, this chocolate fudge cake almost couldn't get any better. That is, until you ice it with my delicious buttercream frosting! Tofu replaces eggs in the cake, and a little bit of coconut cream is added to the frosting to create that buttery feeling our taste buds crave. Be careful if you're making this for someone's birthday. You're going to have to restrain yourself from eating it before they ever get a chance to blow out the candles. You can easily make this a double layer cake by doubling the cake and frosting recipes.

MAKES 1 CAKE; SERVES 12

Chocolate Fudge Cake

1 cup (250 mL) all-purpose flour

1 cup (250 mL) sugar

⅓ cup (75 mL) cocoa powder

1 teaspoon (5 mL) baking soda

½ teaspoon (2 mL) baking powder

½ cup (125 mL) unsweetened soy milk

½ cup (125 mL) cold coffee

⅓ cup (75 mL) medium-firm water-packed tofu, processed in a food processor until smooth (see Tip)

¼ cup (60 mL) vegetable oil

1½ teaspoons (7 mL) pure vanilla extract

⅛ teaspoon (0.5 mL) white vinegar

Buttercream Frosting

1 cup (250 mL) vegan butter, at room temperature

1 tablespoon (15 mL) pure vanilla extract

4 cups (1 L) icing sugar

2 tablespoons (30 mL) coconut cream (see Tip)

Pinch of sea salt

1. Preheat the oven to 350°F (180°C). Grease an 8-inch (1.2 L) round cake pan with vegetable oil.

2. **MAKE THE CHOCOLATE FUDGE CAKE** Using a large sieve placed over a medium bowl, sift together the flour, sugar, cocoa powder, baking soda, and baking powder.

3. In another medium bowl, whisk together the soy milk, cold coffee, processed tofu, vegetable oil, vanilla, and vinegar until well combined.

4. Add the soy milk mixture to the flour mixture and whisk until no lumps remain, taking care not to overmix or the cake can become tough. Transfer to the prepared cake pan and bake until a toothpick inserted in the centre of the cake comes out clean, about 25 minutes. Remove from the oven and allow to cool completely before removing from the pan, about 1 hour.

5. **MEANWHILE, MAKE THE BUTTERCREAM FROSTING** In a medium deep bowl, combine the butter and vanilla. Add the icing sugar and, using an electric mixer, beat on the lowest speed until just combined. Increase the speed to medium and beat until the sugar and butter are well combined and the mixture is fluffy. Add the coconut cream and salt and mix on medium speed until well combined. The frosting should be thick and creamy but still light and fluffy.

6. **FROST THE CAKE** Spread the frosting over the cooled cake. You should have a layer of frosting about ½ inch (1 cm) thick over the top and sides of the cake. Serve immediately or cover and store in the fridge for up to 3 days.

TIP

1. Soft silken tofu will also work well for this recipe. If you use soft silken tofu, you do not need to process it first. **2.** For this recipe, you can use the thick fat from the top of a can of coconut milk, or you can use actual coconut cream. Coconut cream is similar to coconut milk except that it has a higher fat content. It is available in most grocery stores, in Indian specialty stores, or online.

Carrot Cake with Cream Cheese Frosting

This classic cake is made plant-based by mixing together ground flaxseed and water to make "flax eggs." Don't let the word "carrot" scare you. This delectable dessert is full of subtly sweet flavours, moistness, and spices. Slather the cake with my cream cheese frosting and double up the layers for maximum yumminess. This is definitely the best way to eat a vegetable, if you ask me.

MAKES 1 DOUBLE LAYER CAKE; SERVES 10 TO 12

Carrot Cake

¼ cup (60 mL) ground flaxseed

¾ cup (175 mL) hot water (see Tip)

2½ cups (625 mL) all-purpose flour

1 tablespoon (15 mL) cinnamon

2 teaspoons (10 mL) baking powder

1¼ teaspoons (6 mL) baking soda

1 teaspoon (5 mL) sea salt

½ teaspoon (2 mL) ground nutmeg

Pinch of ground cloves

Pinch of ground ginger

4 cups (1 L) peeled and shredded carrots

2 cups (500 mL) sugar

¾ cup (175 mL) melted vegan butter

Cream Cheese Frosting

¾ cup (175 mL) cold vegan butter, cut into cubes

¾ cup (175 mL) vegan cream cheese

2 teaspoons (10 mL) pure vanilla extract

1 teaspoon (5 mL) freshly squeezed lemon juice

Pinch of sea salt

8 cups (2 L) icing sugar

1. Preheat the oven to 350°F (180°C). Lightly grease two 9-inch (23 cm) round cake pans with vegetable oil.

2. **MAKE THE CARROT CAKE** In a small bowl, whisk together the flaxseed and hot water until well combined. Set aside to soak for 10 minutes so that the flaxseed can swell and absorb the liquid.

3. In a large bowl, combine the flour, cinnamon, baking powder, baking soda, salt, nutmeg, cloves, and ginger. Whisk until well combined and no lumps remain. Add the carrots and stir until well combined.

4. In a food processor fitted with a metal blade, combine the flaxseed mixture and sugar. Process until well combined. With the motor running, pour the melted butter through the feed tube in a slow, steady stream and process until combined. Add the butter and flaxseed mixture to the carrot mixture. Using a spatula, stir until well combined. The mixture should be wet and sticky and hold together when pinched between 2 fingers.

5. Divide the batter evenly between the 2 prepared pans. Bake until a toothpick inserted in the centres of the cakes comes out clean, 25 to 30 minutes. Remove from the oven and place on a rack to cool completely in the pans, about 1 hour. Run a knife around the inside edge of each pan to loosen. Turn out the cakes onto the rack.

6. **MAKE THE CREAM CHEESE FROSTING** In a large bowl, using an electric mixer, mix the butter, cream cheese, vanilla, lemon juice, and salt until well combined and light and fluffy, 2 to 3 minutes. Add the icing sugar, 1 cup (250 mL) at a time, and beat on medium speed until well combined. Transfer to an airtight container and refrigerate until firm, about 30 minutes.

7. **ASSEMBLE THE CAKE** Place one of the cake layers on a serving platter. Place about a third of the frosting on top. Using a small offset spatula, spread the frosting evenly over the layer. Place the second cake layer on top of the iced layer. Cover the top and sides of the cake with the remaining frosting, smoothing it out so that the frosting is flat.

8. Refrigerate the frosted cake for 30 minutes to set. Serve immediately or cover and store in the fridge for up to 3 days.

TIP

Use hot water when making a flax egg, as it is best to help speed up the process of gelling the flax.

Luscious Lemon Meringue Pie

If you are new to the world of plant-based baking, you may hear the word "aquafaba" and wonder what it's all about. Aquafaba is that liquid you find canned legumes, most commonly chickpeas, soaking in. It works wonders as an egg substitute in virtually any baked good recipe, especially when you need to create a frothy or foamy yummy substance. This pie has a light and fluffy topping that is perfectly torched, and a rich tart yet sweet filling that is completely addictive. I promise you will come back not only for seconds, but for thirds and fourths!

MAKES 1 PIE; SERVES 12

Crust

2 cups (500 mL) all-purpose flour, more for dusting

3 tablespoons (45 mL) sugar

¼ teaspoon (1 mL) sea salt

½ cup (125 mL) melted vegan butter

¾ cup (175 mL) ice-cold water

Filling

1 cup (250 mL) firm or extra-firm silken tofu

½ teaspoon (2 mL) lemon zest

½ cup (125 mL) freshly squeezed lemon juice

¼ cup (60 mL) sugar

2 teaspoons (10 mL) cornstarch

1 teaspoon (5 mL) pure vanilla extract

Pinch of ground turmeric

Pinch of sea salt

Meringue

½ cup (125 mL) very cold liquid from canned chickpeas

¼ teaspoon (1 mL) cream of tartar

2 teaspoons (10 mL) pure vanilla extract

6 tablespoons (90 mL) sugar

1. **MAKE THE CRUST** In a medium bowl, whisk together the flour, sugar, and salt until there are no lumps. Add the melted butter and water and stir well. The dough should be slightly sticky, with no lumps. Turn the dough out of the bowl and shape it into a rough disc. Wrap it in plastic wrap and refrigerate for about 30 minutes to rest.

2. On a lightly floured work surface, using a rolling pin, roll the dough into a 12-inch (30 cm) circle, about ¼ inch (5 mm) thick. The rolled-out dough should be about 2 inches (5 cm) bigger in diameter than the pie plate you are using. Check by laying the pie plate face down on top of the dough. Roll the dough loosely around the rolling pin, then carefully unroll it over a 10-inch (25 cm) pie plate. Using your fingers, press the crust firmly against the bottom and sides of the pie plate. Using a paring knife, trim excess dough from the edges of the pie plate. Refrigerate for 15 minutes to rest.

3. Preheat the oven to 350°F (180°C).

4. Using a fork, poke holes in the crust to allow steam to escape. Press a piece of parchment paper into the pie shell. Fill it with 1 cup (250 mL) dried beans or pie weights. Bake for 12 to 15 minutes or until the crust is golden brown. Remove from the oven and carefully lift out the parchment paper with the beans. (Save the beans to use again.) Allow the crust to cool completely, about 1 hour.

5. **MAKE THE FILLING** In a high-speed blender, combine the tofu, lemon zest, lemon juice, sugar, cornstarch, vanilla, turmeric, and salt. Blend on high until completely smooth. Transfer to a small pot.

6. Cook the filling over medium heat, stirring constantly, until it has thickened, 3 to 4 minutes. Remove from the heat and allow to cool slightly, 8 to 10 minutes. Place a piece of plastic wrap over the filling so that a skin does not form. Continue to cool for another 20 minutes.

7. **MAKE THE MERINGUE** Chill the bowl of a stand mixer in the freezer for 30 minutes or overnight. Return the bowl to a stand mixer fitted with the whisk attachment and add the chickpea liquid and cream of tartar. Whisk on high speed for 3 to 4 minutes. Once peaks begin to form, add the vanilla, then add the sugar in a slow, steady stream. Continue to whisk the meringue until firm peaks form.

8. **ASSEMBLE THE PIE** Pour the filling into the cooled pie crust. Top the filling with the meringue. If you have a kitchen torch and know how to use it safely, lightly torch the meringue. Serve immediately or cover and store in the fridge for up to 3 days.

Bodacious Blueberry Pie

You need to try this blueberry pie recipe, whether you're a novice baker or an expert chef. I promise, it will be a piece of . . . well, pie! The perfectly flaky crust will melt in your mouth while the sweet blueberries give your taste buds little explosions of satisfaction. Prepare yourself, because your fingertips and teeth will be covered in purple deliciousness. That's what I like to call the scrumptious aesthetic.

MAKES 1 PIE; SERVES 12

Crust

2 cups (500 mL) pastry flour, more for dusting

1 tablespoon (15 mL) sugar

1 teaspoon (5 mL) sea salt

½ cup (125 mL) cold vegan butter, cut into ½-inch (1 cm) cubes

¼ cup (60 mL) ice-cold water

1 teaspoon (5 mL) white vinegar

Filling

4 cups (1 L) frozen blueberries, divided

½ cup (125 mL) sugar

¼ cup (60 mL) water

2 tablespoons (30 mL) cornstarch

1 teaspoon (5 mL) freshly squeezed lemon juice

Pinch of sea salt

1. **MAKE THE CRUST** In a medium bowl, whisk together the pastry flour, sugar, and salt until there are no lumps. Add the cold butter, water, and vinegar and stir well. The dough should be slightly sticky, with no lumps. Turn out the dough onto a lightly floured work surface and shape into a rough disc. Wrap in plastic wrap and refrigerate for about 30 minutes to rest.

2. On a lightly floured work surface, using a rolling pin, roll the dough into a 12-inch (30 cm) circle, about ¼ inch (5 mm) thick. The rolled-out dough should be about 2 inches (5 cm) bigger in diameter than the pie plate you are using. Check by laying the pie plate face down on top of the dough. Roll the dough loosely around the rolling pin, then carefully unroll it over a 10-inch (25 cm) pie plate. Using your fingers, press the crust firmly against the bottom and sides of the pie plate. Using a paring knife, trim excess dough from the edges of the pie plate. Refrigerate for 15 minutes to rest.

3. Preheat the oven to 375°F (190°C).

4. Using a fork, poke holes in the crust to allow steam to escape. Press a piece of parchment paper into the pie shell. Fill it with 1 cup (250 mL) dried beans or pie weights. Bake until golden brown and flaky, about 30 minutes. Remove from the oven and carefully lift out the parchment paper with the beans. (Save the beans to use again.) Allow the crust to cool completely, about 1 hour.

5. **MAKE THE FILLING** In a medium saucepan, combine 2 cups (500 mL) of the blueberries with the sugar, water, cornstarch, lemon juice, and salt. Bring to a boil uncovered and cook, stirring frequently, until the mixture is thick and shiny, 3 to 4 minutes. Remove from the heat. Using a fork, whisk, or pastry cutter, lightly mash the blueberries. Add the remaining 2 cups (500 mL) blueberries and stir to combine.

6. Pour the filling into the cooled pie crust. Refrigerate for 30 minutes before serving to set. Serve immediately or gently warm in the oven at 350°F (180°C) for 3 or 4 minutes. Cover and store in the fridge for 3 to 4 days.

Pecan Pie

Even though pecan pie is a traditional dessert from southern United States, it's become a staple in my house here in Canada. Flaky pastry crust filled to the brim with a mixture of sweet maple syrup and appetizing pecans is the perfect way to finish off any dinner, especially during the holidays. Instead of using eggs as in most pie recipes, I simply add a little cornstarch to help create the same consistency. Serve up a slice of ooey-gooey goodness, and don't be ashamed to have seconds.

MAKES 1 PIE; SERVES 8 TO 10

Crust

2 cups (500 mL) pastry flour, more for dusting

1 tablespoon (15 mL) sugar

1 teaspoon (5 mL) sea salt

½ cup (125 mL) cold vegan butter, cut into ½-inch (1 cm) cubes

¼ cup (60 mL) ice-cold water, more as needed

1 teaspoon (5 mL) white vinegar

Filling

2 tablespoons (30 mL) vegan butter

1 cup (250 mL) coarsely chopped raw pecans

1 cup (250 mL) finely chopped raw pecans

1 cup (250 mL) unsweetened soy milk

½ cup (125 mL) maple syrup

¼ cup (60 mL) granulated sugar

¼ cup (60 mL) packed brown sugar

3 tablespoons (45 mL) cornstarch

2 teaspoons (10 mL) pure vanilla extract

¼ teaspoon (1 mL) sea salt

1. **MAKE THE CRUST** In a medium bowl, whisk together the pastry flour, sugar, and salt. Add the butter and, using your hands, combine until the mixture is crumbly. Do not overmix. Add the water and vinegar and, using your hands, mix until the dough just begins to form. Do not overmix or the dough can become tough. Add more water, 1 tablespoon (15 mL) at a time, if needed.

2. Dust a work surface with a little flour. Place the dough on the flour. Using your hands, form the dough into a ball. Using a rolling pin, roll out the dough until about ¼ inch (5 mm) thick. Roll the pastry loosely around the rolling pin, then carefully unroll it over a 10-inch (25 cm) pie plate. Using your fingers, press the dough firmly against the bottom and sides of the pie plate. Using a paring knife, trim excess dough from the edges of the pie plate. Refrigerate for 15 minutes to rest.

3. Preheat the oven to 350°F (180°C).

4. **MAKE THE FILLING** In a medium saucepan, melt the butter over medium heat. Add the pecans and cook, stirring constantly, until they are lightly toasted and fragrant, 3 to 4 minutes. Remove from the pan and set aside.

5. In a medium bowl, whisk together the soy milk, maple syrup, granulated sugar, brown sugar, cornstarch, vanilla, and salt until well combined. Transfer to a medium pot and heat just until the sugar has dissolved, 2 to 3 minutes. You do not want to bring the mixture to a boil or simmer but only heat it enough to dissolve the sugar. Add the toasted pecans and stir to combine.

6. Remove the crust from the fridge and pour in the filling. Bake until the middle of the pie jiggles only a little when shaken and the crust is golden brown, about 30 minutes. If the middle is still very soft, bake for another 5 minutes. Remove from the oven and allow the pie to cool before serving, about 1 hour. Cover and store in the fridge for up to 3 days.

Deluxe Banana Split

One of the most iconic desserts is the classic banana split, which has been served in diners across the Western Hemisphere for decades. My deluxe and dairy-free version features a chocolate sauce that's easy to make, strawberry sauce, and whipped cream made from coconut milk. I prefer to make it with my Best Banana Soft Serve (page 235), but any vanilla ice cream will do. Note that you need to chill the coconut milk in the freezer for 2 hours, so plan ahead!

MAKES 2 BANANA SPLITS

Prep ahead
Best Banana Soft Serve
    (page 235)

Chocolate Sauce
6 tablespoons (90 mL) maple
    syrup
6 tablespoons (90 mL) cocoa
    powder
¼ cup (60 mL) melted virgin
    coconut oil
2 tablespoons (30 mL) cold
    water
½ teaspoon (2 mL) pure
    vanilla extract
Pinch of sea salt

Strawberry Sauce
1 cup (250 mL) frozen
    strawberries
1 tablespoon (15 mL) sugar
1 teaspoon (5 mL) pure
    vanilla extract
½ teaspoon (2 mL) freshly
    squeezed lemon juice

Whipped Cream
1 can (14 ounces/398 mL)
    full-fat coconut milk,
    chilled in freezer for
    2 hours (see Tip)
2 tablespoons (30 mL) agave
    nectar or maple syrup
1 teaspoon (5 mL) pure
    vanilla extract

For serving
2 bananas, cut in half
    lengthwise
1 cup (250 mL) Best Banana
    Soft Serve
Fresh strawberries, cut in
    half
Chopped unsalted peanuts

1. **MAKE THE CHOCOLATE SAUCE** In a small bowl, combine the maple syrup, cocoa powder, coconut oil, water, vanilla, and salt. Whisk until well combined; there should be no lumps and the sauce should be smooth and shiny.

2. **MAKE THE STRAWBERRY SAUCE** In a small pot, combine the strawberries, sugar, vanilla, and lemon juice. Bring to a boil uncovered, then reduce the heat to a simmer. Cook, stirring frequently, until the mixture is thick, 10 to 12 minutes.

3. **MAKE THE WHIPPED CREAM** Freeze the can of coconut milk for about 2 hours, or long enough for the fat to separate completely from the liquid. Carefully scoop the solid cream that has separated into the chilled bowl of a stand mixer fitted with the whisk attachment. Reserve the remaining liquid in an airtight container in the refrigerator for up to 3 days.

4. Whip the coconut cream for 4 to 5 minutes, or until soft peaks begin to form. Add the agave and vanilla and whip for 1 to 2 more minutes, or until stiff peaks form. Serve immediately or transfer to an airtight container and store in the fridge for up to 2 days.

5. **MAKE THE BANANA SPLITS** Place 2 banana slices in each serving dish and move them to each side of the dish, leaving room in the middle for the ice cream. Place 3 scoops of ice cream in the middle of each dish. Top with strawberry sauce, chocolate sauce, and whipped cream, then top with fresh strawberries and chopped peanuts. Serve immediately.

TIP

Most commercial coconut milks have some type of emulsifier added. This keeps the fat and water blended but can make whipping it to stiff peaks a little more challenging. If you are using coconut milk that has an added emulsifier, add a pinch of xanthan gum while the cream is mixing. This will help hold the air that has already been incorporated into the cream.

Peanut Butter Buckeyes

I'll be honest, there really isn't a better combination of flavours than chocolate and peanut butter. Better than mac and cheese, better than fries and ice cream (trust me, it's a great combination), these buckeyes hit the bullseye when it comes to nailing a really good dessert. Good news for lazy bakers: these candies are made with only a few ingredients and require no baking time.

MAKES 12 CANDIES

Ingredients

1¼ cups (300 mL) smooth natural peanut butter

¼ cup (60 mL) vegan cream cheese

¼ cup (60 mL) melted vegan butter

2 cups (500 mL) icing sugar

1½ cups (375 mL) semi-sweet dairy-free chocolate chips

1. In a medium bowl, using an electric hand mixer fitted with the beater attachment, combine the peanut butter, cream cheese, and butter. Gradually increase the speed until it is about half strength. Mix until well combined. Add the icing sugar and again gradually increase the speed until it is about half strength and mix until well combined.

2. Divide the mixture into 12 equal portions. Using about 1 tablespoon (15 mL) of the mixture at a time, roll into balls about 1 inch (2.5 cm) in diameter and freeze for 20 minutes on a baking sheet lined with parchment paper.

3. Meanwhile, fill a small pot about one-third full of water, bring to a boil uncovered, then reduce the heat to a simmer. Place the chocolate chips in a metal mixing bowl that is larger than the pot of simmering water. The bowl must be able to sit on top of the pot of simmering water without moving or touching the water. This is called a double boiler. Using a rubber spatula, stir the chocolate chips until they begin to melt. Once the chocolate chips are mostly melted, remove from the heat and continue to stir until completely melted.

4. Stick a toothpick into each buckeye. Dip into the melted chocolate most of the way up the sides of each buckeye, leaving a little space at the top. Place the buckeyes on a baking sheet lined with parchment paper and refrigerate until the chocolate is firm, about 30 minutes. Serve immediately or store in an airtight container in the fridge for up to 2 weeks or in the freezer for up to 2 months.

Churros with Salted Caramel Sauce

When I discovered churros, I immediately fell in love with these delicious sticks of sugary, deep-fried dough made famous in Spain. An easy substitution for the butter in this recipe is coconut oil. Coconut oil is a saturated fat similar to butter, so it helps provide a great mouthfeel. These are crispy on the outside and soft in the middle and pair perfectly with the caramel sauce for dipping.

MAKES 12 CHURROS

Churros
1 cup (250 mL) water

3 tablespoons (45 mL) virgin coconut oil

1 cup (250 mL) all-purpose flour

Sugar and Cinnamon Mix
½ cup (125 mL) sugar

2 teaspoons (10 mL) cinnamon

Pinch of sea salt

Salted Caramel Sauce
1 can (14 ounces/398 mL) full-fat coconut milk

1 cup (250 mL) sugar

1 teaspoon (5 mL) sea salt

1 tablespoon (15 mL) pure vanilla extract

———

4 to 6 cups (1 to 1.5 L) vegetable oil, for frying

1. **MAKE THE CHURROS DOUGH** In a small saucepan, combine the water and coconut oil. Bring to a boil, then reduce the heat to a simmer. Add the flour and, using a wooden spoon, stir until the dough comes away from the sides of the pan, about 2 minutes. Remove from the heat and transfer to a large bowl. Set aside until cool enough to handle.

2. **MAKE THE CINNAMON AND SUGAR MIX** In a small bowl, whisk together the sugar, cinnamon, and salt.

3. **MAKE THE SALTED CARAMEL SAUCE** In a medium pot, combine the coconut milk, sugar, and salt. Bring to a boil uncovered, reduce the heat to a simmer, and cook for 7 to 8 minutes or until reduced by half. Whisk in the vanilla.

4. Heat the vegetable oil in a large pot or small deep fryer to a temperature of 375°F (190°C).

5. **FRY THE CHURROS** Tip out the dough onto a work surface. Roll into 12 small logs, each 3 inches (8 cm) long. Working in batches of 3 to 4 churros, carefully lower the dough into the hot oil. Cook for 3 to 4 minutes, or until the churros are crisp and golden brown. Using a slotted spoon, transfer to the bowl with the cinnamon sugar and toss to coat well. Transfer to a serving plate. Repeat with the remaining batter. Serve immediately with salted caramel sauce for dipping.

VARIATION

Traditionally, churros are made with a star shape. To do this, allow the dough to cool enough to handle. Fill a piping bag fitted with a star-shaped tip with the dough. Working in batches of 2 or 3 churros, squeeze strips of dough 3 inches (8 cm) long into the hot oil. Cook for 3 to 4 minutes, or until the churros are crisp and golden brown. Using a slotted spoon, transfer to the bowl with the cinnamon sugar and toss to coat well. Transfer to a serving plate. Repeat with the remaining batter. Serve immediately with salted caramel sauce for dipping.

Pantry Staples and Condiments

Almond Milk Cheddar Cheese

Cheese is an addictive food staple found in nearly every home in the modern world. It melts, it stretches, and it is rich and creamy, giving our taste buds everything they could ever want. Dairy cheese gets its classic stretch from the protein called casein. In my dairy-free adaptation, I replace casein with tapioca flour, which helps to provide the same effect. A blend of nutritional yeast, lemon, and mustard gives this recipe a cheddar taste that doesn't require kidnapping any baby calves, so you can enjoy it guilt-free. Try all of the variations to figure out which is your favourite! You will need to make your own almond milk for this recipe. Store-bought almond milks contain thickeners and other ingredients that prevent them from setting properly. Make sure to soak the almonds at least 2 hours ahead for this recipe.

MAKES 1½ CUPS (375 ML)

Ingredients

2 cups (500 mL) Homemade Almond Milk (see recipe)

½ cup (125 mL) nutritional yeast

6 tablespoons (90 mL) tapioca starch

6 tablespoons (90 mL) melted deodorized coconut oil

1 tablespoon (15 mL) + 1½ teaspoons (7 mL)freshly squeezed lemon juice

1 tablespoon (15 mL) agar powder

1 teaspoon (5 mL) sea salt

½ teaspoon (2 mL) Dijon mustard

½ teaspoon (2 mL) garlic powder

¼ teaspoon (1 mL) ground turmeric

1. In a blender, combine the almond milk, nutritional yeast, tapioca starch, coconut oil, lemon juice, agar powder, salt, mustard, garlic powder, and turmeric. Blend until completely smooth.

2. Transfer the mixture to a medium pot and bring to a boil uncovered, stirring constantly using a wooden spoon. Switch to using a heat-proof spatula, reduce the heat to medium, and cook the mixture until it is thick and creamy, scraping down the bottom of the pot from time to time. Total cooking time is about 5 to 6 minutes.

3. Transfer the mixture to a container and allow to cool completely. Store in an airtight container in the fridge for up to 1 week.

HOMEMADE ALMOND MILK

1. To make almond milk, soak 1 cup (250 mL) whole raw almonds in 4 cups (1 L) water for at least 2 hours or overnight, covered and stored in the fridge. Drain, discarding the soaking water.

2. Place the soaked almonds in a high-speed blender with 4 cups (1 L) water and blend until no large pieces of almonds remain, the water turns white, and the texture is smooth and creamy, about 2 minutes. Strain the mixture through a nut milk bag, fine mesh strainer, or sieve lined with cheesecloth, reserving the pulp for later use, if desired. Store the almond milk (and pulp) in the fridge for up to 5 days. The leftover pulp can be dried out in the oven or a dehydrator and processed in a food processor or blender into a flour, then used as almond flour in cookies, muffins, cakes, and other baked goods as almond flour.

VARIATIONS

HERBED CHEDDAR Add ½ teaspoon (2 mL) each of dried thyme, dried dill, and dried parsley to the blender in step 1.

SPICY CHEDDAR Add 1 tablespoon (15 mL) chopped jalapeño peppers, 1 teaspoon (5 mL) white wine vinegar, and ½ teaspoon (2 mL) ground cumin to the blender in step 1.

SMOKY CHEDDAR Add 1 teaspoon (5 mL) smoked paprika, 1 teaspoon (5 mL) tamari or soy sauce, a pinch of cayenne pepper, and a dash of liquid smoke to the blender in step 1.

Almond Milk Cheese Curds

In conventional cheese-making, an animal milk is boiled, an acid is added, then some of the protein coagulates, becoming curdled. Vegan cheese can be made in very much the same way using citric acid, except with almond milk instead of dairy milk. Add a little tapioca starch for body, and this cheese is great served fresh on sandwiches or salads, melted on pizza, or in Classic Poutine (page 57).

MAKES 15 SMALL CURDS OR 1½ POUNDS (675 G) CHEESE

Brine

2 cups (500 mL) cold water

2 teaspoons (10 mL) sea salt

Curd

1⅓ cups (325 mL) Homemade Almond Milk (see page 216)

⅓ cup (75 mL) tapioca starch

⅓ cup (75 mL) melted deodorized coconut oil

1 tablespoon (15 mL) agar powder

1 tablespoon (15 mL) nutritional yeast

1¼ teaspoons (6 mL) sea salt

¼ teaspoon (1 mL) citric acid (see Tip)

1. **MAKE THE BRINE** In a medium bowl, whisk together the water and salt. Refrigerate until ready to use.

2. **MAKE THE CURDS** In a blender, combine the almond milk, tapioca starch, coconut oil, agar powder, nutritional yeast, and salt. Blend at the highest speed until smooth.

3. Transfer to a saucepan and heat over medium heat, stirring constantly using a wooden spoon, for 5 to 6 minutes. You want the mixture to be thick and creamy. Remove the pan from the heat and whisk in the citric acid.

4. Remove the cold brine from the fridge. Using a small ice cream scoop or a ¼-cup (60 mL) measuring cup, drop portions of curd mixture directly into the brine until all of the mixture has been used. Refrigerate until the curds are cold, about 3 hours. Remove from the brine using a slotted spoon when ready to use, draining excess liquid on a clean kitchen towel or paper towel. Store the curds, in brine, in an airtight container in the fridge for up to 5 days.

TIP

Citric acid is a weak acid that is most commonly produced from citrus fruit such as lemons and limes. It has a strong tart flavour and is a great addition in making vegan cheeses and other sauces. Make sure to look for food grade citric acid when purchasing.

Cashew Mozzarella

I developed this mozzarella cheese substitute so that it would brown and melt, either in an oven set to at least 400°F (200°C) or under a broiler. The high protein content in dairy cheese helps it melt, but in this cheese I've used protein-rich cashews along with agar powder to help it set, allowing it to firm up so that it can be sliced and shredded. Try it with my French Onion Soup with Melted Mozzarella (page 27) or Cheesy Garlic Bread (page 31).

MAKES 4 CUPS (1 L)

Ingredients

1¼ cups (300 mL) hot water

½ cup (125 mL) agar powder

2 cups (500 mL) raw cashews, soaked and drained (see Tip)

6 tablespoons (90 mL) melted deodorized coconut oil

⅓ cup (75 mL) nutritional yeast

2 tablespoons (30 mL) freshly squeezed lemon juice

1 tablespoon (15 mL) unpasteurized apple cider vinegar

2 teaspoons (10 mL) sea salt

1 teaspoon (5 mL) soy lecithin granules (see Tip)

¼ teaspoon (1 mL) garlic powder

1. In a small saucepan, whisk together the water and agar powder. Bring to a simmer and cook until the agar is dissolved, about 2 minutes.

2. In a high-speed blender, combine the agar mixture, soaked cashews, coconut oil, nutritional yeast, lemon juice, apple cider vinegar, salt, lecithin, and garlic powder. Blend on high speed until smooth and creamy, stopping the machine to scrape down the sides of the blender jar as necessary. Transfer to an 8-inch (2 L) square glass dish, cover, and refrigerate until set, at least 4 hours or overnight. Store in an airtight container in the fridge for up to 10 days.

TIP

1. To soak the cashews, place them in a large bowl and cover with 4 cups (1 L) hot water for at least 1 hour or overnight, covered, and stored in the fridge. Drain and rinse the cashews, discarding the soaking liquid. **2.** Soy lecithin is available in most well-stocked grocery stores or online. It helps emulsify recipes and is beneficial to help hold together the fats and proteins in this recipe, resulting in a cheese that melts and browns very well. You can substitute an equal amount of sunflower lecithin for the soy lecithin in this recipe.

Swiss Cheese

I originally created this Swiss cheese for a deli-style sandwich. Since then, I've used it in other sandwiches like Count of Monte Cristo (page 108), Reuben Sandwiches (page 151), and Croque Monsieur (page 109). Also, it's responsible for the richness and creaminess of my White Widow Mac and Cheese (page 143). This plant-based replacement uses a mixture of apple cider vinegar, tahini, miso, mustard, and white wine to help provide the tang of traditional Swiss cheese. Full of flavour and plant-based—win-win!

MAKES 2 CUPS (500 ML)

Ingredients

1 cup (250 mL) water

1 tablespoon (15 mL) agar powder

1 cup (250 mL) raw cashews, soaked and drained (see Tip)

¼ cup (60 mL) unsweetened almond milk

⅓ cup (75 mL) semi-sweet white wine, such as Riesling

2 tablespoons (30 mL) freshly squeezed lemon juice

2 tablespoons (30 mL) unpasteurized apple cider vinegar

2 teaspoons (10 mL) Dijon mustard

1½ teaspoons (7 mL) nutritional yeast

1½ teaspoons (7 mL) sea salt

1½ teaspoons (7 mL) tahini

¼ teaspoon (1 mL) ground mustard powder

⅛ teaspoon (0.5 mL) brown rice miso

1. In a small pot, combine the water and agar powder. Bring to a boil, reduce the heat to a simmer, and cook until reduced by half, about 10 minutes. Set aside.

2. In a high-speed blender, combine the soaked cashews, almond milk, white wine, lemon juice, apple cider vinegar, mustard, nutritional yeast, salt, tahini, mustard powder, and miso. Blend on high speed until smooth. Add the agar mixture and blend until no lumps remain.

3. Transfer to a shallow container. Refrigerate until set, about 2 hours. Serve immediately or store in an airtight container in the fridge for up to 10 days.

TIP

To soak the cashews, place them in a small bowl and cover with 2 cups (500 mL) hot water for at least 1 hour or overnight, covered, and stored in the fridge. Drain and rinse the cashews, discarding the soaking liquid.

Blue Cheese

When I was a young cook, one of my favourite smells, flavours, and textures was blue cheese. I loved the pungent flavour and its crumbly yet creamy texture. Traditional blue cheese uses the bacteria penicillin to help create its flavour. In my version, I use the bacteria found in miso and sauerkraut to help create the same cheesy tang. Spirulina powder gives it those characteristic streaks of blue, with the benefit of added nutrients.

MAKES 3 CUPS (750 ML)

Ingredients

2 cups (500 mL) raw cashews

⅓ cup (75 mL) unsweetened almond milk

¼ cup (60 mL) sauerkraut liquid from unpasteurized sauerkraut (see Tip)

¼ cup (60 mL) deodorized coconut oil

1 tablespoon + 1 teaspoon (20 mL) sea salt

1 tablespoon (15 mL) red wine vinegar

1 tablespoon (15 mL) white wine vinegar

1 tablespoon (15 mL) agave nectar

1 tablespoon (15 mL) unpasteurized sauerkraut (see Tip)

¼ teaspoon (1 mL) unpasteurized brown rice miso or any unpasteurized miso

¼ teaspoon (1 mL) spirulina powder

1. In a food processor fitted with a metal blade, process the cashews, almond milk, sauerkraut liquid, coconut oil, salt, red wine vinegar, white wine vinegar, agave, sauerkraut, and miso until smooth. You will need to stop the machine once and use a rubber spatula to scrape down the sides of the bowl.

2. Transfer the mixture to a medium bowl and stir in the spirulina with a fork or small whisk. You want to marble the mixture with the spirulina but not make the entire mixture blue.

3. Transfer the mixture to the middle of a triple layer of cheesecloth, about 10 to 12 inches (25 to 30 cm) in diameter. Gather all sides of the cheesecloth and tie the ends together. You want to form a barrier around the cheese.

4. Making space in your fridge, tie the ball of cheese so that it can hang with enough room to place a shallow bowl beneath it. Allow the cheese to hang in the fridge for at least 8 hours or overnight. Hanging the cheese in the cheesecloth allows the bacteria culture found in the miso and sauerkraut to ferment sugars into acids. This helps to give the cheese its flavour. It also allows any excess liquid to slowly drip out of the cheesecloth, which concentrates the sugars naturally, resulting in a great-tasting cheese! Remove the cheese from the cheesecloth and serve immediately or store in an airtight container in the fridge for up to 10 days.

TIP

You will need to use the liquid and sauerkraut from sauerkraut that has not been pasteurized. The pasteurization process kills the beneficial bacteria that help to give this cheese its flavour.

Feta Cheese

I loved Greek salad as a kid, especially the creamy, crumbly, and salty feta cheese. It blew my mind, and I knew when I went vegan that I had to create a version that paralleled the taste and texture! Tofu gives my feta cheese the same crumbly texture you'd expect from dairy feta.

MAKES 1½ CUPS (375 ML)

Ingredients

- 1 pound (450 g) firm or extra-firm vacuum-packed tofu, cut into 1-inch (2.5 cm) cubes
- ¼ cup (60 mL) freshly squeezed lemon juice
- ¼ cup (60 mL) melted coconut oil
- 2 tablespoons (30 mL) nutritional yeast
- 1 tablespoon (15 mL) + 1½ teaspoons (7 mL) sea salt
- ½ teaspoon (2 mL) vegan lactic acid

1. In a food processor fitted with a metal blade, process the tofu until no large pieces remain. You will need to stop the machine once or twice and use a rubber spatula to scrape down the sides of the bowl. You want the tofu to be crumbly and soft to the touch.

2. Add the lemon juice, coconut oil, nutritional yeast, salt, and lactic acid. Process until well combined.

3. Transfer the mixture to an airtight container and gently press into it so that it is firm. Refrigerate for at least 4 hours or overnight. Serve immediately or cover and store in the fridge for up to 2 weeks.

VARIATION

HERBED FETA CHEESE In step 2, add 1 tablespoon (15 mL) dried oregano, 1 teaspoon (5 mL) dried basil, and ½ teaspoon (2 mL) freshly cracked black pepper.

Cream Cheese

Usually, cream cheese is made from a mixture of animal milk and cream. In my veganized version, I use tofu as a stand-in for the milk and coconut oil for the cream. This cheese is perfect to spread on your favourite toasted bagel or to stuff into dishes like my Cage-Free Cheesy Omelette (page 102). So many options, so little stomach.

MAKES ABOUT 2½ CUPS (625 ML)

Ingredients

2 cups (500 mL) firm water-packed tofu, cut into small cubes

¼ cup (60 mL) melted deodorized coconut oil

1 tablespoon + 2 teaspoons (25 mL) freshly squeezed lemon juice

1 tablespoon (15 mL) unpasteurized apple cider vinegar

¾ teaspoon (4 mL) sea salt

¼ teaspoon (1 mL) garlic powder

¼ teaspoon (1 mL) onion powder

1. In a high-speed blender, combine the tofu, coconut oil, lemon juice, apple cider vinegar, salt, garlic powder, and onion powder. Blend until smooth and creamy. You will need to stop the machine once or twice and use a rubber spatula to scrape down the sides of the bowl. The mixture should be smooth but not liquid, so take care not to overblend. Serve immediately or transfer to an airtight container and store in the fridge for up to 1 week.

VARIATIONS

STRAWBERRY CREAM CHEESE Add ⅓ cup (75 mL) chopped hulled fresh strawberries and 2 tablespoons (30 mL) maple syrup to the blender.

GARLIC AND SCALLION CREAM CHEESE Increase the amount of garlic powder to 1 tablespoon (15 mL) and add 3 tablespoons (45 mL) thinly sliced green onion to the blender. After the cream cheese is blended, add another 2 tablespoons (30 mL) thinly sliced green onion to the cream cheese and stir together.

Mac and Cheese Sauce

Nutritional yeast mixed with the starch and fat from squash and potatoes gives this ooey-gooey mac and cheese sauce an incredibly creamy texture. This cruelty-free cheese sauce is sensational served over pasta, as in my Sharp Cheddar Mac and Cheese (page 144), as a thick and rich dip, or even spread on bread.

MAKES 4 CUPS (1 L)

Ingredients

- 2 cups (500 mL) peeled cubed butternut squash
- 1 cup (250 mL) raw cashew pieces
- 1 cup (250 mL) peeled roughly chopped russet potatoes
- ½ cup (125 mL) roughly chopped white onion
- ½ cup (125 mL) peeled roughly chopped carrot
- 1 tablespoon (15 mL) sea salt
- 3 to 4 cloves garlic
- 1 cup (250 mL) nutritional yeast
- ½ cup (125 mL) deodorized coconut oil
- 1 tablespoon (15 mL) Dijon mustard
- 1 teaspoon (5 mL) freshly squeezed lemon juice

1. In a medium pot, combine the squash, cashews, potatoes, onion, carrots, salt, and garlic. Add enough water so that the vegetables are covered by a couple of inches. Cover with a tight-fitting lid and bring to a boil. Remove the lid, reduce the heat to a simmer, and cook until all of the vegetables are soft, about 20 minutes. Do not discard the cooking liquid.

2. In a high-speed blender, add the cooked vegetables and cashews along with half of the cooking liquid. Add the nutritional yeast, coconut oil, mustard, and lemon juice. Blend on high speed until smooth and creamy. If the sauce is too thick, add a little more of the cooking liquid. Serve immediately or allow to cool completely and store in an airtight container in the fridge for up to 1 week.

Nacho Cheese Sauce

When I was starting out as a cook, one of the first dishes I made was nachos. I still remember pouring the nacho cheese powder out of the bag and mixing it with hot water. Even though it was made from a powder, the flavour sticks in my mind to this day. Cheesy, tangy, and full of flavour, I put that sauce on everything! My plant-based version gets its cheesiness from nutritional yeast, its thick and pourable texture from a little arrowroot starch, and its creaminess from cashews. This sauce is a must for my Mile-High Loaded Nachos (page 35) and Fiesta Seven-Layer Dip (page 40).

MAKES 3 CUPS (750 ML)

Ingredients

1 cup (250 mL) peeled and cubed butternut squash

1 cup (250 mL) raw cashews

½ cup (125 mL) roughly chopped white onion

½ cup (125 mL) peeled roughly chopped carrot

½ cup (125 mL) peeled roughly chopped russet potatoes

1 tablespoon (15 mL) freshly squeezed lemon juice

1 tablespoon (15 mL) unpasteurized apple cider vinegar

1 tablespoon (15 mL) sea salt

1½ teaspoons (7 mL) arrowroot starch

1½ teaspoons (7 mL) tomato paste

3 cloves garlic

1½ cups (375 mL) nutritional yeast

¼ cup (60 mL) deodorized coconut oil

1. In a medium pot, combine the squash, cashews, onion, carrots, potatoes, lemon juice, apple cider vinegar, salt, arrowroot, tomato paste, and garlic. Add enough water to cover the vegetables by a couple of inches. Bring to a boil, covered. Remove the lid, reduce the heat to a simmer, and cook until all vegetables are soft, about 20 minutes. Do not discard the cooking liquid.

2. In a high-speed blender, add the cooked vegetables and cashews along with half of the cooking liquid. Add the nutritional yeast and coconut oil. Blend on high speed until smooth and creamy. If the sauce is too thick, add a little more of the cooking liquid. Serve immediately or allow to cool and store in an airtight container in the fridge for up to 1 week.

Tartar Sauce

Fish and chips are not complete without tartar sauce! I highly recommend my plant-based tartar sauce served with my Beer Battered Tempeh and Chips (page 134) or simply as a dip with fresh carrot and celery sticks. Use my Creamy Mayo (page 232) as a base, or if you're crunched for time, you can use any store-bought vegan mayo.

MAKES 2 CUPS (500 ML)

Make ahead

Creamy Mayo (page 232)

Ingredients

1½ cups (375 mL) Creamy Mayo

3 tablespoons (45 mL) finely diced dill pickles

2 tablespoons (30 mL) finely chopped flat-leaf parsley

2 tablespoons (30 mL) roughly chopped fresh dill (see Tip)

2 tablespoons (30 mL) freshly squeezed lemon juice

1 tablespoon (15 mL) + 1½ teaspoons (7 mL) Dijon mustard

½ teaspoon (2 mL) prepared yellow mustard

¼ teaspoon (1 mL) sea salt

1. In a small bowl, combine the creamy mayo, pickles, parsley, dill, lemon juice, Dijon mustard, yellow mustard, and salt. Using a rubber spatula, mix until well combined. Serve immediately or transfer to an airtight container and store in the fridge for up to 10 days.

TIP

Soft herbs like fresh dill or fresh basil should not be chopped too much. They oxidize and turn brown very easily, which makes them lose their flavour. When chopping, try not to bang the blade of the knife on the herbs; instead, rock it back and forth until the herb is cut small enough.

Hollandaise Sauce

Classic hollandaise sauce is made from eggs and butter—essentially the furthest thing from vegan. My version relies on a roux—a sauce made from oil, flour, and milk—to provide the creaminess. Coconut oil is a great replacement for butter and also helps to give the same mouth-watering texture found in a traditional hollandaise sauce. This sauce is fantastic served with my Cage-Free Eggs Florentine (page 118) or, one of my personal favourites, as a dip for my Brunch Club Sandwich (page 113).

MAKES 1½ CUPS (375 ML)

Ingredients

- ½ cup (125 mL) deodorized coconut oil or melted vegan butter
- ⅔ cup (150 mL) all-purpose flour
- ⅛ teaspoon (0.5 mL) ground turmeric
- 6 tablespoons (90 mL) dry white wine, such as Chardonnay
- ¼ cup (60 mL) freshly squeezed lemon juice
- 3 cups (750 mL) unsweetened almond milk, divided
- 2 tablespoons (30 mL) nutritional yeast
- 1 tablespoon (15 mL) Dijon mustard
- 1 teaspoon (5 mL) black salt

1. In a large saucepan, combine the coconut oil, flour, and turmeric over medium heat. Cook, stirring constantly, until the raw flavour of the flour cooks out, 3 to 4 minutes.

2. Stir in the white wine and cook, stirring constantly, until the mixture thickens and forms a paste, about 2 minutes. Stir in the lemon juice and bring to a simmer.

3. Remove the pot from the heat, stir in 1 cup (250 mL) of the almond milk, and use a whisk to remove any lumps. Add another 1 cup (250 mL) almond milk and continue to whisk. Add the remaining 1 cup (250 mL) almond milk and whisk. There should not be any lumps at this point.

4. Return the pot to medium heat, bring to a boil, then reduce the heat to a simmer. Cook uncovered, stirring occasionally with a wooden spoon or heat-proof spatula, for 2 to 3 minutes, until the mixture is thick enough to coat the back of a spoon. Remove from the heat. Stir in the nutritional yeast, mustard, and black salt. If the final sauce has any lumps, add it to a blender and blend for 30 seconds to make it smooth. Serve immediately or allow to cool and store in an airtight container in the fridge for up to 1 week.

TIP

1. If the sauce has lumps in it and you do not have a blender, you can use a fine-mesh sieve to strain the sauce into a bowl or another pot. Discard the solids. 2. If this sauce needs to sit for a period before being used, transfer it to a bowl, cover with plastic wrap (to prevent a skin forming), and set aside.

Honey Garlic Sauce

This sauce made with sweet and sticky agave nectar instead of honey will make you salivate. Don't worry, you won't know the difference, but you'll rest easy knowing that you're not eating bee vomit. I like to serve it with crispy tofu, tempeh, and vegetables, but if you really want to impress people, make it as a sauce for my Boneless Wings (page 24).

MAKES 1 CUP (250 ML)

Ingredients

2 tablespoons (30 mL) vegetable oil

2 tablespoons (30 mL) minced garlic

1 cup (250 mL) agave nectar

1 tablespoon (15 mL) tamari or soy sauce

1 teaspoon (5 mL) white sesame seeds

½ teaspoon (2 mL) freshly squeezed lemon juice

¼ teaspoon (1 mL) sea salt

1. In a small pot, heat the vegetable oil over medium heat. Add the garlic and cook, stirring constantly, until fragrant and lightly brown, about 2 minutes. Be careful that the garlic does not burn.

2. Add the agave, tamari, sesame seeds, lemon juice, and salt. Bring to a simmer and cook for 8 to 10 minutes or until the mixture has reduced slightly. Serve immediately or cool and store in an airtight container in the fridge for up to 1 month.

Buffalo Sauce

Toss my Boneless Wings (page 24) in this fiery sauce for the ultimate appetizer. Great for game night or anytime you are craving some crispy, fiery wings.

MAKES 4 CUPS (1 L)

Ingredients

2 cups (500 mL) melted vegan margarine

½ cup (125 mL) hot cayenne pepper sauce

1 teaspoon (5 mL) vegan Worcestershire sauce

1 teaspoon (5 mL) garlic powder

1 teaspoon (5 mL) cornstarch

1. Place all the ingredients in a small pot, bring to a simmer, and whisk to remove lumps. Set aside to cool. Store, covered, in the fridge for up to 2 weeks.

Anytime Gravy

Warning: this gravy is so good, you're going to want to drink it straight from the gravy boat—all year round, not just on holidays. In fact, if I had my way, gravy would be its own food group! Make sure you save some to drizzle on my Perfect French Fries and Seasoning Salt (page 64) or Classic Poutine (page 57).

MAKES 6 CUPS (1.5 L)

Ingredients

¼ cup (60 mL) deodorized coconut oil or vegan butter

1 cup (250 mL) finely diced onion

⅓ cup (75 mL) all-purpose flour (see Tip)

2 tablespoons (30 mL) tomato paste

2 tablespoons (30 mL) minced garlic

¾ cup (175 mL) dry red wine

¾ cup (175 mL) tamari (see Tip)

1 tablespoon (15 mL) chopped fresh thyme leaves

6 cups (1.5 L) water

1. In a medium pot, heat the coconut oil over medium heat. Add the onions and cook, stirring frequently, until golden brown, 4 to 5 minutes.

2. Add the flour, tomato paste, and garlic and cook, stirring frequently, for 3 to 4 minutes. Add the red wine and cook until the wine has reduced by half, about 5 minutes

3. Remove the pot from the heat. Using a whisk, add the tamari, thyme, and water and whisk until no lumps remain. Return the pot to medium-high heat and bring to a boil. Reduce the heat to a simmer and cook, stirring frequently, for about 10 minutes. Serve immediately or cool and store in an airtight container in the fridge for up to 10 days.

TIP

1. Make this recipe gluten-free by substituting an equal amount of gluten-free all-purpose flour blend for the all-purpose flour. 2. Tamari is preferred over soy sauce for this recipe because of its richer, bolder flavour.

Whipped Butter

Yes, it melts and spreads just like the real thing! This plant-based whipped butter is creamy and rich like traditional butter, and perfect for your morning toast, sandwiches, sauces, baking, and more. You will need to make your own cashew milk; cashew milk, as opposed to other nut milks, is the creamiest and therefore ideal for this recipe. Store-bought cashew milks contain thickeners and other ingredients that prevent them from setting properly. Put in the extra effort; it will be worth it.

MAKES 3 CUPS (750 ML)

Ingredients

1 cup (250 mL) Homemade Cashew Milk (see recipe)

2 tablespoons (30 mL) unpasteurized apple cider vinegar

1 tablespoon (15 mL) freshly squeezed lemon juice

1¼ cups (300 mL) melted deodorized coconut oil

2 tablespoons (30 mL) vegetable oil

2 tablespoons (30 mL) soy lecithin granules

½ teaspoon (2 mL) ground golden flaxseed

¼ teaspoon (1 mL) sea salt

1. In a medium bowl, combine the cashew milk, apple cider vinegar, and lemon juice. Set aside so that the milk can curdle slightly, about 10 minutes.

2. In a food processor fitted with a metal blade, combine the curdled milk mixture, coconut oil, vegetable oil, lecithin, flaxseed, and salt. Process until well combined and the lecithin has dissolved, about 2 minutes. You will need to stop the machine once and use a rubber spatula to scrape down the sides of the bowl.

3. Transfer to an airtight container and refrigerate until firm, at least 3 hours or overnight. When ready to use, remove from the fridge and use whatever amount you need. Store in an airtight container in the fridge for up to 1 month.

HOMEMADE CASHEW MILK

1. To make the cashew milk, soak 1 cup (250 mL) whole raw cashews in 4 cups (1 L) hot water for at least 1 hour or overnight, covered, and stored in the fridge. Drain and rinse, discarding the soaking water.

2. Place the soaked cashews in a blender with 4 cups (1 L) water and blend for 2 minutes on high speed. Strain the mixture through a nut milk bag, fine mesh strainer, or sieve lined with cheesecloth, reserving the pulp for later use. Store the cashew milk (and pulp) in the fridge for up to 5 days. The leftover pulp can be dried out in the oven or a dehydrator and processed in a food processor or blender into a flour, then used as cashew flour in cookies, muffins, cakes, and other baked goods.

Garlic Butter

Everyone loves garlic butter slathered over a piece of perfectly toasted baguette or smothering a steamy baked potato. Made with my Whipped Butter (page 229), the trick to making great garlic butter is to cook the minced garlic first. Cooking the garlic intensifies its flavour and prevents your friends from eating chunks of raw garlic! It also helps make the garlic butter last longer, as raw garlic spoils more quickly. Don't be afraid to cook tons of it.

MAKES 1 CUP (250 ML)

Prep ahead
Whipped Butter (page 229)

Ingredients

2 tablespoons (30 mL) vegetable oil

½ cup (125 mL) minced garlic

1 cup (250 mL) Whipped Butter, at room temperature for 15 minutes

1 teaspoon (5 mL) garlic powder

1 teaspoon (5 mL) finely grated lemon zest

¼ cup (60 mL) tightly packed finely chopped flat-leaf parsley

Pinch of sea salt

Pinch of freshly cracked black pepper

1. In a medium frying pan, heat the vegetable oil over medium-high heat. Add the garlic and cook, stirring frequently, until lightly browned and fragrant, 3 to 4 minutes. Set aside to cool.

2. In a small bowl, combine the cooked garlic, softened butter, garlic powder, lemon zest, parsley, salt, and pepper. Using a rubber spatula, mix until well combined. Serve immediately or store in an airtight container in the fridge for up to 1 week.

Sour Cream

Growing up, my absolute favourite condiment was sour cream. Full of flavourful fat and tang, sour cream is perfect served on a baked potato, a bowl of chili, nachos, or my personal favourite, mashed potatoes! Traditional sour cream is made from cream and a bacterial culture such as lactic acid, but equally as pleasing vegan sour cream uses the fat from two plant-based staples—tofu and raw cashews. Dollop it on top of virtually any meal for some extra satisfaction.

MAKES 2 CUPS (500 ML)

Ingredients

1½ cups (375 mL) firm vacuum-packed tofu, cut into small cubes

¼ cup (60 mL) raw cashews, soaked and drained (see Tip)

3 tablespoons (45 mL) freshly squeezed lemon juice

2 tablespoons (30 mL) water

2 tablespoons (30 mL) deodorized coconut oil

1 tablespoon (15 mL) + 1½ teaspoons (7 mL) unpasteurized apple cider vinegar

½ teaspoon (2 mL) sea salt

1. In a high-speed blender, combine the tofu, soaked cashews, lemon juice, water, coconut oil, apple cider vinegar, and salt. Blend until smooth and creamy. You will need to stop the machine once or twice and use a rubber spatula to scrape down the sides of the bowl. It will take a bit of time to blend until smooth (especially if you are not using a high-speed blender), so blend for as long as needed, up to about 5 minutes. Serve immediately or transfer to an airtight container and store in the fridge for up to 1 week.

TIP

To soak the cashews, place them in a small bowl with 1 cup (250 mL) hot water for at least 1 hour or overnight, covered, and stored in the fridge. Drain and rinse, discarding the soaking liquid.

Creamy Mayo

In traditional mayonnaise, eggs are used because they're high in protein and work well to emulsify the oil with the liquids. In my plant-based mayonnaise, the eggs are replaced with tofu, which emulsifies the oil in the same way the egg would because it is high in protein. Try my mayo as a spread on sandwiches or as a base for dips, spreads, salad dressings, and more!

MAKES 4 CUPS (1 L)

Ingredients

- 1 block (24 ounces/680 g) firm or extra-firm silken tofu (see Tip)
- 2 tablespoons (30 mL) freshly squeezed lemon juice
- 1 tablespoon (15 mL) agave nectar
- 1 tablespoon (15 mL) Dijon mustard
- 1 teaspoon (5 mL) sea salt
- ½ teaspoon (2 mL) unpasteurized apple cider vinegar
- ¼ teaspoon (1 mL) garlic powder
- 2 cups (500 mL) vegetable oil
- ½ cup (125 mL) extra-virgin olive oil

1. In a high-speed blender (see Tip), combine the tofu, lemon juice, agave, mustard, salt, apple cider vinegar, and garlic powder. Blend until smooth and creamy.
2. With the blender running on the lowest setting, drizzle the vegetable oil through the feed tube in a slow, steady stream. At first, you want to pour the vegetable oil in very slowly to help build the emulsification. After you have poured about ½ cup (125 mL) of the vegetable oil through the feed tube, you can increase the blender speed to medium. Add the olive oil after all the vegetable oil has been added.
3. Transfer to an airtight container and refrigerate for 1 hour to allow the mayonnaise to set. Serve immediately or store in an airtight container in the fridge for up to 1 week.

TIP

1. Silken tofu comes in specialty ascetic packs that are shelf stable and do not require refrigeration until they have been opened. This is different from vacuum- or water-packed tofu. **2.** If you are using a high-speed blender, make sure not to blend the mayonnaise at a high speed. This can cause the mayo to get too hot, which can cause it to split. Mayonnaise is an example of an emulsion. Sometimes emulsions can split. Various factors affect the science behind an emulsion, including temperature of the ingredients and speed of the blender. If the mayonnaise splits, remove it from the blender and add a little more tofu and about 2 tablespoons (30 mL) of cold water and blend until smooth. Return the broken mayo slowly to the puréed tofu as you would if it were pure oil. Blend until smooth and creamy.

VARIATIONS

ROASTED RED PEPPER MAYO Once the mayo has cooled, transfer to a medium bowl. Add ½ cup (125 mL) puréed roasted red peppers, 2 tablespoons (30 mL) nutritional yeast, and 1 teaspoon (5 mL) dried basil. Mix with the mayo until well combined.

HERBED OLIVE MAYO Once the mayo has cooled, transfer to a medium bowl. Add ⅓ cup (75 mL) finely chopped pitted Kalamata olives, 1 teaspoon (5 mL) dried oregano, and a pinch of finely grated lemon zest. Mix with the mayo until well combined.

CHIPOTLE AIOLI Once the mayo has cooled, transfer to a medium bowl. Add 3 tablespoons (45 mL) Dijon mustard, 3 tablespoons (45 mL) freshly squeezed lemon juice, 2 teaspoons (10 mL) dried chipotle powder, ½ teaspoon (2 mL) smoked paprika, and ¼ teaspoon (1 mL) sea salt. Mix with the mayo until well combined.

Classic Vinaigrette

A good vinaigrette is a perfect example of a well-balanced recipe. All great recipes work best when all of the right flavours come together in perfect balance. These flavours are usually sweet, salt, acid, and fat. In my version, tahini helps create creaminess and is mixed with tamari and tart apple cider vinegar for that yummy umami flavour.

MAKES 1¾ CUPS (425 ML)

Ingredients

¾ cup (175 mL) extra-virgin olive oil

½ cup (125 mL) water

¼ cup (60 mL) unpasteurized apple cider vinegar

¼ cup (60 mL) tahini

2 tablespoons (30 mL) tamari or soy sauce (see Tip)

1½ teaspoons (7 mL) sea salt

1 to 2 cloves garlic

1. In a blender, combine the olive oil, water, apple cider vinegar, tahini, tamari, salt, and garlic. Blend until smooth and creamy. Serve immediately or store in an airtight container in the fridge for up to 2 weeks.

TIP

Tamari has a bolder, more robust flavour than soy sauce as it is generally made only from soybeans, water, and salt. Soy sauce generally contains a grain such as wheat. I prefer to use tamari in my recipes, especially when used as an ingredient in sauces, dressings, dips, and marinades. Soy sauce will work as a substitute for tamari, but the flavour will not be as rich and pronounced.

Ranch Dressing

Ranch dressing is making a comeback, and for good reason. It's a savoury dressing that's great for salads, dips, and more. I like to serve it with my Boneless Wings (page 24) and Crispy Dillies (page 74). This easy-to-make dressing uses Creamy Mayo (page 232) mixed with Sour Cream (page 231) as a base. In a pinch, any store-bought vegan sour cream and mayo will do.

MAKES 2½ CUPS (625 ML)

Prep ahead

Sour Cream (page 231)

Creamy Mayo (page 232)

Ingredients

2 cups (500 mL) Sour Cream

½ cup (125 mL) Creamy Mayo

1 tablespoon (15 mL) finely chopped flat-leaf parsley

1 tablespoon (15 mL) roughly chopped fresh dill or 1 teaspoon (5 mL) dried dill

2 teaspoons (10 mL) onion powder

1 teaspoon (5 mL) freshly cracked black pepper

1 teaspoon (5 mL) garlic powder

½ teaspoon (2 mL) ground mustard powder

¼ teaspoon (1 mL) sea salt

1. In a medium bowl, combine the sour cream, creamy mayo, parsley, dill, onion powder, pepper, garlic powder, mustard powder, and salt. Using a rubber spatula, mix until well combined. You do not want any large lumps of spices or herbs left in the sauce. Serve immediately or store in an airtight container in the fridge for up to 10 days.

Russian Dressing

Russian dressing is served on deli sandwiches like my Reuben Sandwiches (page 151), but it is also great on salads, as a spread on all kinds of sandwiches, or as a dip. I like to think of a good Russian dressing as a foolproof way to make any sandwich taste good. I use my Creamy Mayo (page 232) as a base, but you can use any store-bought vegan mayo.

MAKES 2½ CUPS (625 ML)

Prep ahead

Creamy Mayo (page 232)

Ingredients

2 cups (500 mL) Creamy Mayo

½ cup (125 mL) ketchup

¼ cup (60 mL) finely diced pickles

2 tablespoons (30 mL) finely diced red onion

1 tablespoon (15 mL) Dijon mustard

¼ teaspoon (1 mL) garlic powder

¼ teaspoon (1 mL) sea salt

1. In a medium bowl, combine the creamy mayo, ketchup, pickles, red onion, mustard, garlic powder, and salt. Using a rubber spatula, mix until well combined. You do not want any large lumps of spices or herbs left in the dressing. Serve immediately or store in an airtight container in the fridge for up to 10 days.

Best Banana Soft Serve

This soft serve is so simple to make, and its creaminess could fool any dairy lover. It is sweet, rich, creamy, and truly decadent. It does make an ice cream that is closer to soft serve in texture, but if you want it to be a little firmer, just pop it in the freezer for 30 minutes before serving. Go ahead and try it; you will be blown away!

MAKES 2 CUPS (500 ML)

Ingredients

2 cups (500 mL) chopped very ripe frozen bananas (see Tip)

3 tablespoons (45 mL) unsweetened almond milk or soy milk

1 tablespoon (15 mL) maple syrup

1 teaspoon (5 mL) pure vanilla extract

1. In a food processor fitted with a metal blade, combine the bananas, almond milk, maple syrup, and vanilla. Process until the bananas are crumbly, about 2 minutes. Using a rubber spatula, scrape down the sides of the bowl. Process again until the bananas start to become somewhat smooth, about 1 more minute.

2. Scrape down the sides of the bowl again. Process until the bananas are smooth, creamy, and look and feel like soft serve ice cream. Serve immediately or freeze for 30 minutes. You will need to eat the ice cream almost right away because it does not keep well frozen for long periods like traditional ice cream usually does.

TIP

It is best to make this ice cream with frozen bananas that are very ripe and covered in brown spots. Firmer green bananas will not break down and become smooth and creamy.

VARIATION

CHOCOLATE PEANUT BUTTER FUDGE SOFT SERVE In step 1, add ¼ cup (60 mL) smooth natural peanut butter and 2 tablespoons (30 mL) cocoa powder, and increase the maple syrup to 2 tablespoons (30 mL). Process it as you would in the recipe above and enjoy right away or freeze for 30 minutes.

Acknowledgements

We get one shot at life, and we need to do our best to make and inspire change for the better. I truly feel that without inspiring others, our lives would not be complete. There are some people in my life who I need to thank and acknowledge for being part of my story, inspiring me, or simply teaching me a life lesson.

To my wife, Candice, from falling asleep with you while watching *The Office* to our silly banter and even our arguments, thank you for believing in me and us. I would not have it any other way, with anyone else on this planet.

To everyone at Penguin Random House Canada, especially Andrea Magyar, thank you for believing in me and for the opportunity. Publishing a cookbook is no easy feat, and it really does take a whole team to make it happen.

To Nicole, thank you for capturing my food on camera and having it stand out. You are truly gifted.

To Walker and Carol, thank you for embracing my inner Ray Charles!

To Hellenic, thank you for the ride and all you do for the animals.

To anyone who has ever believed in me, supported what I do, or been part of the process, thank you. Without you I would not be where I am today, and for that I am forever grateful.

Index

A

agar powder
  Cashew Mozzarella, 218
  Deviled Eggs, 81
agave nectar: Honey Garlic Sauce,
  227
almond flour
  Parmesan Cheese, 85–86
  Parmesan Cheese (with basil),
  139–40
almond milk (as ingredient)
  Best Banana Soft Serve, 235
  Blooming Onion, 44
  Blue Cheese, 220
  Butter Tofu, 171
  Cheesy Béchamel, 180
  Chickpea Pot Pie, 133
  Count of Monte Cristo, 108
  Eggplant Parmesan, 183–84
  Hollandaise Sauce, 226
  Mornay Sauce, 109–10
  Swiss Cheese, 219
  White Widow Mac and
    Cheese, 143
Almond Milk Cheddar
  Cheese, 216
Almond Milk Cheese Curds, 217
Almond Milk, Homemade, 216
Anytime Gravy, 228
appetizers
  Blooming Onion, 44
  Boneless Wings, 24
  Caprese Stacks, 52
  Cashew Mozzarella Sticks, 28
  Cheesy Garlic Bread, 31
  Cheesy Tex-Mex Quesadillas, 32
  Crispy Corn and Squash Hush
    Puppies, 51
  Crispy Mushroom Calamari, 23
  Gooey Cheese Fondue, 39
  Killer Crispy Latkes with Sour
    Cream and Chives, 55–56
  Mile-High Loaded Nachos, 35

  South of the Border Jalapeño
    Poppers, 43
  Stuffed to the Rim Skins, 36
apple juice: Herbed Holiday
  Stuffing, 70
apples
  Apple Crisp, 189
  Waldorf Salad, 87
avocados
  Chopped Salad, 90
  Cobb Salad, 82
  Fiesta Seven-Layer Dip, 40
  Mile-High Loaded Nachos, 35

B

Bacon Double Cheeseburgers,
  137–38
bacon (vegan) see also pork (vegan)
  Coconut, 85–86
  Seitan, 105
  Tempeh, 113
Baked Crab Dip, 58
bananas
  Best Banana Soft Serve, 235
  Deluxe Banana Split, 208
Bangers and Mash, 145
basil
  Caprese Stacks, 52
  Tomato Sauce, 157
beans see also chickpeas
beans, black
  Chopped Salad, 90
  Fiesta Chili, 179
  Shepherd's Pie, 165
beans, navy: Maple Baked Beans, 68
beans, pinto
  Cheesy Tex-Mex Quesadillas, 32
  Tortilla Bake, 180
beef/steak (vegan) see also ground
  meats (vegan)
  Chickpea Salisbury Steak, 146
  No-Beef Stroganoff, 162

  The NY Strip, 129
  Philly Cheesesteak Sandwiches, 152
  Reuben Sandwiches, 151
beer
  Beer Battered Tempeh and
    Chips, 134
  Cashew Mozzarella Sticks, 28
  Crispy Dillies with Ranch
    Dressing, 74
beet juice
  Holiday Ham, 166
  Marinade for Croque
    Monsieur, 109–10
  Marinade for Reuben
    Sandwiches, 151
bell peppers see green peppers; red
  peppers
Best Banana Soft Serve, 235
biscuits and breads
  Biscuits, 120
  Breakfast in Bed Scones, 104
  Cheesy Garlic Bread, 31
  Cheesy Scramble Biscuits, 122
  Stuffed and Stacked French
    Toast, 99
Bisque, Creamy Tomato, 45
black beans
  Chopped Salad, 90
  Fiesta Chili, 179
  Shepherd's Pie, 165
Blooming Onion, 44
blueberries
  Bodacious Blueberry Pie, 206
  Buttermilk Blueberry Pancakes, 95
  Muesli and Cashew Yogurt
    Parfait, 100
Blue Cheese, 220
Boneless Wings, 24
breads see biscuits and breads
breakfasts
  Breakfast in Bed Scones, 104
  Buttermilk Blueberry Pancakes, 95
  Cage-Free Cheesy Omelette, 102

The Classics Veganized

Cage-Free Eggs Florentine, 118
Cheesy Scramble Biscuits, 122
Dirty South Sausages and Biscuits
    with Gravy, 120
Downhome Fries, 116
Muesli and Cashew Yogurt
    Parfait, 100
No Bull Breakfast Links, 121
Peanut Butter Fudge and
    Chocolate Waffles, 96
Perfect Vegan Scramble, 115
Quiche Lorraine, 107
Seitan Bacon, 105
Shakshuka, 123
Stuffed and Stacked French
    Toast, 99
Sunny Side Up Vegan Eggs with
    Yolks, 114
broccoli: Eggplant Parmesan, 183–84
broths
    for Boneless Wings, 24
    for Buttermilk Fried Chicken, 117
    for Croque Monsieur, 109–10
    for Dirty South Sausages and
        Biscuits with Gravy, 120
    for Hickory Smoked Ribs, 167
    for Holiday Ham, 166
    for The NY Strip, 129
    for Reuben Sandwiches, 151
    Smoky, 105
Brunch Club Sandwich, 113
Buffalo Sauce, 227
Buttercream Frosting, 202
Buttermilk Blueberry Pancakes, 95
Buttermilk Fried Chicken, 117
Buttermilk Onion Rings, 78
butternut squash
    Crispy Corn and Squash Hush
        Puppies, 51
    Mac and Cheese Sauce, 223
    Nacho Cheese Sauce, 224
butters
    Garlic, 230
    Whipped, 229
Butter Tofu, 171

C

Caesar Dressing, 85–86
Cage-Free Cheesy Omelette, 102
Cage-Free Eggs Florentine, 118
cakes
    Carrot Cake with Cream Cheese
        Frosting, 203
    Chocolate Fudge Cake with
        Buttercream Frosting, 202
    Coffee Cake, 200
    Everyday Pound Cake, 195
    Molten Lava Chocolate Brownie
        Cakes, 196
    New York Style Cheesecake, 199
    Pineapple Upside Down Cake, 192
capers
    Remoulade Sauce, 176
    Shakshuka, 123
Caprese Stacks, 52
carrots
    Carrot Cake with Cream Cheese
        Frosting, 203
    Chickpea Pot Pie, 133
    Creamy Tomato Bisque, 45
    Drunken Vegan Chicken Stew, 175
    Herbed Holiday Stuffing, 70
    Home-Style Meatloaf, 130
    Lentil Ragout, 148
    Mac and Cheese Sauce, 223
    Nacho Cheese Sauce, 224
    Shepherd's Pie, 165
    Smoked Carrot Lox Pinwheel
        Wrap, 154
    Un-Chicken Noodle Soup, 48
Cashew Mozzarella Sticks, 28
cashews
    Blue Cheese, 220
    Butter Tofu, 171
    Cashew Mozzarella, 218
    Cashew Yogurt, 100
    Creamed Garlic Spinach, 73
    Creamy Tomato Bisque, 45
    Fettuccini Alfredo, 158
    Gooey Cheese Fondue, 39
    Herbed Cashew Cheese, 183–84

Homemade Cashew Milk, 229
Mac and Cheese Sauce, 223
Mascarpone, 99
Nacho Cheese Sauce, 224
Sour Cream, 231
Swiss Cheese, 219
Cauliflower, Tandoori, 185
celery
    Baked Crab Dip, 58
    Chickpea Pot Pie, 133
    Crab Cakes with Remoulade
        Sauce, 176
    Drunken Vegan Chicken Stew, 175
    Fiesta Chili, 179
    Herbed Holiday Stuffing, 70
    Home-Style Meatloaf, 130
    Lentil Ragout, 148
    Shepherd's Pie, 165
    Ultimate Vegan Caesar, 125
    Un-Chicken Noodle Soup, 48
    Waldorf Salad, 87
Change Your Life Chana with
    Tandoori Cauliflower, 185
Cheeseburgers, Bacon Double, 137–38
Cheesecake, New York Style, 199
cheeses (vegan)
    Almond Milk Cheddar
        rCheese, 216
    Almond Milk Cheese Curds, 217
    Blue Cheese, 220
    Cashew Mozzarella, 218
    Cream Cheese, 222
    Feta Cheese, 221
    Herbed Cashew Cheese, 183
    Mascarpone, 99
    Swiss Cheese, 219
Cheesy Béchamel, 180
Cheesy Chickpeas, 82
Cheesy Garlic Bread, 31
Cheesy Rice, 148
Cheesy Scramble Biscuits, 122
Cheesy Tex-Mex Quesadillas, 32
chicken (vegan)
    Boneless Wings, 24
    Buttermilk Fried Chicken, 117

Drunken Vegan Chicken Stew, 175

Un-Chicken Noodle Soup, 48

chickpea liquid: Luscious Lemon
     Meringue Pie, 205

chickpeas

Chana Masala, 185

Cheesy Chickpeas, 82

Chickpea Pot Pie, 133

Chickpea Salisbury Steak, 146

Chopped Salad, 90

Hickory Smoked Ribs, 167–68

Chili, Fiesta, 179

chives: Killer Crispy Latkes with
     Sour Cream and Chives, 55–56

chocolate/chocolate chips

Chocolate Fudge Cake with
     Buttercream Frosting, 202

Chocolate Sauce, 96, 208

Crunchy Chocolate Chip
     Cookies, 190

Molten Lava Chocolate Brownie
     Cakes, 196

Peanut Butter Buckeyes, 211

Chopped Salad, 90

Churros with Salted Caramel
     Sauce, 213

cilantro

Chana Masala, 185

Fiesta Seven-Layer Dip, 40

Classic Poutine, 57

Classic Vinaigrette, 233

cloves

Broth for Croque
     Monsieur, 109–10

Broth for Reuben Sandwiches, 151

Cobb Salad, 82

Coconut Bacon, 85–86

coconut milk

Salted Caramel Sauce, 213

Whipped Cream, 208

Coffee Cake, 200

Collard Greens, Slow-Cooked
     Southern-Style, 77

condiments see also dips

Creamy Mayo, 232

Garlic Butter, 230

Seasoning Salt, 64

Sour Cream, 231

Whipped Butter, 229

Whipped Cream, 208

Cookies, Crunchy Chocolate
     Chip, 190

corn

Chopped Salad, 90

Crispy Corn and Squash Hush
     Puppies, 51

Fiesta Chili, 179

Shepherd's Pie, 165

cornmeal

Blooming Onion, 44

Crispy Mushroom Calamari, 23

Eggplant Parmesan, 183–84

South of the Border Jalapeño
     Poppers, 43

Count of Monte Cristo, 108

crab (vegan)

Baked Crab Dip, 58

Crab Cakes with Remoulade
     Sauce, 176

Cream Cheese (recipe for), 222

cream cheese (vegan, as ingredient)

Cream Cheese Frosting, 203

New York Style Cheesecake, 199

Peanut Butter Buckeyes, 211

Creamed Garlic Spinach, 73

Creamiest Cream of Mushroom
     Soup, 47

Creamy Caesar Salad, 85–86

Creamy Mayo, 232

Creamy Risotto, 71

Creamy Sauce for Perfect Vegan
     Scramble, 115

Creamy Tomato Bisque, 45

Crisp, Apple, 189

Crispy Corn and Squash Hush
     Puppies, 51

Crispy Dillies with Ranch
     Dressing, 74

Crispy Mushroom Calamari, 23

Croque Monsieur, 109–10

Croutons, 85–86

Crunchy Chocolate Chip
     Cookies, 190

cucumbers: Greek Salad, 89

D

Deluxe Banana Split, 208

Deviled Eggs, 81

Dijon mustard see mustard, Dijon

dill

Baked Crab Dip, 58

Crispy Dillies with Ranch
     Dressing, 74

Crispy Mushroom Calamari, 23

Ranch Dressing, 233

Tartar Sauce, 225

dips see also condiments

Baked Crab Dip, 58

Fiesta Seven-Layer Dip, 40

Guacamole, 40

Salsa, 40

Dirty South Sausages and Biscuits
     with Gravy, 120

Downhome Fries, 116

dressings and vinaigrettes see also
     marinades; sauces

Caesar Dressing, 85–86

Classic Vinaigrette, 233

for Cobb Salad, 82

for Greek Salad, 89

Ranch Dressing, 233

Russian Dressing, 235

for Waldorf Salad, 87

Drunken Vegan Chicken Stew, 175

E

Eggplant Parmesan, 183–84

eggs (vegan)

Cage-Free Cheesy Omelette, 102

Cage-Free Eggs Florentine, 118

Cheesy Scramble Biscuits, 122

Perfect Vegan Scramble, 115

Quiche Lorraine, 107

Sunny Side Up Vegan Eggs with
Yolks, 114
Vegan Egg Wash, 104, 133
Everyday Pound Cake, 195

F

Feta Cheese, 221
Fettuccini Alfredo, 158
Fiesta Chili, 179
Fiesta Seven-Layer Dip, 40
flaxseed: Carrot Cake with Cream
Cheese Frosting, 203
flaxseed, golden
Bacon Double Cheeseburgers,
137-38
Cage-Free Cheesy Omelette, 102
Crispy Corn and Squash Hush
Puppies, 51
Crunchy Chocolate Chip
Cookies, 190
Herbed Holiday Stuffing, 70
Home-Style Meatloaf, 130
Killer Crispy Latkes with Sour
Cream and Chives, 55-56
Meatballs, 139-40, 157
Fondue, Gooey Cheese, 39
French Onion Soup with Melted
Mozzarella, 27
French Toast, Stuffed and
Stacked, 99
fried foods
Bangers and Mash, 145
Beer Battered Tempeh and
Chips, 134
Blooming Onion, 44
Buttermilk Fried Chicken, 117
Buttermilk Onion Rings, 78
Cashew Mozzarella Sticks, 28
Churros with Salted Caramel
Sauce, 213
Crispy Corn and Squash Hush
Puppies, 51
Crispy Dillies with Ranch
Dressing, 74

Crispy Mushroom Calamari, 23
Killer Crispy Latkes with Sour
Cream and Chives, 55-56
South of the Border Jalapeño
Poppers, 43
Stuffed to the Rim Skins, 36
fries
Classic Poutine, 57
Downhome Fries, 116
Perfect French Fries, 64
frostings
Buttercream, 202
Cream Cheese, 203

G

garbanzo beans see chickpeas
garlic
Buttermilk Fried Chicken, 117
Cheesy Garlic Bread, 31
Creamed Garlic Spinach, 73
Creamiest Cream of Mushroom
Soup, 47
Creamy Tomato Bisque, 45
Fettuccini Alfredo, 158
Fiesta Chili, 179
Garlic Butter, 230
General Tso Tofu, 172
Honey Garlic Sauce, 227
No-Beef Stroganoff, 162
The NY Strip, 129
Refried Pinto Beans, 32, 180
General Tso Tofu, 172
ginger
Butter Tofu, 171
General Tso Tofu, 172
Maple Baked Beans, 68
Gooey Cheese Fondue, 39
grapes, red: Waldorf Salad, 87
Gravy, Anytime, 228
Greek Salad, 89
green peppers
General Tso Tofu, 172
Philly Cheesesteak Sandwiches,
152

ground meats (vegan) see also
beef/steak (vegan)
Bacon Double Cheeseburgers,
137-38
Chickpea Salisbury Steak, 146
Home-Style Meatloaf, 130
Meatballs, 139-40, 157
Guacamole, 40

H

hearts of palm
Baked Crab Dip, 58
Crab Cakes, 176
Herbed Cashew Cheese, 183
Herbed Holiday Stuffing, 70
Hickory Smoked Ribs, 167-68
Holiday Ham, 166
Hollandaise Sauce, 226
Homemade Almond Milk, 216
Homemade Cashew Milk, 229
Home-Style Meatloaf, 130
Honey Garlic Sauce, 227
horseradish
Remoulade Sauce, 176
Ultimate Vegan Caesar, 125

I

ice creams
Best Banana Soft Serve, 235
Deluxe Banana Split, 208

J

jalapeño peppers
Butter Tofu, 171
Chana Masala, 185
Fiesta Seven-Layer Dip, 40
Slow-Cooked Southern-Style
Collard Greens, 77
South of the Border Jalapeño
Poppers, 43

K

kale: Eggplant Parmesan, 183–84
ketchup
  Bacon Double Cheeseburgers,
    137–38
  Home-Style Meatloaf, 130
  Maple Baked Beans, 68
  Russian Dressing, 235
Killer Crispy Latkes with Sour
  Cream and Chives, 55–56

L

Lasagna, Mushroom and Spinach, 161
lemon juice/zest
  Almond Milk Cheddar Cheese, 216
  Cashew Mozzarella, 218
  Cashew Yogurt, 100
  Crab Cakes with Remoulade
    Sauce, 176
  Cream Cheese, 222
  Creamy Caesar Salad, 85–86
  Creamy Mayo, 232
  Feta Cheese, 221
  Fiesta Chili, 179
  Guacamole, 40
  Herbed Cashew Cheese, 183
  Hollandaise Sauce, 226
  Luscious Lemon Meringue
    Pie, 205
  Mascarpone, 99
  Mile-High Loaded Nachos, 35
  New York Style Cheesecake, 199
  Sour Cream, 231
  Swiss Cheese, 219
  Tartar Sauce, 225
  Ultimate Vegan Caesar, 125
lentils, green
  Home-Style Meatloaf, 130
  Meatballs, 139–40, 157
lentils, red
  Creamiest Cream of Mushroom
    Soup, 47
  Gooey Cheese Fondue, 39
  Lentil Ragout, 148

lettuce, Boston: Waldorf Salad, 87
lettuce, iceberg: Cobb Salad, 82
lettuce, romaine
  Chopped Salad, 90
  Creamy Caesar Salad, 85–86
  Greek Salad, 89
lime juice
  Butter Tofu, 171
  Chana Masala, 185
  Mile-High Loaded Nachos, 35
  Salsa, 40
Luscious Lemon Meringue Pie, 205

M

Mac and Cheese Sauce, 223
macaroni
  Sharp Cheddar Mac and
    Cheese, 144
  White Widow Mac and
    Cheese, 143
Maple Baked Beans, 68
maple syrup
  Cashew Yogurt, 100
  Coconut Bacon, 85–86
  Deluxe Banana Split, 208
  Fiesta Chili, 179
  General Tso Tofu, 172
  Holiday Ham, 166
  Maple Baked Beans, 68
  Mascarpone, 99
  Peanut Butter Fudge and
    Chocolate Waffles, 96
  Pecan Pie, 207
  Seitan Bacon, 105
  Tempeh Bacon, 113
  Vegan Egg Wash, 104, 133
marinades see also dressings and
    vinaigrettes; sauces
  for Beer Battered Tempeh and
    Chips, 134
  for Croque Monsieur, 109–10
  for The NY Strip, 129
  for Reuben Sandwiches, 151
  for Seitan Bacon, 105

Mascarpone, 99
Mayo, Creamy, 232
Meatballs, 139–40, 157
Meatball Sub, 139–40
Meatloaf, Home-Style, 130
Mile-High Loaded Nachos, 35
milks
  Homemade Almond, 216
  Homemade Cashew, 229
millet
  Bacon Double Cheeseburgers,
    137–38
  Home-Style Meatloaf, 130
miso, dark: Sharp Cheddar Mac and
    Cheese, 144
miso, white: Cheesy Béchamel, 180
molasses, blackstrap/fancy
  Maple Baked Beans, 68
  Seitan (Corned Beef) Dough, 151
Molten Lava Chocolate Brownie
    Cakes, 196
Mornay Sauce, 109–10
Mozzarella, Cashew, 218
Muesli and Cashew Yogurt
    Parfait, 100
Mushroom and Spinach Lasagna, 161
mushrooms, button
  Bacon Double Cheeseburgers,
    137–38
  Chickpea Salisbury Steak, 146
  Creamiest Cream of Mushroom
    Soup, 47
  Drunken Vegan Chicken Stew, 175
  Lentil Ragout, 148
mushrooms, cremini: No-Beef
    Stroganoff, 162
mushrooms, oyster: Crispy
    Mushroom Calamari, 23
mushrooms, portobello: Creamiest
    Cream of Mushroom Soup, 47
mustard, Dijon
  Blooming Onion, 44
  Buttermilk Fried Chicken, 117
  Buttermilk Onion Rings, 78
  Cobb Salad, 82

Crab Cakes with Remoulade
  Sauce, 176
Croque Monsieur, 109-10
Eggplant Parmesan, 183-84
Fettuccini Alfredo, 158
Holiday Ham, 166
Philly Cheesesteak
  Sandwiches, 152
Reuben Sandwiches, 151
Seitan (Sausage) Dough, 120
South of the Border Jalapeño
  Poppers, 43
mustard, yellow: Deviled Eggs, 81

N
Nacho Cheese Sauce, 224
Nachos, Mile-High Loaded, 35
navy beans: Maple Baked Beans, 68
New York Style Cheesecake, 199
No-Beef Stroganoff, 162
No Bull Breakfast Links, 121
nutritional yeast
  Almond Milk Cheddar Cheese, 216
  Almond Parmesan Cheese, 85-86
  Boneless Wings, 24
  Brunch Club Sandwich, 113
  Buttermilk Fried Chicken, 117
  Cashew Mozzarella, 218
  Cashew Mozzarella Sticks, 28
  Cheesy Béchamel, 180
  Cheesy Rice, 148
  Chickpea Pot Pie, 133
  Cobb Salad, 82
  Creamiest Cream of Mushroom
    Soup, 47
  Creamy Caesar Salad, 85-86
  Creamy Risotto, 71
  Eggplant Parmesan, 183
  Feta Cheese, 221
  Fettuccini Alfredo, 158
  Gooey Cheese Fondue, 39
  Hickory Smoked Ribs, 167-68
  Lentil Ragout with Cheesy
    Rice, 148

Mac and Cheese Sauce, 223
Mornay Sauce, 109-10
Mushroom and Spinach
  Lasagna, 161
Nacho Cheese Sauce, 224
Parmesan Cheese, 139-40
Perfect Vegan Scramble, 115
Quiche Lorraine, 107
Seitan Bacon, 105
Sharp Cheddar Mac and
  Cheese, 144
Sunny Side Up Vegan Eggs with
  Yolks, 114
Twice Baked Vegan Taters, 63
Un-Chicken Noodle Soup, 48
White Widow Mac and Cheese, 143
nuts see cashews; pecans; walnuts
The NY Strip, 129

O
oats
  Apple Crisp, 189
  Buttermilk Blueberry Pancakes, 95
  Hickory Smoked Ribs, 167-68
  Muesli, 100
olives, Kalamata
  Caprese Stacks, 52
  Greek Salad, 89
Omelette, Cage-Free Cheesy, 102
onions
  Drunken Vegan Chicken Stew, 175
  Fiesta Chili, 179
  French Onion Soup with Melted
    Mozzarella, 27
  Herbed Holiday Stuffing, 70
  Hickory Smoked Ribs, 167-68
  Philly Cheesesteak
    Sandwiches, 152
  Quiche Lorraine, 107
  Stuffed Grilled Cheese
    Sandwiches, 149
onions, green
  Cobb Salad, 82
  Fiesta Seven-Layer Dip, 40

General Tso Tofu, 172
Remoulade Sauce, 176
Twice Baked Vegan Taters, 63
onions, red
  Baked Crab Dip, 58
  Crab Cakes, 176
  Greek Salad, 89
  Russian Dressing, 235
  Smoked Carrot Lox Pinwheel
    Wrap, 154
onions, Vidalia
  Blooming Onion, 44
  Buttermilk Onion Rings, 78
orange juice: Fiesta Chili, 179

P
Pancakes, Buttermilk Blueberry, 95
panko crumbs
  Buttermilk Onion Rings, 78
  Crab Cakes with Remoulade
    Sauce, 176
  Crispy Dillies with Ranch
    Dressing, 74
  White Widow Mac and Cheese, 143
Parmesan Cheese, 85-86, 139-40
parsley
  Baked Crab Dip, 58
  Cheesy Garlic Bread, 31
  Garlic Butter, 230
  Greek Salad, 89
  Meatballs, 139-40, 157
  Smoked Carrot Lox Pinwheel
    Wrap, 154
  Tartar Sauce, 225
  Un-Chicken Noodle Soup, 48
pastas
  Fettuccini Alfredo, 158
  Mushroom and Spinach
    Lasagna, 161
  Sharp Cheddar Mac and
    Cheese, 144
  Spaghetti and Meatballs, 157
  White Widow Mac and Cheese, 143
Peanut Butter Buckeyes, 211

Index

Peanut Butter Fudge and Chocolate
    Waffles, 96
peas: Chickpea Pot Pie, 133
pecans
    Muesli, 100
    Pecan Pie, 207
peppers *see* green peppers; jalapeño
    peppers; red peppers
Perfect French Fries and Seasoning
    Salt, 64
Perfect Vegan Scramble, 115
Philly Cheesesteak Sandwiches, 152
pickles, dill
    Crispy Dillies with Ranch
        Dressing, 74
    Remoulade Sauce, 176
    Russian Dressing, 235
    Tartar Sauce, 225
pies
    Bodacious Blueberry, 206
    Chickpea Pot, 133
    Luscious Lemon Meringue, 205
    Pecan, 207
    Shepherd's, 165
pineapples/pineapple juice
    Holiday Ham, 166
    Pineapple Upside Down Cake, 192
    Seitan (Ham) Dough, 109-10
pinto beans
    Cheesy Tex-Mex Quesadillas, 32
    Tortilla Bake, 180
pork (vegan) *see also* bacon (vegan)
    Bangers and Mash, 145
    Count of Monte Cristo, 108
    Croque Monsieur, 109-10
    Dirty South Sausages and Biscuits
        with Gravy, 120
    Hickory Smoked Ribs, 167-68
    Holiday Ham, 166
    No Bull Breakfast Links, 121
    Quiche Lorraine, 107
potatoes, fingerling: Smashed
    Taters, 67
potatoes, red-skin: Downhome
    Fries, 116

potatoes, russet
    Bangers and Mash, 145
    Deviled Eggs, 81
    Gooey Cheese Fondue, 39
    Killer Crispy Latkes with Sour
        Cream and Chives, 55-56
    Mac and Cheese Sauce, 223
    Nacho Cheese Sauce, 224
    Perfect French Fries and
        Seasoning Salt, 64
    Shepherd's Pie, 165
    Stuffed to the Rim Skins, 36
    Twice Baked Vegan Taters, 63
potatoes, yellow: Creamy Tomato
    Bisque, 45
Poutine, Classic, 57
pumpkin seeds: Muesli, 100

Q

Quesadillas, Cheesy Tex-Mex, 32
Quiche Lorraine, 107
quinoa, white: Crispy Corn and
    Squash Hush Puppies, 51

R

raisins: Muesli, 100
Ranch Dressing, 233
red peppers
    Baked Crab Dip, 58
    Chopped Salad, 90
    Crab Cakes with Remoulade
        Sauce, 176
    Fiesta Chili, 179
    Greek Salad, 89
    Shakshuka, 123
    Tomato Sauce, 139, 157, 183-84
Refried Pinto Beans, 32, 180
Remoulade Sauce, 176
Reuben Sandwiches, 151
Ribs, Hickory Smoked, 167-68
rice, arborio/carnaroli
    Creamy Risotto, 71
    Gooey Cheese Fondue, 39

Rice, Cheesy, 148
rosemary
    Chickpea Pot Pie, 133
    Herbed Holiday Stuffing, 70
Russian Dressing, 235

S

sage: Herbed Holiday Stuffing, 70
salads
    Chopped, 90
    Cobb, 82
    Creamy Caesar, 85-86
    Greek, 89
    Waldorf, 87
Salsa, 40
Salt, Seasoning, 64
Salted Caramel Sauce, 213
sandwiches
    Brunch Club Sandwich, 113
    Count of Monte Cristo, 108
    Croque Monsieur, 109-10
    Meatball Sub, 139-40
    Philly Cheesesteak
        Sandwiches, 152
    Reuben Sandwiches, 151
    Smoked Carrot Lox Pinwheel
        Wrap, 154
    Stuffed Grilled Cheese
        Sandwiches, 149
sauces *see also* dressings and
    vinaigrettes; marinades
    Anytime Gravy, 228
    Buffalo Sauce, 227
    Cheesy Béchamel, 180
    Chocolate Sauce, 96, 208
    Creamy Sauce for Perfect Vegan
        Scramble, 115
    Hollandaise Sauce, 226
    Honey Garlic Sauce, 227
    Mac and Cheese Sauce, 223
    Mornay Sauce, 109-10
    Nacho Cheese Sauce, 224
    Remoulade Sauce, 176
    Salted Caramel Sauce, 213

Sauce for Butter Tofu, 171
Sauce for General Tso Tofu, 172
Strawberry Compote, 99
Strawberry Sauce, 208
Tartar Sauce, 225
Tomato Sauce, 139, 157, 183–84
sauerkraut
    Blue Cheese, 220
    Reuben Sandwiches, 151
sausages (vegan)
    Bangers and Mash, 145
    Dirty South Sausages and Biscuits
        with Gravy, 120
    No Bull Breakfast Links, 121
Scones, Breakfast in Bed, 104
Seasoning Salt, 64
seeds *see* flaxseed; flaxseed, golden;
    pumpkin seeds; sunflower
    seeds
seitan doughs
    Bacon, 105
    Chicken, 117, 175
    Corned Beef, 151
    Ham, 109–10, 166
    Sausage, 120
    Steak, 129
    Wings, 24
Shakshuka, 123
Sharp Cheddar Mac and Cheese, 144
Shepherd's Pie, 165
sides
    Creamed Garlic Spinach, 73
    Creamy Risotto, 71
    Deviled Eggs, 81
    Herbed Holiday Stuffing, 70
    Maple Baked Beans, 68
    Perfect French Fries and
        Seasoning Salt, 64
    Slow-Cooked Southern-Style
        Collard Greens, 77
    Smashed Taters, 67
    Twice Baked Vegan Taters, 63
Slow-Cooked Southern-Style
    Collard Greens, 77
Smashed Taters, 67

Smoked Carrot Lox Pinwheel
    Wrap, 154
Smoky Broth for Seitan Bacon, 105
soups and stews
    Creamiest Cream of Mushroom
        Soup, 47
    Creamy Tomato Bisque, 45
    Drunken Vegan Chicken Stew, 175
    French Onion Soup with Melted
        Mozzarella, 27
    Un-Chicken Noodle Soup, 48
Sour Cream (recipe for), 231
sour cream (vegan, as ingredient)
    Fiesta Seven-Layer Dip, 40
    Killer Crispy Latkes with Sour
        Cream and Chives, 55–56
    New York Style Cheesecake, 199
    Twice Baked Vegan Taters, 63
South of the Border Jalapeño
    Poppers, 43
soy milk
    Best Banana Soft Serve, 235
    Buttermilk Fried Chicken, 117
    Buttermilk Onion Rings, 78
    Coffee Cake, 200
    Everyday Pound Cake, 195
    Molten Lava Chocolate Brownie
        Cakes, 196
    Pecan Pie, 207
    Whipped Cream, 208
soy sauce *see* tamari/soy sauce
spaghetti
    Spaghetti and Meatballs, 157
    Un-Chicken Noodle Soup, 48
spinach
    Cage-Free Eggs Florentine, 118
    Mushroom and Spinach
        Lasagna, 161
spinach, baby: Creamed Garlic
    Spinach, 73
squash *see* butternut squash
strawberries
    Muesli and Cashew Yogurt
        Parfait, 100
    Strawberry Compote, 99

Strawberry Sauce, 208
Stuffed and Stacked French
    Toast, 99
Stuffed Grilled Cheese
    Sandwiches, 149
Stuffed to the Rim Skins, 36
Stuffing, Herbed Holiday, 70
sunflower seeds
    Bacon Double Cheeseburgers,
        137–38
    Chopped Salad, 90
    Meatballs, 139–40, 157
    Muesli, 100
Sunny Side Up Vegan Eggs with
    Yolks, 114
sweet potatoes
    Chopped Salad, 90
    Creamy Tomato Bisque, 45
    Lentil Ragout, 148
Swiss Cheese, 219

T
tahini
    Classic Vinaigrette, 233
    Creamy Risotto, 71
tamari/soy sauce
    Anytime Gravy, 228
    Bacon Double Cheeseburgers,
        137–38
    Creamiest Cream of Mushroom
        Soup, 47
    Croque Monsieur, 109–10
    Dirty South Sausages and Biscuits
        with Gravy, 120
    Drunken Vegan Chicken Stew, 175
    Fiesta Chili, 179
    French Onion Soup with Melted
        Mozzarella, 27
    General Tso Tofu, 172
    Home-Style Meatloaf, 130
    Lentil Ragout, 148
    No-Beef Stroganoff, 162
    The NY Strip, 129
    Philly Cheesesteak Sandwiches, 152

Reuben Sandwiches, 151
Seitan Bacon, 105
Shepherd's Pie, 165
Tempeh Bacon, 113
Tandoori Cauliflower, 185
tapioca starch
  Almond Milk Cheddar
    Cheese, 216
  Almond Milk Cheese Curds, 217
Tartar Sauce, 225
tempeh
  Bacon Double Cheeseburgers,
    137–38
  Beer Battered Tempeh and
    Chips, 134
  Fiesta Chili, 179
  Tempeh Bacon, 113
thyme
  Boneless Wings, 24
  Chickpea Pot Pie, 133
  Creamiest Cream of Mushroom
    Soup, 47
  Drunken Vegan Chicken Stew, 175
  French Onion Soup with Melted
    Mozzarella, 27
  Herbed Cashew Cheese, 183
  The NY Strip, 129
tofu, firm/extra-firm
  Bangers and Mash, 145
  Butter Tofu, 171
  Cage-Free Cheesy Omelette, 102
  Cheesy Tex-Mex Quesadillas, 32
  Cream Cheese, 222
  Feta Cheese, 221
  General Tso Tofu, 172
  Hickory Smoked Ribs, 167–68
  Luscious Lemon Meringue
    Pie, 205
  Mushroom and Spinach
    Lasagna, 161
  No Bull Breakfast Links, 121
  Seitan Bacon, 105
  Sour Cream, 231
  Stuffed and Stacked French
    Toast, 99

tofu, medium-firm
  Brunch Club Sandwich, 113
  Cage-Free Eggs Florentine, 118
  Chocolate Fudge Cake with
    Buttercream Frosting, 202
  Coffee Cake, 200
  Everyday Pound Cake, 195
  Perfect Vegan Scramble, 115
tofu, silken
  Creamy Mayo, 232
  Deviled Eggs, 81
  Quiche Lorraine, 107
  Sunny Side Up Vegan Eggs with
    Yolks, 114
tofu, soft: Count of Monte
    Cristo, 108
tomatoes
  Butter Tofu, 171
  Caprese Stacks, 52
  Chana Masala, 185
  Cheesy Tex-Mex Quesadillas, 32
  Creamy Tomato Bisque, 45
  Fiesta Chili, 179
  Salsa, 40
  Shakshuka, 123
  Tomato Sauce, 139, 157, 183–84
  Tortilla Bake, 180
tomatoes, cherry
  Chopped Salad, 90
  Cobb Salad, 82
tomatoes, sun-dried: Creamy Caesar
    Salad, 85–86
tomato purée: Maple Baked
    Beans, 68
Tortilla Bake, 180
TVP (texturized vegetable protein)
  No-Beef Stroganoff, 162
  Shepherd's Pie, 165
Twice Baked Vegan Taters, 63

U
Ultimate Vegan Caesar, 125
Un-Chicken Noodle Soup, 48

V
Vegan Egg Wash, 104, 133
vinaigrettes see dressings and
    vinaigrettes
vital wheat gluten flour see seitan
    doughs
vodka: Ultimate Vegan Caesar, 125

W
Waffles, Peanut Butter Fudge and
    Chocolate, 96
Waldorf Salad, 87
walnuts
  Meatballs, 139–40, 157
  Muesli, 100
  Waldorf Salad, 87
Whipped Butter, 229
Whipped Cream, 208
White Widow Mac and Cheese, 143
wine, red
  Anytime Gravy, 228
  Chickpea Salisbury Steak, 146
  Drunken Vegan Chicken Stew, 175
  The NY Strip, 129
  Shepherd's Pie, 165
wine, white
  Cheesy Béchamel, 180
  Creamy Risotto, 71
  French Onion Soup with Melted
    Mozzarella, 27
  Gooey Cheese Fondue, 39
  Hollandaise Sauce, 226
  Mornay Sauce, 109–10
  Swiss Cheese, 219
  White Widow Mac and
    Cheese, 143
Wings, Boneless, 24

Y
Yogurt, Cashew, 100